Diary *of an* Invalid

Diary *of an* Invalid

Journal of a Tour in Pursuit of Health
1817-1819

Henry Matthews

Sketched by L. Gruner.

NONSUCH

First published 1820
Copyright © in this edition 2005
Nonsuch Publishing Ltd

Nonsuch Publishing Limited
The Mill, Brimscombe Port, Stroud, Gloucestershire, GL5 2QG
www.nonsuch-publishing.com

British Library Cataloguing in Publication Data.
A catalogue record for this book is available from the British Library.

ISBN 1-84588-017-X

Typesetting and origination by Nonsuch Publishing Limited
Printed in Great Britain by Oaklands Book Services Limited

CONTENTS

Introduction to the Modern Edition		7
Preface		11
I	Lisbon	13
II	Pisa and Florence	33
III	Arrival in Rome	57
IV	Christmas in Rome	71
V	Sightseeing in the New Year	91
VI	Festival and Carnival	111
VII	Naples	133
VIII	Roman and Modern Sights	155
IX	From Rome to Florence	177
X	Venice and Buonaparte	197
XI	Milan to Lausanne	225
XII	Tour of Switzerland	249
XIII	Journey to Nismes	269
XIV	Montpellier	289
XV	Toulouse	303
XVI	Church and State	323
XVII	Bourdeaux to Versailles	341
XVIII	Paris and Home	357

INTRODUCTION TO THE
MODERN EDITION

Henry Matthews was born in 1789 in Herefordshire, the fifth son of John Matthews, a physician and poet, and was educated at Eton College and King's College, Cambridge. In 1817 ill-health forced him to seek a warmer climate, and he left England for the Continent. Over the next two year his 'wild goose chase after health' would take him to Portugal, Italy, Switzerland and France and he would visit many major European cities, including Lisbon, Florence, Rome, Venice, Bern, Geneva, Lyons, Toulouse and Paris. He would see some of the continent's greatest artistic treasures, most important archaeological discoveries and grandest architecture, while his status as an Englishman would allow him to mix with the highest society in many of the places where he stopped. Yet he would always 'exult in the reflection that [he] was born an Englishman'.

Matthews is an observant and perceptive diarist, and very little escapes his notice. The landscape, the buildings, the people and their customs are all described objectively and with attention to detail. Unlike many Englishmen abroad in the nineteenth century, however, he does not assume an air of superiority: he has an open mind and does not look down upon the Portuguese, the Italians, the Swiss and the French. That is not to say that he is not critical of them when he believes that their behaviour warrants criticism, but neither does he withold praise where it is due. And, although an Anglican and, therefore, a Protestant, he appears

to hold the Roman Catholic Church in far greater esteem than
many of his co-religionists.

His visit to Portugal, during which he spent most of his time
in Lisbon, was relatively short, and he did not especially enjoy
his stay there: he found the smell of the city overpowering and
left 'without one feeling of regret' having been 'fairly stunk out.'
Italy, however, was much more to his taste, and he seemed to
find endless enjoyment visiting the art galleries and ancient ruins.
He describes in great detail the paintings and sculptures he saw,
including works by Michaelangelo, Raphael and Titian, recording
his own thoughts and opinions on these great works, and he is
awed by the sheer size of St Peter's Basilica in the Vatican. The
Roman Forum and Colosseum and the excavations at Pompeii
especially delight him because of his evident reverence for the
ancient world.

While Matthews in general enjoyed his stay in Italy, where
he remained much longer than he did in Portugal, he was less
impressed with Switzerland. He remarks that 'Swiss honesty is a
phrase that is much used ... but it is an article that seems to be
cultivated solely for exportation, and none is retained for home
consumption.' He was, however, very taken with the scenery of
the Swiss Alps. France, like Switzerland, is a country for which
he had mixed feelings. As an Englishman making such a journey
not very long after the British victory over the French in the
Napoleonic Wars, some of the French people he encountered
were not very well disposed toward him, and his opinion of them
was not as high as it might otherwise have been. Nonetheless, he
was not blinded by prejudice, and was still able to recognise the
good qualities in the people he met, regardless of his observations
on the nation as a whole, and opines that '[i]n comparing French
and English cookery, ... the balance is greatly in favour of the
former.'

When Henry Mattews set out in 1817 he was not certain that
his health would allow him ever to see England again. Yet he
returned in 1819 none the worse for the trip, despite the fact that
his search for a warmer climate than England had not always been

entirely successful; indeed, he often thought that he might have been warmer if he had stayed at home. He was called to the Bar in 1821 and appointed advocate-fiscal of Ceylon (Sri Lanka) in the same year. He married Emma, daughter of William Blount, of Herefordshire, and their only child, Henry (who would go on to become Home Secretary and a viscount), was born in 1826. Henry Matthews the elder was appointed a judge in Ceylon in 1827 and died there in 1828.

PREFACE

The following pages may seem to require some apology, being, as they are, the transcript of a Journal written to amuse the hours of indisposition, without any idea of publication.

From these materials, I was induced, upon my return to England, to begin an account of my travels in a more serious and sustained style of composition; but my work was arrested by hearing, from those to whose judgment I have deferred, that I was labouring only to deprive my Journal of almost all that made it interesting in its original form;—like an indifferent artist, whose finished picture has often less to recommend it, than his first rough sketch from nature. Though this may be no excuse for publishing a Volume at all; yet it will at least serve to explain why that volume has appeared in its present shape.

In preparing it for the press, I have been less solicitous to add, than to take away: but in adhering to the original Diary, it was impossible to avoid frequent egotism; so that if I should be found on many occasions, uninteresting, or even impertinent, I fear I have nothing to plead in my excuse, but must throw myself entirely on the charitable consideration of the Reader.

ADVERTISEMENT TO THE SECOND EDITION

The immediate demand for a new edition of "The Diary of an Invalid," has furnished the author with a fresh inducement to endeavour, as far as the time would permit, to render it less unworthy of public attention.

Some passages have been altered, and some additions made; and, with a view to facilitate the task of perusal, the narrative has been broken into chapters; in order that the reader may be conducted by easier stages, from one end of the volume to the other.

Without interruptions of this kind, indeed, as Fielding says, the best narrative must overpower every reader; for nothing short of the everlasting watchfulness which Homer has ascribed to Jove himself, can he proof against a continued newspaper.

ADVERTISEMENT TO THE THIRD EDITION

The progress of a third edition through the press affords me another opportunity for revisal and correction, of which I would willingly make greater use, if I were not called away from the task of superintendence to a distant part of the globe. No man but he who has tried the experiment knows how difficult it is to be accurate. A Book of Travels must always be more or less a volume of inaccuracies; and I fear that had my endeavours to weed out such imperfections been much more minute and prolonged, enough would have still remained to exercise the patience and require the indulgence of the reader.

H.M.

London, 29*th October*, 1821.

I

LISBON

September 6th, 1817

I believe it is Horace Walpole who says,—quoting a remark of Gray,—that if any man would keep a faithful account of what he had seen and heard himself, it must, in whatever hands, prove an interesting one. The observation would perhaps be strictly true, if nothing were recorded but what really appeared at the time to be worth remembering; whereas, I believe, most writers of Journals keep their minds upon the stretch to insert as much matter as possible.

It is not without the fear of affording an exception to Mr. Gray's observation, that I begin a brief chronicle of what I may think, see, and hear, during the pilgrimage which I am about to undertake.

In obedience to medical advice, I have at last determined to set out upon a wild goose chase after health, and try, like honest Tristram Shandy, whether it be possible to run away from death;— and, in spite of Horace's hint of *Mors et fugacem persequitur virum*, I have this day completed the first stage of my journey.

Who has not experienced the bitter feelings with which one turns round on the last height that commands the last view of home? This farewell look was longer than usual, for in my state I can scarcely hope ever to see it again. But if, as Pope says,

> Life can little more supply
> Than just to look about us and to die,

I certainly have no time to lose.

7th

My flight has been necessarily too rapid to allow any time for the gratification of curiosity on this side of the water; and I have passed through Gloucester, Bath, and Exeter, without seeing more of those places than might be viewed from the coach window.

8th

All I saw of Plymouth was in rowing across the Hamoaze, in my way to Tor Point, from whence the mail-coach starts. The harbour, full of three-deckers, presents a glorious sight; which an Englishman cannot look at without feeling that inward glorying, and exultation of soul, which Longinus describes as the effect of the sublime. At Tor Point we found the mail-coach, and after a tedious drag, accomplished sixty-five miles in twelve hours.

Everything in this district savours of the sea. The inhabitants are a sort of amphibious race. The very coachman partook of the marine nature; and the slang peculiar to his calling was tempered with sea-phrases. The coach was to be under sail at such an hour, and it was promoted from the neuter to the feminine gender, with as much reason perhaps as the ship. At Falmouth I found my brother[1] waiting my arrival;—whose anxiety respecting my health, as it had led him to urge the trial of a voyage, determined him also to accompany me across the sea.

10th and 11th.

Agonies of deliberation upon my future plans.—

Too much deliberation is certainly worse than too little. This difficulty of deciding arises perhaps from the wish to combine advantages which are incompatible. A man is too apt to forget that in this world he cannot have everything. A choice is all that is left him. The world was all before me where to choose;—but the difficulty of the choice was increased by the arrival of a packet from Lord Viscount S., whose obliging kindness, of which I am happy to have an occasion of expressing my grateful sense, furnished me with passports and letters to various quarters;—for this, by enlarging the scope, embarrassed the decision of my plans.

At last I resolved to embark in the Malta packet, with the option of determining my bargain with the captain at the first port at which he might touch.

12th

Received a hasty summons at seven o'clock in the evening. The post from London brought orders that the Malta packet should carry out the Lisbon as well as the Mediterranean mails. In a moment all was "bustle! bustle!" On a fine starlight evening, the boatmen came to carry us and our baggage on board.—Kissed the last stone of granite, from which I stepped into the boat, with affection and regret. All the pains of parting were renewed at this moment;—but, luckily, at such a moment, one had scarcely leisure for the indulgence of any feelings. In a few minutes we were on board;—at ten o'clock the Princess Charlotte packet slipped from her moorings,—and we were fairly off.

13th

At daybreak we found ourselves off the Lizard, in a dead calm, with a heavy swell. Here began the horrors of sea-sickness!

Mind cannot conceive, nor imagination paint the afflicting agonies of this state of suffering. I am surprised the poets have made no use of it in their descriptions of the place of torment; for it might have furnished an excellent hint for improving the punishments of their hells. What are the waters of Tantalus, or the stone of Sisyphus, when compared with the throes of sea-sickness?

14th

Still in hell.—Here the poor devil is confined in a dark and dismal hole, six feet by three, below the level of the water; with the waves roaring in his ears—raging as it were to get at him—from which he is only protected by a single plank, and with the noises of Pandemonium all round him.

The depression and despondency of spirit which accompany this sickness deprive the mind of all its energy, and fill up the last trait in the resemblance, by taking away even the consolations of hope—that last resource of the miserable which comes to all—but the damned and the sea-sick.

16th

Gleam of comfort!—Began to be reconciled to the motion of the vessel. Though in the hour of sickness I had vowed, as is usual, that if fortune should once set me on shore at Lisbon, nothing should ever tempt me on shipboard again, I now began to contemplate a voyage to Malta with some degree of pleasure, and thought no more of my vow—than the Devil did of his sick resolution to turn Friar.

17th

A fresh breeze. Our progress has been hitherto most favourable. If Neptune himself had been shoving us along with his trident, we could not have proceeded more directly in our course. It must be confessed that a journey by water has some advantages over a journey by land. You move along without the jolting of ruts, and your progress is not impeded by the incidents of eating, drinking, and sleeping. But then, nothing can be less interesting than the dull uniformity of the sea scene. The view, when out of sight of land, is much less vast than I had expected. The panorama is limited to a little circle of water, seven miles all round us. Within the limits of this circle we move along, day after day, without the least variety of prospect or incident.

We have not yet encountered a single sail; and I had imagined that, in so beaten a track as we are pursuing, we should have met ships as thick as stage-coaches on the Bath road.

18th

The wind died away last night. A dead calm.—Got up to see the sun rise. Much has been said of the splendour of this sight at sea: but I confess I think it inferior to the same scene on shore. There is indeed plenty of the—"dread magnificence of Heaven,"—but it is all over in a moment. The sun braves the east, and carries the heavens by a *coup-de-main*; instead of approaching gradually, as he does on land, preceded by a troop of rosy messengers that prepare you for his arrival. One misses the charming variety of the terrestrial scene;—the wood and water;—the hill and dale;—the "babbling brook;"—the "pomp of groves and garniture of fields." At sea, too, all is inanimate; for the gambols of the fishes if they do gambol at their matins are out of sight; and it is the effect of morning on living sentient beings that constitutes its great charm. At sea, there is—"no song of earliest birds;"—no "warbling woodland;"—no "whistling plough-boy:"—nothing, in short, to awaken interest or sympathy. There is magnificence and splendour—but it is solitary splendour.

Let me rather see—"the morn, in russet mantle clad, walk o'er the dew of yon high *Malvern* hill." But, alas!—when am I likely to behold this sight again?

In the evening, I sat on the deck to enjoy the moonlight. If the sunrise be best seen on shore, the moonlight has the advantage at sea. At this season of repose, the absence of *living* objects is not felt. A lovely night.—The moon, in this latitude, has a silvery brightness which we never see in England.—It was a night for romance;—such as Shakspeare describes, when Troilus sighed his soul to absent Cressid;—the sea, calm and tranquil as the bosom of innocence;—not a breath of air;—while the reflection of the moon and stars, and the gentle rippling of the water against the sides of the vessel, completed the magic of the scene.

Sat with my face turned towards England, absorbed in the reflections which it is the effect of such a night to encourage;—and indulged in that secret devotion of the heart, which, at such seasons particularly, the heart loves to pay to the absent objects of its affections.

19th
A foul wind. A poor little bird, of a species unknown in England, alighted on the steers-man's shoulder, quite spent with fatigue,

and allowed itself to be taken. Probably making its way from America to Portugal. To-day, saw a sail, for the first time.

20th

The foul wind still continues. Here we are within a hundred miles of Lisbon, and yet without a hope of getting there, till it shall please the wind to change. I remember Lord Bacon says, "'Tis a strange thing, that in sea voyages, where there is nothing to be seen but sky and sea, men should make diaries." But it is a strange thing to me the Viscount of St. Alban's should not perceive, that where there is nothing to be *seen*, there is little *done*; and that a man must needs scribble in his own defence, though it be but to register the winds, and chronicle the clouds.

In adjusting the balance between land and water carriage, I had till to-day been in some doubt; but four-and-twenty hours of beating to windward have put the question beyond all doubt; for though you may *move along* without fatigue, it is terribly fatiguing to *stand still*;—especially with the wind in your teeth. So long, therefore, as the wind "bloweth where it listeth," I believe we must agree that old Cato's repentance was well founded.

Sunday, *21st*

To-day we have again a breeze in our favour. All the crew are busily employed. This demand for hands prevents the celebration of Church Service, which was read by the Captain last Sunday.

The deck of a ship, out of sight of land, with nothing above but the—"brave o'erhanging firmament,"—with its—"majestical roof fretted with golden fire,"—is better calculated to inspire feelings of devotion, than the proudest temple that was ever dedicated to the worship of the Supreme Being.

22nd

Once more welcomed the sight of land! Indeed, I believe we did catch a glimpse of Cape Finisterre in our passage, but it might have been a "camel" or a "whale;"—this morning, however, the rock of Lisbon rose with clouded majesty within a few miles of us.

At eleven o'clock we fired a gun, and hoisted a signal for a pilot. A number of boats immediately put off to us, and the quickest sailer obtained the job.

Our first interview with the natives has not prepossessed us in their favour. From an uncouth clumsy boat we have taken in a meagre swarthy fellow, with a face as red as Kean's in Othello.

He soon gave us a sample of the choleric disposition of his nation. The captain seemed to doubt his skill, and sending below for his pistols, he intimated to the pilot that if he should get his ship a-ground, he would, on that account, shoot him through the head. The fellow was transported with indignation at this menace; and, though alone amongst strangers, he drew his knife, and threatened to revenge himself for the insult.

We crept along the shore at a snail's pace, and did not anchor within the bar of the harbour till ten at night.

23d

Beautiful day. Sailed up the Tagus. The view is certainly magnificent; but it has, I think, been over-rated by travellers. He who has seen London from Greenwich Park, may survey without any great astonishment the capital of Portugal. The finest feature is the river, compared with which the Thames sinks into insignificance. Each side has its peculiar beauties, and I doubt whether the left bank, with its vineyards and orange groves, does not attract the eye as much as the right, on which the town stands.

The entire absence of smoke is a striking novelty to an English eye, and at first gives an idea that the town must be without inhabitants.

Being tired of the sea, I resolved to stay at Lisbon;—almost the only place for which I had no passport. Some little difficulties occurred in consequence;—but these were soon removed; and after a broiling walk in search of lodgings, we subsided at last in Reeves's hotel, Rua do Prior, Buenos Ayres;—an excellent house, kept by an Englishman, full of cleanliness and comfort;—and these are qualities which one appreciates at their just value, after a walk through the streets of Lisbon.

Though travellers may have exaggerated the beauties of the view, I have seen no description that does justice to the indescribable nastiness of the town. I have spoken of the view from the river as *magnificent*, but I believe the true epithet would have been *imposing*; for it is mere deceit and delusion: the *prestige* vanishes at once on landing; and the gay and glittering city proves to be a painted sepulchre. Filth and beastliness assault you at every turn—in their most loathsome and disgusting shapes. In yielding to first impressions, one is generally led to exaggerate; but the abominations of Lisbon are incapable of exaggeration.

24th and 25th

Jaunted about Lisbon by land and water carriage. To *walk* about the streets is scarcely possible for an invalid. A clumsy sort of carriage on two wheels, driven by a postilion, with a pair of mules, is to be hired by the day, or the half day;—but not at a cheaper rate than one might hire a coach in London. A good idea of these carriages will be formed from the prints in the old editions of Gil Blas, since whose time no improvement seems to have taken place in vehicular architecture.

I have already experienced the truth of Mr. Bowdler's remark,—"that in Lisbon, under a scorching sun, you are constantly exposed to a cold wind." The Portuguese guard against this by a large great coat, worn loose like a mantle, with hanging *sinecure* sleeves, and which they wrap round them when, in turning a corner, they encounter the wind. The use of this sweltering surtout, in some shape or other, is universal, even in the hottest weather;—but the remedy is perhaps worse than the disease.

There is something in the appearance of Lisbon that seems to portend an earthquake; and, instead of wondering that it was once visited by such a calamity, I am rather disposed to consider its daily preservation as a standing miracle. Repeated shocks have been felt of late years; and to an earthquake it may look, as its natural death. From the vestiges which the indolence of the people has allowed to remain, one might fancy the last convulsion had taken place but a few months. Many ruins are now standing just as the earthquake left them.—Gorgeous Palaces and solemn Temples now totter in crumbling ruins, an awful monument of the fatal wreck. There are some streets, built since the earthquake, with trottoirs on each side, which make a handsome appearance; and, with any industry on the part of the people, the whole town might be made one of the most cleanly in Europe;—the undulating nature of the ground being so well calculated for carrying away all impurities.

At present, the only scavengers are the dogs, which roam about the streets in hordes, without homes or masters, seeking what they may devour. And indeed, where all sorts of filth and offal are thrown into the street, till they shall be carried by the next shower into the Tagus, the dogs are not without their use; and the legislature has not been wholly inattentive to their accommodation. There is an old law obliging certain trades to keep a vessel of water at the doors of their houses for the refreshment of these freebooters. Canine madness is, I am told, almost unknown here; and it is well that it is so. Upon the whole, the dogs behave very well,—except to one another; but it is up-hill work to a new settler, for he must fight his way. They are *strict preservers*;—if any dog is caught out of the limits of his own manor, he is proceeded against as a wilful trespasser without any *notice*.

26th

Rose at daybreak, and set out in a cabriolet with a stout pair of mules for Cintra. The scarcity of gold, and the depreciation of their vile paper money, exposed me to the inconvenience of carrying about a travelling treasury of silver crusadoes in a green baize bag, heavy with the weight of 150,000 *rees*. How rich this sounds!—but alas, the high-sounding sesterces of the Romans are nothing to the paltry pomposity of Portuguese arithmetic,—for the *ree* is little more than the fourth of a farthing.

The road to Cintra carried me near to the great aqueduct of Alcantara,—the work of Manuel de Maya, in 1738,—which

stretches across a wide and deep valley, by a range of thirty-five
arches. The centre one of these is said to be the highest arch in
the world, and the view from the ground, looking upwards at it,
is beyond measure grand and imposing. The width is 107 French
feet, and the height 230. I paced the whole range of the aqueduct,
upon which there is a fine stone walk of about three-quarters of
a mile, protected by a parapet. This vast work, while it remains
a monument of the industry of the Portuguese, would lead one
to believe that they were—as the ancients also are supposed
to have been—ignorant of the first principles of hydraulics,
which have every where else superseded the necessity of such
stupendous structures. Still, in point of architectural grandeur and
magnificence, it is a just source of national pride; and in a country
where so few great undertakings, unconnected with religion, are
brought to perfection, it stands like the giant Gulliver amongst
the pigmies of Lilliput. Apropos of giants;—whole armies of
windmills are seen here on every side;—and it is well observed
by Semple, that Don Quixote's mistake, which is too absurd if
judged by English windmills, is rendered probable by the sight of
these, which look like good sturdy giants of ten feet high.

Great attention seems every where paid to the preservation
of water in this country. Fountains of marble, of neat and often
elegant architecture, with large troughs, are constructed on the
roadside, for the use of the traveller and his beasts. My postilion,
however, having accomplished one-half of his journey, seemed
to think that his mules, or himself or both, for they fared alike,
required something better than water; so he stopped at the half
way house, with *"Vinho do Porto, Carcavelos, Colares, &c. &c.,"*
inscribed on its front, and there fed himself and his beasts with
bread soaked in wine. By virtue of this restorative we contrived to
reach Cintra; having consumed nearly five hours in a stage of not
more than sixteen English miles;—though it must be confessed
that the road was so rough, that greater speed might have been
disagreeable.

I can add little to the warm tints of description that have
been so justly lavished upon Cintra, the beauties of which are

heightened by the contrast of the barren and uninteresting country all around it. I should compare it with Malvern;—but to the heights of Malvern must be added some hundred feet of perpendicular rock. The summits are composed of huge masses of stone, which seem to have been thrown up in some great convulsion of nature. On one of the peaks are the ruins of an old Moorish castle, the bath of which still remains in excellent preservation, and shows how attentive to cleanliness these Moors were. On the highest point of the ridge is the convent of Penha, the existence of which, on such a spot, is so wonderful, that I am surprised the monks have not attributed it to the same kind of assistance which brought our Lady's Chapel to Loretto. It commands a most extensive prospect;—but however superior Cintra may be to Malvern in itself, the view from it is much less pleasing. Instead of the fertile valleys of Worcestershire, the eye has nothing to repose on, but a dreary and barren waste. The village of Cintra stands half-way up—nestled as it were in the bosom of the hill—amidst groves of pine and cork orange and lemon trees, with a profusion of geraniums and evergreens of all kinds. This is the very region of romance. The sun is less hot, and the wind less cold, than at Lisbon. The mildness of the evening is charming, and there is neither damp nor chill to prevent your indulging in all the luxuries of a moonlight walk.

27th and 28th

Fell in with Mr. Ward, Chargé d'Affaires, an old Cambridge acquaintance. Excursion to Penha. The convent, high as it is, was not out of the reach of French rapacity. They robbed the church and the altar of every thing worth taking. All they spared was a plated candle-stick, and the ornaments of the Virgin:—and here I suspect it was not their *piety* that restrained them—for the Virgin's habiliments have not the appearance of being very costly. She wears a flaxen powdered wig, and her diamond ornaments savour strongly of Birmingham jewellery.

Upon my return to my hotel, I found two old Etonians waiting for me, who, having heard from Mr. Ward of the arrival of an old schoolfellow at Cintra, were kind enough to come and claim acquaintance with me.

Dined, and passed a pleasant evening with one of them—Colonel Ross, of the Portuguese service. Nearly twenty years had elapsed since he left school, but we could just make out that we had been contemporaries. Without acquaintanceship, however, there is a sort of freemasonry among Etonians, which, I have ever found, disposes them to be friendly to one another, whenever they may happen to meet:—and it is, indeed, a pleasant thing to meet, wherever you go, with some face that you are acquainted with, without the ceremony of introduction, from the common relationship of schoolfellow.

29th, 30th, and 31st

Still at Cintra. My land-lady, Mrs. Dacey, an old Irish woman, above eighty years old, is now quite blind; but she remembers perfectly the great earthquake, and describes the horrors of that awful event. Her house is generally full of holiday-folks from Lisbon; especially from Saturday till Monday. Cintra is to Lisbon what Richmond is to London; and the Lisbon cockneys are glad to escape from their counting-houses for a few hours of fresh air. The accommodations of her house are good, and the table d'hôte excellent. The charge for board and lodging is 2,000 *rees* per day—about eleven shillings English. This does not include wine, so that Cintra is not cheaper than Cheltenham.

A wolf sometimes makes its appearance here;—and one has lately been very mischievous.

Walked over the Royal Palace. They show the room where Sebastian held his last council, before he set out on that fatal expedition, from which he has not yet returned: but the Portuguese have not abandoned all hopes of seeing him again; and the lower orders expect him with about as much confidence as the Jews expect their Messiah. Hard by is the palace of the Marquis Marialva, famous for the Cintra convention. The ink which was spilt on this memorable occasion is still visible on the floor—scattered, as it is said, by Junot, in an ebullition of spleen, when he put his name to the instrument:—but surely *he* had not the most cause for vexation

Returned in the evening to Lisbon. Cattle much used here for draught. Met abundance of ox-wains—the wheels of a singular construction;—circular pieces of board, solid and entire, though very narrow. The creaking of these is intolerable, and the noise as disagreeable as the sharpening of a saw.

Thursday, 1st October
Made a bargain with my landlord, to board and lodge me for 25 *crusadoes* a week—about 3*l.* 10*s.* English. For this I have three rooms, and two meals per day, but no wine. The cheapest thing in Lisbon is the fruit. Grapes are bought at three half-pence a pound, quinces at a shilling a hundred, and other things in proportion; but the flavour of the fruit in general is not equal to our own. Because Nature has done so much, these lazy rascals seem determined to do nothing. Peaches, nectarines, and apricots are left to take their chance, without pruning or training. Grapes are treated with more care, and melons are very abundant. One sees them piled up in heaps in the streets, and sold out retail by the slice.

Walked in the gardens of the Convent dos Necessidades, of great extent, and some beauty. At least they afford shade and retirement, and—what is extraordinary in Lisbon—you are admitted for nothing.

Made inquiries in vain for a vessel bound to Italy. To contemplate a residence here for the winter would be enough to make a healthy man sick; and the *désagrémens* of the place strike with exaggerated impression on the irritable nerves of an invalid. There is not a room in the hotel where I am that has a fire in it, except the kitchen. A grate indeed is a rarity in Lisbon. In winter this inconvenience must be severely felt; it is obviated, as well as it can be, by a brazier of coal placed in the middle of the room.—So much for comfort:—then, the disposition of the people towards us offers no inducement to stay. There is no doubt of the fact, that neither the generosity and good faith of the British, nor the blood

profusely shed in defence of their country, have endeared us to
our Portuguese allies. They dislike us mortally. How is this to he
explained? Is it that malicious sentiment of envy, which seems to
have overspread the whole Continent, at the prodigious elevation
to which England has arisen: or is it the repulsive, unaccom-
modating manners which an Englishman is too apt to carry with
him into all countries, which make even a benefit from him less
binding than the winning urbanity by which the French contrive
to render confiscation and robbery palatable?

The Portuguese are full of discontent; and their long intimacy
with us has spread far and wide amongst them the lights of
information. Indeed, it is no wonder that they should be
discontented, abandoned as they are by their sovereign, who has
converted the mother-country into a province, from which men and
money are drawn for the support of his transatlantic dominions;
whilst the command of their national army, and the principal
situations of power and profit, are in the hands of foreigners. The
greatest unwillingness now prevails among the soldiers to embark
for America. I have seen some hundred deserters chained together,
and marched down to the bank of the river.

2d.

Drank tea with Mr. M——, and from thence went to see the
funeral procession of one of the Members of the Regency, who
was understood to be chief of the anti-British party; but he
has probably left his mantle behind.—Saw nothing.—Heard
discharges of artillery in abundance, and this was all.—Nothing
can be more dreary than the streets of Lisbon at night. No part of
the town is regularly lighted. The Virgin and the Saints engross
the few lamps which here and there give a gleam of light. Amongst
dirt, dogs, and darkness, it is easy to imagine how it fares with the
stranger groping his way through the streets at night.

The police of Lisbon, as far as it affects the suppression
of disturbances in the streets, and the maintenance of public
decency, is extremely good. One is struck with the entire absence
of all external symptoms of the vices and immoralities that

might be expected to prevail in a metropolis, and sea-port, in this southern latitude. These regulations, though they may not be sufficient to counteract the vicious propensities of human nature, must be of some use; and I think we should do well to imitate them in our own metropolis: for—"how oft the sight of means to do ill deeds makes ill deeds done!" Thus far the police is good; but for the prevention of crimes, or for inquiry into the perpetrators of them, it is of little service. The lower orders are in the habit of carrying a large clasp knife, with the open blade concealed under the right sleeve, and, as it may be supposed, assassinations are by no means uncommon.

The Inquisition is still an object of mysterious dread. And, truly, the sight of its gloomy prison—*triplici circumdata muro*—is sufficient to suggest the idea of that Infernal Tribunal of which *Tisiphone* kept the gate, and *Rhadamanthus* administered the laws:

> —stat ferrea turris ad auras;
> Tisiphoneque sedens, pallâ succincta cruentâ,
> Vestibulum insomnis servat noctesque diesque.
> Hinc exaudiri *gemitus*, et sæva sonare
> *Verbera*;—tum *stridor ferri* tractæque *catanæ.*
> Gnossius hæc Rhadamanthus habet durissima regna,
> Castigatque, auditque dolos, *subigitque fateri.*

A young man of considerable fortune disappeared about a year ago, and it was supposed for some time that he was murdered. A large reward was offered for the discovery of his body; but the river was dragged, and every well and hole in the town explored without success. It is the opinion of many that he is now immured in the prisons of the Inquisition. By-the-by, I have not yet mentioned the priests;—and for aught I know, they are more numerous than the dogs. Doghood and Priesthood are certainly the most thriving trades in Lisbon. It is an humiliating spectacle to see the abject superstition in which the people are sunk and brutified. As the best things, by being corrupted, become the worst, so here Christianity exhibits a system of idolatry much more revolting than the old Pagan worship. One cannot help feeling some regard for the ancient mythology, which is as amusing as Mother Bunch, illustrated and adorned too, as it was, by such divine statues. Besides—the heathens had not the means of knowing better; but who that has read the New Testament can tolerate the contemptible mummeries which are here practised under the name of religion? The religion of the heathens was as superior to this, as the statues of Phidias excel in beauty the tawdry and disgusting images to which these poor creatures bow down with such humble prostrations.

In the meantime, however, the priests thrive and fatten. I will not say, with Semple, that they are the *only* fat people in Portugal, but I will vouch for their universal *embonpoint*.

This to be sure is only the outward and visible sign;—but it tends to give credibility to the tales in vogue, of the sloth and good cheer, the licentious feastings and debaucheries, which take place in the convents, or rather the castles of indolence, in which these portly monks are lodged. The French, who hated a monk and the smell of a monk, as much as Walter Shandy, that is—"worse than all the devils of hell"—while they bayoneted the dogs without mercy, made the monks lay aside the crucifix to brandish the besom, and fairly set them to sweep the streets; but the French are gone—and the monks and the dogs have resumed their usual occupations.

The nunneries enjoy a better reputation, and are said to be filled with sincerely pious women, who have been led, from perhaps a mistaken sense of religion, to bury themselves in the unprofitable seclusion of a convent. This is, however, a delicate question, and I leave it in the uncertainty in which it has been left by the sage in Rasselas.

3d, 4th, and 5th
Passed over to the left bank of the river, which, in the broadest part, is about four miles across. The view from the opposite side is very beautiful; and from the absence of smoke, the whole of

the town in all its details is distinctly visible. The indolence of the people is most striking;—you can scarcely get a shopkeeper to give himself the trouble to serve you. It pervades all classes:—arts, science, literature—every thing languishes at Lisbon.

The Portuguese are worthy of better things; but they are bowed down by a despotic government, and hood-winked by a besotted superstition. The priests seem to fear that the growing spirit of inquiry will destroy the foundations of their power; and therefore they do all they can to keep the people in a state of ignorance, in which they are supported by the Inquisition, which prohibits the circulation of all writings tending to excite religious investigation.

The government, on the other hand, takes equal care that no political disquisitions shall be introduced to disturb the quiet slavery to which the people seem at present constrained to submit. The suppression of the late conspiracy will contribute to strengthen the hands of government; and the indolence of the people may help to continue the present state of things some time longer;—but a change must take place sooner or later.

6th

Every thing warns me to depart. I have to-day been attending as pall-bearer at the funeral of one of my fellow passengers from England: He was in the last stage of a decline, and might as well have been suffered to lay his bones in his own country. The funeral of a young countryman in a foreign land must always be an affecting ceremony; and my own situation perhaps—for philosophers assure us that self is the foundation of sympathy—made it still more impressive. It may be my turn next:—*mea res agitur, paries cum proximus ardet.*—He lodged next door.

The English burying-ground is pleasantly situated, and well shaded with fine cypresses. I looked in vain for the grave of Fielding. They do indeed pretend to point out the spot; but to the reproach of the English factory be it said, there is no stone to indicate where his remains lie.

It does really concern the honour of the nation that some monument should be erected to his memory; and it is a pity that Mr. Canning, during his embassy to Lisbon, was not solicited to prepare a suitable inscription; whose truly classical pen would have done full justice to the subject.

After the ceremony, went to the church of St. Roque, which contains some fine specimens of mosaic. The altar is surrounded by a railing of verd antique, and displays a profusion of porphyry, lapis lazuli, amethyst, &c. &c.

The friars would have you believe they contrived to persuade the French that the immense candle sticks, which are really silver gilt, were made of brass.

7th to 12th

Still in Lisbon;—though daily becoming more impatient to leave it. Amongst the minor plagues of the place, I ought to mention the flies. The rooms are full of them. They attack you in countless myriads and their annoyance is intolerable. With what different feelings would one read the story of Domitian, in England and Lisbon!—There I sympathized with the flies; here with Domitian;—whose hostility seems very justifiable, and whose expertness is the daily subject of my emulation.

13th

Visited the botanical gardens, where there is a museum, containing a good collection of curiosities in all the departments of nature. At the entrance of the garden, are placed two military statues, of rude and uncouth workmanship. These were dug up some years ago at Montalegre, and are supposed to belong to a period anterior to the Carthaginian conquest of Spain. They afford a curious and interesting specimen of the first essays of a barbarous people in the art of sculpture, to perpetuate the memory of their chiefs.

Went to mass, where I liked nothing but the music. There certainly seems to be one convenience in the Catholic worship:— for those who attend might, with Friar John in Rabelais, compare their prayers to stirrup leathers—which are made short or long at pleasure.

Took leave of my brother, whose kindness has been unremitting, and who this evening went on board the packet upon his return to England.

14th

Found a ship bound to Leghorn,—the Fanny,—a small trading vessel, of about 140 tons burthen. The captain asked me twenty guineas for my passage and would fain have persuaded me that his demand was just. I knew it to be too much by half, and when he saw me resolved not to give more than ten, he acceded to my terms with scarcely a decent demur.

I am to find my own sea-stock and bedding.

15th and 16th

Busily employed in preparations for my voyage. Mr. Ward kindly sent me his boat to make use of in conveying my various stores on board.

Took a farewell stroll through Lisbon.—Of the Portuguese women I have said nothing, though I have seen some fine specimens of face and figure. It is in expression of countenance and gracefulness of carriage that their charm consists, for to complexional beauty they have no claims. The hair is profusely ornamented with gold combs, artificial flowers, or precious stones of various colours. The women in walking the streets never wear a hat or bonnet, but cover the head with a white handkerchief. And, let the weather be ever so hot, an immense cloak, or rather great coat—often of red cloth—is thrown over their shoulders.

As I was returning from my stroll, I sat down to rest on the steps of a statue; but was hurried away by observing a man ridding himself of a numerous retinue of vermin on the other side of the pedestal—and cracking them by dozens on the steps.

And so much for the Lusitanian, or—as it might with more propriety be called—the Lousitanian Metropolis. I shall quit it

without one feeling of regret. In fact, to remain in it is impossible:
—I am fairly stunk out.

1. The Rev. AM.

II

PISA AND FLORENCE

Friday, 17th
My fat landlord, Mr. Reeves, whom I strongly recommend to all visitors to Lisbon, entered my room before day-break, to announce that the Fanny was making preparations for weighing anchor. Went on board as the sun rose. We weighed anchor immediately; and with a fine breeze from the northward, and the tide in our favour, glided rapidly down the Tagus.

18th and 19th
Sick as a dog!

20th
Mounted the deck with a firm step.—Passed over the scene of the battle of Trafalgar.—To-morrow is the anniversary of the death of Nelson.—Sung *Rule Britannia*, with enthusiasm; as the most appropriate requiem to the memory of the immortal Admiral.

About dinner-time we arrived at the mouth of the Strait, or, as the sailors call it, the Gut of Gibraltar.—The view strikingly grand. The African side much more bold and lofty than the European. Attempted to sketch the rock of Gibraltar, which is less remarkable for its height, than for its singularly detached situation, which has all the appearance of an island in rough weather.

We passed up the Strait with a fresh breeze; and I do not remember to have ever seen a more magnificent prospect. As we sailed onwards, the view was enlivened by constant variety;—the rock of Gibraltar changing its appearance as we shifted our ground, and caught it in different points of view.

21st
To-day at noon saw Cape de Gata. Flew onwards on the pinions of the finest breeze imaginable. I find I have committed a great mistake in the laying in of my sea-stock. Wishing to try the effect of an abstemious diet, I resolved to compel an adherence to it, and therefore contented myself with a goat to furnish me with milk, confining the remainder of my stores to biscuit, rice, potatoes, cocoa, and arrow root. I mention this to warn any invalid who may chance to read my Journal from following my example. For milk will be found of little use, unless a man have the stomach of a sailor; and the want of something in the shape of broth or soup will be severely felt. Though my poor Nanny is a most entertaining companion on deck, she is of no further use. Her society, however, is worth a good deal. She is an old sailor, and so accustomed to the sea, that the voyage has not at all diminished her supply of milk.

My only other fellow passenger is a Genoese—the supercargo of the vessel;—between whom and the Captain I am obliged to act as interpreter.

22d
Out of sight of land. The last point we saw was Cape Palos. The southern coast of Spain presents an inaccessible barrier of mountains covered with snow.

Our voyage had hitherto been most prosperous;—but soon after I retired to bed, a sudden squall came on, and the wind shifted round to the east ward. The squall was accompanied with thunder, lightning, rain, and the usual symptoms of a storm. Whilst all was confusion on the deck, the cabin-window immediately behind my berth was driven in, and we shipped a sea, that fairly washed me out of bed. The supercargo joined me in roaring out lustily for help;—for, to say the truth, I believe we both thought that we were going to the bottom. The fact was, that, in consequence of the very favourable weather, we had neglected to put up the dead lights; and the squall came on so suddenly, that before the sails could be taken in, the ship was driven backwards against the heavy sea, which had been rolling us along since we entered the Mediterranean.

It was some time before any one could be spared from the deck to attend to the state of affairs below; and if, in the mean time, we had shipped another sea, the consequence would have been more serious.

As it was, my situation was sufficiently deplorable; and my only choice was between salt-water in the cabin, or rain on deck.—Passed the remainder of the night like a half-drowned rat.—The squall soon subsided; and the wind returned to its old quarter in our favour.

23rd

Breeze still steady. Fine weather, but cold. The sea of a fine dark indigo. Quantities of fish sporting about the vessel. A strange sail to the southward of a suspicious appearance, which seemed to savour of Algiers.

24th

I begin to suspect that all I shall gain by my voyage will be the conviction that a man who travels so far from home, in pursuit of health, travels on a fool's errand. The crosses he must meet on his road will do him more injury, than he can hope to compensate by any change of climate. I am told that a sea-voyage, to be of any benefit to an invalid, should be made in a frigate, or other vessel of equal size; but of this I doubt;—for all comfort is so entirely out of the question at sea, that I think the difference of as little importance as the choice of a silken or hempen rope would be to a man at the gallows. I am sure, however, that the fatigue and discomfort of such a little cock-boat as this, is much the same thing as if one were to be tossed in a blanket during one-half of the day, and thrown into a pigsty for the remainder.

I nunc, et ventis animam committe dolato
Confisus ligno, digitis à morte remotus
Quatuor, aut septem—si sit latissima teda.

26th
Saw land again at a distance on the western coast of Corsica.

27th
The wind, which had hitherto been blowing steadily in our favour, now slackened. At noon we were becalmed, with a very heavy swell. A storm came suddenly on. While we were standing on the deck, the ship received a violent blow on the stern, which threw the captain, the supercargo, and myself, on our faces. It is such an accident as this, according to the captain, that, in rough weather, sometimes sends a ship in a moment to the bottom. The boat was knocked away, and we heard another crash in the cabin. It was a repetition of the affair of Wednesday, with this difference, that on this occasion it was on the supercargo's side. As I saw his bed brought up to be dried, I never felt so strongly Rochefoucault's meaning, in his memorable maxim about our *neighbours' misfortunes*. This storm ended as the last, and the wind returned to its old quarter in our rear with greater violence than before; and we made all sail for Leghorn.

Tuesday, 28th
Italiam! Italiam! At eight o'clock this morning we were within eighteen miles of Leghorn near the little island of Gorgona, with Elba on our right, and the smiling land of Italy spread out before us. Achates himself could not have been more rejoiced than I was at this sight; and it is not the "*humilem Italiam*" which Æneas describes, but the high ground behind Leghorn, with the bold outline of the Apennines in the background.

If the wind had continued three hours longer, we should have breakfasted at Leghorn. But, within sight of port, the wind has chopped about, and, for the first time since we left Lisbon, we have begun to tack. The view is, however, full of interest, and

I have no right to complain of the wind, considering what a galloping voyage we have made.

29th

After tacking against a foul wind throughout the whole of last night, we entered the road of Leghorn at nine o'clock this morning, having completed the passage from Lisbon in twelve days.

A boat from the Health-office hailed us immediately, and we were ordered to perform a quarantine of ten days.

Thus it seems that, before we enjoy the delights of an Italian Paradise, we are to be subjected to a purgatory of purification; such as Virgil describes:

> Aliæ panduntur inanes
> Suspensæ ad ventos:
> Donec longa dies, perfecto temporis orbe,
> Concretam exemit labem, purumque reliquit.

Our passage has been so short, that these ten days might well be added to the account, without exciting much impatience—but it is always difficult to submit quietly to unnecessary restraint.

30th

Weighed anchor, and were permitted to go within the mole into the harbour. The last ten days of all quarantines are performed here; and as we had a clean bill of health, and there was, in fact, no real ground for putting us under quarantine at all, we proceeded at once to this destination. Two officers of the Health-Office were put on board to prevent all intercourse with us. As soon as we were safely moored within the harbour, a boat full of musicians made its appearance under the cabin-window, and we were serenaded with "Rule Britannia," and "God save the King." It is the custom to celebrate in this manner the arrival of every new comer, and to welcome him with the national airs of the country to which he belongs. A few hours afterwards, an American came to an anchor very near us, and we had then to listen to *Yankee Doodle's March*, with some other airs not at all tuneable to an English ear. This serenading is probably the remains of an old custom, when a voyage was considered an adventure of great danger, and the return of a ship an event worthy of extraordinary celebration.

Boats are constantly plying with supplies of all sorts of provisions from the shore; and it is perhaps worth while to fast for ten days, in order to enjoy in perfection the true relish of beef.

Saturday, 1st Nov. to 7th
The days of quarantine pass heavily along. The value of liberty can only be known by those who have been in confinement for:

> It so falls out
> That what we have we prize not to the worth,
> While we enjoy it; but when 'tis lack'd and lost,
> Why, then we rack the value; then we find
> The virtue, that possession would not shew us
> Whiles it was ours.—

The quarantine laws, like most others, though originally intended for the general good, come at last to be perverted to private purposes. This is the history of all human institutions. Our quarantine has been manifestly a mere matter of form. Whenever there is any apprehension of infection, the suspected ship is obliged to remain in the open roads. But here we are with a multitude of vessels of all nations packed together, higgledy-piggledy, as close as sheep in a pen;—a rare precaution against infection. The true cause of these strict regulations, I believe, is the emolument derived from them by the Health-Office. A number of men are thus kept in employment at the expense of those whom they are appointed to guard;—for our Captain is obliged to pay his gaolers. In the mean time, we poor travellers suffer. These officers prevent all communication between the natives and us, and between the inhabitants of one ship and another, though we absolutely touch our next-door neighbour.

As a proof of the rigorous observance of these regulations,—a fowl from our ship flew into the rigging of that alongside us; and it was determined—after a grave debate—that the fowl must remain where it was, till the quarantine of our neighbour had expired.

Our captain, who was tolerable as long as we were at sea, now, in a state of idleness, proves a most unmanageable brute.

Letters from my old friend C., who promised to meet me at Pisa.

Saturday, 8th

At last came the day of our deliverance. Johnson says, that no man ever does any thing for the last time, without some feeling of regret. The last day of quarantine might form an exception to this observation. Early this morning the boat of the Health-Office came alongside:—the crew were mustered on the deck;—and the examination was begun and concluded in a moment. Thus ended the farce of quarantine. I lost no time in getting myself and my baggage on shore; and after a short ramble through the streets of Leghorn, hired a cabriolet to carry me to Pisa.

Perhaps the most interesting sight in Leghorn is the English burying-ground. Smollett was buried here, affording in his death, as in his writings, a parallel to Fielding;—both being destined to find their last home in a foreign land.

Excellent road from Leghorn to Pisa, through the fertile plain of the Arno. At the gate of Pisa, I first encountered the restraints of continental travelling, in the examination of my passport and baggage.

Found my friend C. at the "Tre Donzelle." Passed a long evening in chatting over the tales of former times.—Disgusted at the mode of salute in use amongst Italians. They kiss each other in the street—first, on one cheek, then on the other, and lastly, lip to lip.

Pisa has a gloomy and deserted appearance, as if it had once seen better days. The inn—cold and comfortless—with brick floors, and without carpets.

The cathedral—a venerable pile of party-coloured marble. The first impression of this style of building is unfavourable; but this may be the mere effect of novelty. One seldom likes what one is not accustomed to.

The leaning tower at first sight is quite terrific, and exceeds expectation. There is, I believe, no doubt of the real history of this tower. The foundation-ground gave way during the progress of the building, and the architect completed his work in the direction thus accidentally given to it. Accordingly, we find in the construction of the upper part, that the weight is disposed in a way to support the equilibrium.

Upon the whole, it is a very elegant structure; and the general effect is so pleasing, that—like Alexander's wry neck—it might well bring leaning into fashion amongst all the towers in Christendom.

9th

Finding I could not establish myself immediately *en pension*, I resolved to accept C.'s offer of a seat in his carriage to Florence.

Whenever the Grand Duke of Tuscany moves about his dominions, all the post-horses on his route are put under *taboo* for his exclusive use.

Unluckily for us, he was to-day on his road from Pisa to Florence. It was necessary, therefore, to hire a *Vetturino*, who undertakes to transport your carriage, in a certain time, for a certain sum.

Left Pisa at noon. Soon after our departure the rain came down in torrents. The horses knocked up; and the vetturino was half-drowned. The post-master refused to let us have horses;—and as he had no beds to offer us—there was every prospect of our passing the night in the carriage. S., who was with us, smoked his pipe:—I swore in English;—and C. out-swore, out-argued, and out-joked the post-master and all his crew in their native tongue. At last, by dint of his arguments and humour, for which the Italians have a keen relish, the difficulties were got over; though we did not reach Florence till after midnight.

10th to 20th

Travellers generally exaggerate most outrageously;—but they
have hardly done justice to Florence. It may well be called—Fair
Florence.—The Arno runs through it with a turbid, but rapid,
and therefore cheerful, stream, forming as it were the middle of
the principal street. Between the lines of houses and the river
is a broad quay, serving for carriages and foot-passengers. Four
bridges at short distances connect the two sides of the street, and
add to its beauty. The absence of smoke, and the clearness of the
atmosphere, enable you to see the surrounding country distinctly,
from all parts of the town.

The views up and down the river are beautiful; and the
immediate environs are ornamented with undulating shrubberies
and villas without number.

The prospect from these environs is rich beyond description.
Florence is laid out at your feet—and the Arno winds through a
golden and fertile plain, till the scene is closed by the bold and
rugged range of the Apennines—

gaudetque nivali
Vertice se attollens Pater Apenninus ad auras.

Such is the first view of Florence;—and within its walls is all
that can conduce to gratify the senses, or delight the imagination.
The wonders of ancient and modern art are all around you, and
furnish an inexhaustible field of occupation and amusement.

Schneiderf's hotel is a magnificent establishment; and though
Florence may be better calculated for a summer residence, yet it is
well provided with winter comforts;—and the comforts of a place
are as important to an invalid as the climate.

The daily charge at Schneiderf's, if you have only one
room—which in Italy may serve for all purposes—is seven pauls
for lodging, ten pauls for dinner, and four pauls for breakfast—
altogether about ten shillings English. For this, you have a good
room, an excellent dinner of two courses, with a dessert, and as
much of the wine of the country as you like.—If a man wishes to

drink genuine liquor—let him always drink the common wine of the country in which he happens to be. Mould candles are also thrown into the bargain;—if you burn wax you pay for them, and an extra charge is made for fire. The dinner alone in England would cost more than the whole daily expenditure.

The English abound so much in Florence, that a traveller has little occasion for any other language. At all the hotels, there is some one connected with the house that can speak English. English shops abound with all sorts of knickknacks—from Reading sauce to Woodstock gloves;—and the last new novels stare you in the face at the libraries.

The first thing every man goes to see in Florence is—the Gallery. It is thrown open to the public every day except Sundays and holydays, which last, by-the-by, occur too often in Italy, to the great interruption of business. The attendants are always civil and obliging, and without any interested motive, for notices are affixed to the doors to request that nothing may be given to them. Upon the same principle that a child picks out the plums, before he eats the rest of his pudding, I hurried at once to the Sanctum Sanctorum of this Temple of Taste—the Tribune;—a small octagon room, the walls of which are decorated with a select few of the best paintings of the best masters, and in the area of the apartment are five of the most admired pieces of ancient sculpture.

First and foremost amongst these is—"the statue that enchants the world"—the unimitated, inimitable Venus. She has now resumed her old station after her *second* visit to Paris;—for I am surprised the French did not argue that her adventure with the shepherd on Mount Ida was clearly typical of her late trip to their metropolis.

One is generally disappointed after great expectations have been raised, but in this instance I was delighted at first sight, and each succeeding visit has charmed me more. It is indeed a wonderful work in conception and execution—but I doubt whether *Venus* be not a misnomer. Who can recognize in this divine statue any traits of the queen of love and pleasure? It seems rather intended as a personification of all that is elegant, graceful, and beautiful; not only abstracted from all human infirmities, but elevated above all human feelings and affections;—for, though the form is female, the beauty is like the beauty of angels, who are of no sex. I was at first reminded of Milton's Eve; but in Eve—even in her days of innocence before "she damned us all"—there was some tincture of humanity, of which there is none in the Venus; in whose eye[1] there is no heaven, and in whose gesture there is no love.

Immediately behind the statue is the most famous of all the famous Venuses of Titian, who has represented the Goddess of Pleasure in her true character—the Houri of a Mahometan paradise;—and a most bewitching picture it is. But the triumph of the statue is complete;—there is an all-powerful fascination about it that rivets the attention, and makes the spectator turn away from the picture—like Hercules from the voluptuous blandishments of the Goddess of Pleasure—to devote an exclusive adoration to the celestial purity of her rival;—for celestial she certainly is.

The peculiar attribute of her divinity is, not its ubiquity, but its individuality.—It seems impossible to transfer any portion of her "glorious beauty" to a copy.—None of the casts give any idea of the nameless grace of the original.—This incommunicable essence is always the criterion of transcendent excellence.

The arms are modern, and very inferior to the rest of the work. There is something finical and affected in the turn of the fingers, wholly at variance with the exquisite simplicity of the rest of the figure.

I must record,—though I would willingly forget,—the only traces of humanity in the Venus; which escaped my notice in the first fervour of admiration. Her ears are bored for ear-rings, which probably once hung there; and her arm bears the mark of having been compressed by a bracelet. This last ornament might perhaps be excused, but for the other barbarous trinkets—what can be said? I would wish to think they were not the work of the original sculptor; but that they might have been added by some later proprietor, in the same taste that the Squire in Smollett bestows full-curled periwigs, by the hand of an itinerant limner, at so much per head, on the portraits of his ancestors painted by Vandyke.

Having said so much of the Venus, the others may be soon despatched.

The *Apollino* is a model of symmetry. The *Wrestlers* are admirable: but I should like them better if there were more contrast between the figures;—for they are so alike, that they might be supposed to be twins. The arm of the vanquished is out of joint, from the violence of his overthrow.

The *Knife Grinder*, as it is called, may be anybody. None of the suggestions that have yet been made are completely satisfactory.

The *Faun* is principally remarkable, as exhibiting the best instance of Michael Angelo's skill in restoration. He has added a new head, and I doubt if the original could have excelled the substitute. Besides these, which are in the Tribune,—there is the *Hermaphrodite*;—the attitude of which is an exquisite specimen of the skill of the ancients in imitating the ease and simplicity of nature. The disposition of the reclining figure is so delightfully natural, that you feel afraid to approach it, lest you should disturb its sleep. This felicity in catching the postures of nature is still more happily illustrated in *The Shepherd* extracting a thorn from his foot. The marble is actually alive. *Venus* rising from the sea, which is in one of the corridors, deserves a place in the Tribune.

The head of *Alexander* is worthy of the son of Ammon, and the conqueror of the world. The figures in the group of the Niobe are of very unequal merit. Perhaps the taste of the whole is rather too theatrical. Niobe herself, and two of her children, are very superior to the rest. The agony of maternal affection is beautifully expressed in the figure of Niobe. Did Ovid borrow his affecting description from the statue, or did the sculptor take his idea from Ovid?

> Ultima restabat, quam toto corpore Mater,
> Totâ veste tegens, unam, minimamque relinque;
> De multis minimam posco, clamavit, et unam!

However this be, the statue and the verses form an excellent commentary upon each other:

> The verse and sculpture bore an equal part,
> And art reflected images to art.

Amongst the modern statues there are but few to admire. Michael Angelo's *Bacchus* will have no incense from me;—and his unfinished *Brutus* has all the air of a blacksmith. By the way, this is not intended, as it has been often supposed, for Marcus Brutus. It is a portrait of one of the *Medici*, who assassinated his uncle, and was called the Florentine Brutus; but proving afterwards the oppressor, and not the liberator, of his country, M. Angelo laid aside his unfinished bust in disgust. The head of a *Satyr*—his first essay in sculpture as a boy of fourteen—is a truly wonderful performance; but there is nothing of M. Angelo's in the Gallery that will compare with the *Rape of the Sabines*, or the bronze *Mercury* of John of Bologna. The *Mercury* is standing on one leg, upborne by the breath of a Zephyr. It is a figure of ethereal lightness and might "bestride the gossamer, that idles in the wanton summer air."

So much for the sculpture of the Gallery; and it is equally rich in paintings. In addition to the two Venuses of Titian, which exhibit in the highest perfection all the glowing beauties of that painter, there are also in the Tribune some of the choicest works of Raphael. *St. John* in the Wilderness, and the portrait of *Fornarina*, are in his last and best manner, without any trace of that hard dry style derived from his master Perugino, from which he so happily lived to emancipate himself. I must also mention a portrait of Cardinal Aguechia by Domenichino, which is worthy of being compared with the noble picture of Charles V on horseback, by Vandyke, that hangs opposite to it;—and this is praise enough. There are some fine bold sketches of Salvator Rosa, in the ante-rooms of the Tribune, which will well repay the trouble of hunting them out;—and the famous head of Medusa, by Leonardo da Vinci, must not be overlooked.

These are the *plums* of the Gallery; I leave it to guides and catalogues to discuss the rest of *the pudding*.

Sunday 16th

This evening, Sunday, I was presented to the Grand Duke. The Pitti Palace was thrown open to receive the congratulations of the public on the marriage of the Grand Duke's eldest son to a Princess of Saxony.—The bride, an elegant, interesting girl of seventeen, paid her compliments to the company with affability and grace;—the Grand Duke and his family played at cards; and every thing went off very well;—but for my part, I could not help thinking we were all *de trop*—as the marriage had only taken place in the morning.

The palace, spacious and splendid. The state-rooms were thrown open, and we roamed about without restraint, and were regaled with all kinds of refreshments. The boudoir, in the centre of which stands Canova's Venus, brilliantly illuminated, and lined with mirrors, reflected the beauties of her figure in all directions, and exhibited the statue to the highest advantage. This is the statue which occupied the pedestal of the Medicean Venus, during her flight to Paris:—but I can find nothing *divine* about Canova's Venus. She is not worthy to officiate as chambermaid to the Goddess of the Tribune. It is simply the representation of a modest *woman*, who seems to shrink from exposure in such a dishabille; while her Grecian prototype, in native innocence and simplicity—scarcely conscious of nakedness—seems to belong to an order of beings to whom the sentiment of shame was as yet unknown.

The attitude of Canova's is constrained, and perhaps even awkward. This may arise from the manner in which she compresses that scanty drapery which the sculptor has given her—intended, I suppose—"to double every charm it seeks to hide." 'The symmetry too is by no means perfect. The head is manifestly too large. It is perhaps unfair to attribute to the sculptor the faults of the marble, but it is impossible not to remark that even if the work had been more perfect than it is, the unfortunate flaws, just in those places where they are most *mal-à-propos*, must still have detracted much from its beauty. Many of the copies of this statue seem to me quite equal, if not superior to the original; an infallible proof, if the remark be correct, of its mediocrity of merit.

The Princess wished us good night at ten o'clock;—and we were all bowed out.

Monday, 17th
A long morning amongst the pictures in the Pitti Palace. A magnificent collection. Their value may be estimated by the fact of the French, who certainly had the knack of finding out what was worth stealing, taking no less than sixty-three to the Louvre. These are now returned.

Tuesday, 18th
This evening the city of Florence gave a masked ball, at the rooms of the *Belle Arti*, to which the Grand Duke and all the Court were invited. The Italians have been celebrated for their masquerading talents;—but if this ball were taken as a sample, a masquerade is a duller thing in Italy than in England. I believe it is never entertaining but in a novel—and there very seldom.

The young bride, in a room set apart for the purpose, opened a select ball; and I was pleased that she chose our old-fashioned, well-behaved country dance.

19th
Another morning in the Pitti;—but more of the pictures hereafter.—Strolled carelessly through the rooms, without any guide of any kind, trusting to first impressions. When one has thus, by two or three visits, become familiarized with what one likes, and what one does not, it is useful to get a catalogue, and compare one's sensations with *authority*. Protect me from the tiresome flippancy of a professed Cicerone—who takes you round a gallery of pictures, like the showman of a collection of wild beasts.

Thursday, 20th

In the evening, a masqued ball at the *Cascine Rooms*, to which
the Court and the English were invited; but as I have already had
a peep at these gew-gaws, which I consider only as *Lions* to be
seen with the other raree-shows of a foreign country, I prefer the
"society of solitude" in my own arm-chair.

21st

This evening brought the news of the Princess Charlotte's death,
creating a sensation which has seldom been produced by any
public disaster. It seemed to be felt by all the English as a domestic
calamity. The *Chargé d'Affaires* wrote to the Grand Duke, on the
part of the English, to excuse their attendance at a ball and supper,
which had been fixed for the ensuing Sunday at the Pitti Palace.

  The Duke, we are told, was much pleased with the feeling that
gave rise to this note, and exclaimed, "*Voilà de l'esprit vraiment
national!—cela leur fait beaucoup d'honneur.*" All the English put
on deep mourning. Poor Charlotte! and Poor Leopold! and poor
England!—but all public feelings are absorbed in lamenting her
fate as a woman, a wife, and a mother.

22d

To the Laurentian library, which is one of the raree-shows of
Florence;—but a library is not a thing to be stared at. Here they
show you the famous copy of the Pandects—for which you will
not be a wit the wiser; and one of the oldest manuscripts extant
of Virgil, written in a very beautiful character, in which I neither
found the *Culex*, nor the four lines "*Ille ego qui quondam*," usually
prefixed to the Æneid. There is a Petrarch, too, ornamented with
portraits of the poet, and his Laura, taken, as it is said, from the
life.—I looked with more interest at the finger of Galileo, which
is here preserved under a glass case—pointing with a triumphant
expression to those heavens which he was condemned to a
dungeon for having explored.

  Adjoining is the church of St. Lorenzo; and the mausoleum of
the Medici—a splendid piece of nonsense which has never been

completed. The church is full of the works of Michael Angelo;— but it is no easy matter to comprehend *allegorical* statues.

Countess of Albany's party in the evening. She still maintains the form and ceremony of Queen-Dowager, wearing the arms of England on her carriage, and receiving a circle every Saturday evening, with a strictness of etiquette exceeding that of the Grand Duke's court. She was almost the only person out of mourning. This was, to say the least of it, bad taste. If there is no alliance of blood, there is a pecuniary relationship between her and the English government—from which she receives an annual pension of fifteen hundred pounds—that might well have afforded a black gown. It would be difficult to trace in her present appearance any remains of those charms that could attract and attach the fiery and fastidious Alfieri.

Sunday, 23d

To mass in the cathedral. Of the churches of Florence I say little. The subject is endless—if indeed Eustace have not exhausted it. It is impossible not to admire the magnificence of their internal decorations;—but it is a magnificence that fatigues, and perhaps disgusts a Protestant, unaccustomed to the pomp and pageantry of Catholic worship. External modes however are, after all, mere matters of taste, about which there is no disputing;—and the Italians seem to be attracted by splendour. One thing however, at least, must be remarked in favour of the churches—they are always open. Piety will never, in this country, find the church doors shut in her face. Service seems to be going on all day and every day. The favourite altar at this time—for the altar itself is not exempt from the influence of fashion—is at the S. Nunziata. In asking my way to La Santa Nunziata, I was often corrected with "*Caro lei, la* Santissima *Nunziata è di là*"—as if the omission of the *superlative* had given offence;—but the attraction even of an altar has its day.

24th

Again to the Pitti. A catalogue of pictures is a sad dull business;— and I must rather endeavour to record my own sentiments and reflections. The cant of criticism, and the dogmatism of knowledge, would confine all right of judgment upon painting and sculpture to those alone who have been duly initiated in the mysteries of virtù; whereas it seems to me, that it is with painting and sculpture—as Johnson has pronounced it to be with poetry—it is by the *common sense* of mankind, after all, that the claims to excellence must finally be decided.

Painting, considered as a fine art, is principally valuable, as it is historical, or poetical; by which terms I would not be understood to signify the ideas usually attached to them;—but by an *historical* picture, I mean one which represents the subject as it really was; by a *poetical*—one which represents the subject as it existed in the mind of the painter. Mere excellence of execution is, I think, the lowest claim a painter can advance to admiration. As well might a literary production rest its pretensions upon the mere beauties of the style. If the composition neither please the imagination, nor inform the understanding, to what purpose is its being written in elegant language? In the same manner, drawing and colours—the language of painting—can as little, of themselves, form a title to praise.

When I visit collections of paintings, I go to have my understanding instructed, my senses charmed, my feelings roused, my imagination delighted or exalted. If none of these effects be produced, it is in vain to tell me that a picture is painted with the most exact attention to all the rules of art. At such pictures I look without interest, and turn away from them with indifference. If any sensation be excited, it is a feeling of regret that such powers of *style* should have existed without any sparks of that Promethean heat, which alone confers upon them any real value. If this be wanting, it is in vain that a connoisseur descants upon the merits of the drawing, the correctness of the perspective, and the skill of the arrangement. These are mere technical beauties, and may be interesting to the student in painting; but the liberal lover of the arts looks for those higher excellencies, which have placed painting in the same rank with poetry. For what, in fact, are the works of Michael Angelo—Raphael—Murillo—Salvator

Rosa—Claude—Nicholas Poussin and Sir Joshua Reynolds, but the sublime and enchanting—the terrific and heart-rending conceptions of a Homer—a Virgil—a Shakspeare—a Dante—a Byron—or a Scott, "turned into shapes!"—They are the kindred productions of a congenial inspiration.

Yet, I would not be understood to deny *all* merit to mere excellence of execution. I would only wish to ascertain its true place in the scale. The perfect imitation of beautiful nature in the landscapes of Hobbima or Ruysdaal—the blooming wonders that expand under the pencil of Van-Huysum—and the exquisite finishing of Gerhard Douw's laborious patience—cannot be viewed with absolute indifference. Still less would I wish to deny the praise that is due to the humorous productions of Teniers, Hogarth, or Wilkie. These have a peculiar merit of their own, and evince the same creative powers of mind which are exhibited by the true *vis comica* in the works of literature.

The collection in the Pitti abounds in every variety of excellence. There are eight Raphaels. It is difficult to speak with moderation of *Raphael*. Those who undervalue him rate him by his worst productions, of which there are some to be found of a very ordinary merit;—those who admire him look only to his best—and these are above all praise. The character of his genius was extraordinary. Most painters may almost be said to have been born so; and I think Sir Joshua Reynolds and Mr. West have expressed something like a feeling of humiliation, upon finding, at threescore, how very little they could add to the first juvenile productions of their pencils. Raphael was a genius of a slower growth; and it would be difficult to discover, in the hard dry outlines of his first manner, any indication of that felicity of conception and execution which is so conspicuous in his maturer works. His females are beings of an exclusive species; and if he painted from nature, he was fortunate in his acquaintance. The Madonna is a subject which he has appropriated and made his own:—it is only tolerable in his hands;—or, at least, after seeing his, there is no tolerating any other;—Guido's sky-blue draperies to the contrary notwithstanding.

Raphael's *Madonna della Seggiola* unites the most opposite graces;—there is a refined elegance, joined to a diffident simplicity, with a gentle tenderness pervading the whole expression of her figure, which realizes all one's conceptions of that mother from whom the meek Jesus—who, in the agonies of death, offered up a prayer for his executioners—derived his human nature. His portraits too are excellent, combining the force and the richness of the Flemish and Venetian schools, and are second only to the happiest efforts of Vandyke.

Vandyke must ever be the prince of portrait painters. He is at once *historical* and *poetical*. Any dauber may paint a sign-post likeness; but a portrait must have spirit and character as well as resemblance. Vandyke seems to embody, in one transient expression of the countenance—which is all that a painter can give—the whole character of his subject. The *Bentivoglio* is a magnificent specimen of his talent in this way. The subject is worthy of his pencil, and seems to have pleased him. It is a full length dressed in a Cardinal's robes. The head in Lavater was probably taken from this picture, but it has lost a great deal by being separated from the figure;—the attitude and commanding air of which are admirable.

Salvator Rosa is to me the most *poetical* of all painters; by which I mean, not only that he possesses that *mens divinior*, that mysterious power over the grand, the sublime, and the terrible, which constitutes the soul of a poet;—but also, that he ministers more than any other painter to the imagination of the spectator. There is always a something more than meets the eye, in his wild and romantic sketches, which awakens a train of associations, and sets in motion the airy nothings of the fancy. You may look at his pictures for ever, without feeling the least satiety. There is a battle of his in the Pitti, which might serve as a study to all the poets who have sung of battles—from Homer down to Walter Scott. What a picture he would have made of the witches in Macbeth, which Sir Joshua Reynolds has managed so unhappily;—or of Meg Merrilies hurling her parting imprecations upon the Laird of Ellangowan! He seems to be in painting what Byron is in poetry, or Kean in acting; and it would be difficult to praise him more. There is a portrait of himself, by himself; that promises all the genius which is exhibited in his works.

The *Four Philosophers*—a splendid picture by Rubens—worthy of the master of Vandyke.

The *Fates*—one of the few oil paintings that Michael Angelo has given us—are finely conceived—

——facies non omnibus una,
Nec diversa tamen, qualem decet esse sororum.

The features remind one of the portrait of Dante. There is something quite appalling in the solemn severity—the terrible gravity of their demeanour. They might stand for the weird sisters of Shakspeare, if the witches be indeed sublime;—but I fear that "*mouncht and mouncht and mouncht*," brings them down to the level of old women.

Luther and Calvin, by Giorgioni, detained me a long while, though perhaps more from the interest of the subject than the merit of the painting. I fancied I read in the harsh lines of Calvin's countenance that brutal spirit which could enjoy the spectacle of the sufferings of his victim Servetus, and find materials for ridicule in the last afflicting agonies of affrighted nature.

A *St. John* in the Wilderness, by *Andrea del Sarto*, in the last room, is the only picture I have seen that might form an exception to Forsyth's character of that painter; who says "He has neither poetry in his head, nor pathos in his heart."—But enough of pictures for the present.

25th

Visited the *Gabinetto Fisico*. This is a shockingly accurate imitation of dissected subjects, in wax. I went in immediately after breakfast, and was as much discomposed as I could have been by so many real carcasses. It is too horrible, and, it might be added, too indecent an exhibition for miscellaneous admission. Yet all the world, men and women, lounge there;—though all that is revolting and disgusting in disease or deformity is laid bare and exposed, with a nakedness that can only be gratifying to the eye of science. The commencement and progress of the fatal plague at Florence is represented in miniature; and, from the effect produced by looking at it, I am inclined to believe what is said that if it had been made as large as life, it would have been too horrible for exhibition. Gallery again.

26th

The most interesting church here is the *S. Croce*—the Westminster Abbey of Florence—for here are the bones and the tombs of Galileo, Machiavelli, Michael Angelo, and Alfieri. Machiavelli's epitaph is a good specimen of that brevity, which, when well managed, makes an epitaph so impressive—

> Tanto nomini nullum par elogium.
>> Nicholaus Machiavelli.

Michael Angelo is buried, according to his own desire, so that his grave might command a view of the cupola of the Cathedral—the work of Brunnelleschi; which suggested to him the idea of his own grander work at St. Peter's.

The Florentines would, gladly have recovered the bones of Dante, whom they exiled, to die at Ravenna; and they point with pride to an original picture of him in fresco on the wall of the cathedral.

27th

Bitterly cold. A Siberian wind from the Apennines cuts one to the heart. This is no place for the winter. The scene must be changed,—but whither?—Pisa will never do, after Florence. It is as well to die of consumption as of ennui. All the world is going to Rome—and every body says that Rome is a charming place in the winter. What every body says must be true;—and I shall swim with the stream.

28th to 5th December

Very unwell. My surgeon attributes my illness to the water, which, he says, is very noxious here. I believe it has more to do with the air, for it is more cold than ever I felt it in England, whatever the thermometer may say to the contrary.

6th

A long morning at Morghen's;—the first engraver in the world. His Last Supper, from the picture of Leonardo da Vinci, is the triumph of engraving. It is pity that he did not engrave the *Madonna della Seggiola* at a later period, in his best and softest manner. How could he throw away his time and his labour on the *Madonna del Sacco*;—the fresco daub of Andrea del Sarto? Gallery again.

Met a funeral procession with a military guard. Upon inquiry, I found the defunct was a Jew, and that the precaution was necessary as a protection against the insults of the populace.

Sunday 7th

Bertolini's Studio. There is no sculptor of eminence now at Florence. Bertolini is an excellent workman, and takes admirable likenesses; and if he were employed less in this way, might succeed in original composition. It is now the fashion among the English to sit to him; and you find all your acquaintance drawn up in fearful array; in hard marble;—some at full length! If this fashion hold, it will give posterity some trouble. Family *pictures* are easily put out of the way; but family *statues* would be sadly durable lumber—unless, indeed, they found their way to the limekiln.

The cheapness of sculpture here must injure our English artists. Casts have been imported from London of the busts of the King, Fox, Pitt, Nelson, Perceval, and many others. These Bertolini reproduces in marble, and sends back to London, all expenses of carriage included, for twenty-two pounds each.

Made a circuit of the palaces. The *Corsini* and *Gerini* have each of them a fine collection of pictures. I was particularly struck with two, by Carlo Dolci, whose productions are generally too cloying for my taste. The first is the figure of *Poetry* in the Corsini palace—one of the most beautiful countenances I ever saw;—the charms of which are lighted up by that indefinable expression, which makes the face the index of the mind, and gives the assurance, at the first glance, of intellectual superiority. The other is the *Martyrdom of St. Andrew* in the Gerini palace; a most affecting picture;—the impression of which is aided by every excellence of arrangement, contrast, and colouring.

At the Mozzi palace is Benvenuto's picture of the Saxons taking the Oath of Confederation, after the battle of Jena. The figure of Napoleon is admirable; and is said to be one of the best portraits extant of that extraordinary being.

Vespers at the Duomo;—afterwards to the Cascine, the public drive and promenade—in a word—the Hyde-park of Florence.

1. This passage has been censured as inconsistent and contradictory. If there be any inconsistency, it is in speaking of the *eye* of the Venus at all; as, in point of fact, the eye of the statue is nothing but a cold and colourless blank.

III

ARRIVAL IN ROME

Monday, 8th December
Left Florence with a friend, who had a seat to let in his *calèche*;—and we agreed to travel together. Having met with a courier, who was working his way home and offered to serve us for his expenses, we engaged him to accompany us;—though nothing but our complete inexperience of Italian travelling would have reconciled me to such an ostentatious piece of extravagance.

This man's business is to ride on before you; get the horses ready at the post-houses; and prepare for your reception at the inns where you may be inclined to halt. Carlo, I believe, protects us from much imposition; and as he conducts all the disbursements and disputes on the road, which are in fact synonymous terms—for every bill is a battle—what he saves us in breath and temper is incalculable.

The road to Sienna is hilly and tedious, and we did not arrive till after dark.

9th
Left Sienna long before it was light in the morning; being in some anxiety about passing the Ricorsi, a mountain-torrent, which, at this season, is very liable to be swollen by the rains, and has sometimes detained travellers on the road for many days. The Guide Book informs you, quaintly enough, that you will have to pass it four times—if you are not swallowed up in either of the first three. Having safely forded this stream, we arrived, at the close of evening, at Acquapendente. The accommodations here

were so uninviting, that we proceeded on to S. Lorenzo; and as it was now quite dark, my companion would insist upon taking a small escort of cavalry. This I thought unwise;—it was making sure of being pillaged by the soldiers;—whereas the danger from robbers was only contingent.

At S. Lorenzo we found that we had fallen from the frying-pan into the fire. The inn had a most unfrequented appearance, and our arrival was the signal of destruction to some poor fowls, who were quietly at roost—dreaming of that to-morrow which was never to come.

10th
We rose early again, and breakfasted at Bolsena, on the borders of the lake. The inhabitants bear ample testimony, by their pale and sickly appearance, to the existence of the *malaria*. Throughout this day, the road was beautiful;—commanding every variety of prospect;—hill and dale, wood and water.

The environs of Viterbo, bold and beautiful.—Halted for the night at Baccano;—the inn of which has been undeservedly denounced by Forsyth. Whatever may be said of the roast beef of old England, I think we might learn much from our neighbours in the science of good living. The inns in Italy are generally better than those of an equal class in England. What can a traveller hope to find, at a country-inn in England but the choice of a beef-steak, a mutton-chop, or a veal-cutlet? For one of these, with, some bad beer, or worse wine, he will be charged more than he will pay in Italy, for an abundance and variety of dishes. The wines of the country are light, pleasant, and wholesome; and in that great article of a traveller's comfort—his bed—Italy has again the advantage. Instead of the suffocating feather-beds of England, you find every where an elastic refreshing mattress, which will conduce to ensure a good night's sleep, in spite of the dreary unfurnished room in which it is placed.

11th

We rose early, in order to reach Rome in good time. It was a rainy day; so that when we ascended the hill about two miles from Baccano, from which we ought to have seen Rome—we saw nothing. The approach to Rome is as all travellers have described it. You pass over miles of a barren common, much like Hounslow Heath; and when, at last, you arrive at the gate of the Eternal City, the first impression is, I think, a feeling of disappointment. But this, perhaps, may be referred to the exaggerated expectations, in which, till philosophy and experience have given sobriety to our views, we are all too prone to indulge. We have only to consider the limited powers of man, and to examine what he has been able to do, with a reference to his means of performance, and the tone of our expectations will be lowered to a just level. We were soon in the *Piazza di Spagna*—the focus of fashion, and the general resort of the English. Some travellers have compared it to Grosvenor-square; but the Piazza di Spagna is little more than an irregular open space, a little less nasty than the other piazzas in Rome, because the habits of the people are in some measure restrained by the presence of the English. Still, there is quite enough left to make me believe the Romans the nastiest people in Christendom—if I had not seen the Portuguese.

The English swarm every where. We found all the inns full. It seemed like a country town in England at an assizes. To look for lodgings was impossible, for it rained unmercifully. By the way, when it does rain here, it pours with a downright vehemence, that we are but little accustomed to in England. We got a resting-place for the night with some difficulty, at the Hotel de Paris. Dear and bad.

12th

Signed the articles of a triumvirate with two friends, who were on the same pursuit after lodgings with myself. Established ourselves at No. 43, *Via degli Otto Cantoni, Corso*. This situation is bad. There are two fish-stalls under my window, the people belonging to which commence their vociferations as soon as it is light. There is, however, at least, more variety in these cries than in the perpetual "All alive ho!" of London. The Italian fishmonger displays all the humour he is master of to get rid of his stock, and he will sometimes apostrophize his stale mullet with ludicrous effrontery;—"*Pesci! cosa fate? Pesci! statevi cheti!*" But the worst objection to our lodgings is their height. We are on the *quarto piano*;—a hundred and four steps from the ground—though this objection relates only to convenience; for it is by no means *mauvais ton* in Rome, to live in the upper story, which does not at all answer to our garret. Here—your approach to heaven does not in the least detract from your gentility.

Our lodgings consist of two sitting-rooms, three bed-rooms, servant's room, and kitchen; for which we pay thirty sequins, about fifteen pounds English, per month. The charge of a traiteur for supplying you with dinner at home, varies from six to ten pauls per head. We get Orvietto wine at something less than two pauls a bottle. This wine is pleasant, though it is said to be very unwholesome. But the wine of wines is *Velletri*, which costs us little more than a paul a bottle; and a bottle holds nearly two English quarts. The paul is something less than sixpence, forty-four being the value of a pound sterling, when the exchange is at par.

December 13th to 25th
Sight-seeing. Of the sights at Rome it is impossible to say nothing—and it is difficult to say any thing new. What so many have told, who would tell again?—I must be content to record first impressions.

There are two modes of seeing Rome—the *topographical*—followed by Vasi, who parcels out the town into eight divisions, and jumbles every thing together—antiquities, churches, and palaces—if their situation be contiguous;—and the *chronological*—which would carry you regularly from the house of Romulus to the palace of the reigning Pontiff. The first mode is the most expeditious, and the least expensive;—for even if the traveller walk a-foot, the economy of time is worth considering;—and, after all that can be urged in favour of the chronological order, on the score of reason, Vasi's plan is perhaps the best. For whatever is worth seeing at all is worth seeing twice. Vasi's mode hurries you through every thing, but it enables you to select and note down those objects that are worthy of further examination, and these may be afterwards studied at leisure. Of the great majority of sights, it must be confessed that all we obtain for our labour is the knowledge that they are not worth seeing;—but this is a knowledge that no one is willing to receive upon the authority of another, and Vasi's plan offers a most expeditious mode of arriving at this truth by one's own proper experience. His plan is indeed too expeditious, for he would get through the whole town, with all its wonders, ancient and modern—in eight days! This might suit Young Rapid exactly, but I am content to follow the course he has chalked out at a more leisurely pace.

As a guide to Rome, Vasi's book is worth all the books of travels put together. It is all that it professes to be, and no more—a mere catalogue; but it is comprehensive and accurate. There is nothing to direct the taste or influence the judgment; but a traveller should observe for himself, and it is much better that he should not see through the eyes of others. Forsyth's book is a mine of original remarks, expressed in the most forcible language; but one laments that the author did not live to complete a work, of which his present volume is little more than the Text-Book.

Eustace, notwithstanding the many charms of his book, is not the most accurate of all travellers; and one is sometimes led to doubt whether he really ever saw the places he describes.

If a book of travels must be taken as a guide, *Lalande's* is perhaps the best, which is full of lore and learning: but it is as dull and dry as Vasi's Catalogue—and a great deal longer.

Some remains of the Palatine—the Capitoline—the Celian— the Aventine—the Quirinal—the Viminal—and the Esquiline Hills—are still to be distinguished. The most interesting relics will be found on the two first—the oldest establishments of Rome; for the first foundations of Romulus were limited to the Palatine Hill.

——Porta est, ait, ista, Palati;
Hic stator, hoc primum coudita Roma loco est.

OVID

The best view of the site of ancient Rome is from the tower of the modern capitol. The modern city has been so much elevated by the rubbish and dilapidation of centuries, that it is matter of surprise the shape and situation of the ancient hills still remain so visible. The pavement of old Rome is often discovered at a depth of forty feet. Every thing is developed by excavation; and the Coliseum itself loses much of its effect by the mound of earth accumulated around it. One may judge of the greatness of the wreck, from the effects thus produced by its overthrow. Still, however, we shall be at a loss to find room for the three millions, which is not the highest estimate that is given, as the amount of the ancient population. It is rather the quality of what remains, than the quantity, that impresses one with an idea of the grandeur and magnificence of ancient Rome. There is the fragment of a cornice, lying in the gardens of Colonna Palace, which looks as if it had been brought from the land of Brobdignag;—for no pillars of present existence could support an entablature of such gigantic proportions, as that of which this cornice must have formed a part. One might imagine some great convulsion of nature had swallowed up the city, and left a few fragments to tell the tale of its existence to other times.

One of my first excursions was to the *Forum*. It is difficult to conceive, and impossible to describe, the effect produced by the *admonitus locorum* of this memorable scene—reduced as it now is again to something like the state which Virgil describes, in the days of Evander;—

Passimque armenta videbant,
Romanoque foro et lautis mugire Carinis.

The Roman forum is now the *Campo Vaccino*, the papal Smithfield; but it is still the finest walk in the world; and I doubt whether, in the proudest days of its magnificence, it could have interested a spectator more than it now does—fallen as it is from its high estate. Nothing can be more striking, or more affecting, than the contrast between what it was—and what it is. There is enough in the tottering ruins which yet remain, to recall the history of its ancient grandeur; while its present misery and degradation are obtruded upon you at every step. Here Horace lounged;—here Cicero harangued;—and here now, the modern Romans count their beads—kill their pigs—cleanse their heads—and violate the Sanctity of the place by every species of abomination.

The walk from the Capitol to the Coliseum comprises the history of ages. The broken pillars that remain of the Temple of Concord, the Temple of Jupiter Tonans, and the Comitium, tell the tale of former times, in language at once the most pathetic and intelligible;—it is a mute eloquence, surpassing all the powers of description. It would seem as if the destroying angel had a taste for the picturesque;—for the ruins are left just as the painter would most wish to have them.

The arches of the emperors scarcely appear in harmony with the rest of the scene, and do not accord with the magnificent scale of all around them. I doubt whether Titus's arch be wider or higher than Temple Bar.

The Duchess of Devonshire is excavating round Phocas's Pillar;—re-making the gulf which Curtius closed. Criminals in chains are employed in this work, under the superintendence of a military guard;—but, if patriotism and virtue be again necessary to fill up the chasm, where shall we find the materials here?

Of the Coliseum more hereafter;—for the first impression of the *Via Sacra* is so overwhelming, that the mind is lost in its own reflections, and has no leisure for the examination of details.

Marius, in his exile, sitting amongst the ruins of Carthage, must have been an affecting spectacle. Napoleon, amongst the ruins of Rome, would perhaps afford as striking a picture;—but Napoleon never was in Rome. If he had returned victorious from Russia, it is said that he had intended to make a triumphal entry into the Eternal City, and to be crowned in St. Peter's.

The Palace of the Cæsars. The whole of this region, comprehending all that remains of the residence of the emperors, and the golden house of Nero, is now a desert, full of ruins, and fragments of temples, and baths—presenting an awful picture of fallen greatness. The spot is beautiful, and commands a fine view of Rome. The soil seems rich, if one may judge from the crops of cabbages and artichokes, which it is now made to produce. Great part, however, of this vast tract is covered with wild brushwood, where you may easily lose yourself, if you will. In my last stroll through this wilderness, I encountered a Fox, who paused for a moment to stare at me;—as if he were doubting which of the two was to be considered as the intruder. This Fox seems to be the genius of the place, and delights to show himself to all travellers. There are some remains of a terrace, overlooking the *Circus Maximus*, from which the emperors gave the signal for the commencement of the games.

In another quarter are three rooms, discovered about forty years ago. These chambers are in good preservation and afford a sample of the ancient Roman taste in the construction and proportions of their apartments. They seem to have received their light, like the Pantheon, from a hole in the ceiling; and instead of the formal square which so much prevails in modern rooms, each of the four sides in these is broken into a circular recess or bow. The same accumulation of soil seems to have taken place here, on the Palatine Hill, as elsewhere; for these chambers, which must have been once on the surface, are now thirty feet below ground. These rooms appear to me to be models of proportion, and the effect of the loose flowing outline, produced by the hollowing out of the sides into recesses, is much more pleasing than the harsh angular preciseness of a parallelogram.

Dec. 20th

The more I see of Italy, the more I doubt whether it be worth while for an invalid to encounter the fatigues of so long a journey, for the sake of any advantages to be found in it, in respect of climate, during the winter. To come to Italy, with the hope of *escaping* the winter, is a grievous mistake. This might be done by alternately changing your hemisphere, but in Europe it is impossible; and I believe that Devonshire, after all, may be the best place for an invalid during that season. If the thermometer be not so low here, the temperature is more variable, and the winds are more bitter and cutting. In Devonshire too, all the comforts of the country are directed against cold;—here, all the precautions are the other way. The streets are built to exclude as much as possible the rays of the sun, and are now as damp and cold as rain and frost can make them. And then, what a difference between the warm carpet, the snug elbowed chair, and the blazing coal-fire of an English winter evening, and the stone staircases, marble floors, and starving casements of an Italian house!—where every thing is designed to guard against the heat of summer; which occupies as large a proportion of the Italian year, as the winter season does our own. The only advantage of Italy then is, that your penance is *shorter* than it would be in England; for I repeat that, during the time it lasts, winter is more severely felt here than at Sidmouth, where I would even recommend an Italian invalid to repair, from November till February—if he could possess himself of Fortunatus's cap, to remove the difficulties of the journey.

Having provided myself with a warm cloak, which is absolutely necessary where the temperature varies twenty degrees between one street and another, I have been proceeding leisurely through the wonders of Rome. In travelling round the circuit of the antiquities, it is curious to remark how the scale of buildings gradually increases, from the little modest temple of *Vesta* to the temple of *Fortuna Virilis*, and the other works of the republic, till they swell out into colossal magnificence, in the vast works of Nero, Vespasian, and Caracalla.

The same remark may be extended to the tombs; and the same growing taste for ostentation may be traced from the earlier days of the republic to the tomb of Cæcilia Metella, the wife of Crassus. Augustus carried this taste farther in his mausoleum;—though he was at least social enough to admit his family. Adrian, at last, outdid all former outdoings, and constructed that enormous pile, which is now the Castle of St. Angelo, for the exclusive accommodation of his own single carcass.

Dec. 21st
The Tiber has been very differently described by different writers. Some have degraded it to a ditch; while others have exalted it to an equality with the finest rivers in Europe. There are those again, who, admitting its pretensions in other respects, find fault with its *colour*—"fluere hunc *lutulentum*." The first sight of it has, I believe, generally occasioned a feeling of disappointment. But when we come to admeasurement, we find that at the *Pons Ælius*, now the *Ponte S. Angelo*, the breadth is about 212 English feet. This is the narrowest point; and certainly if we apply to *this* part of the river Horace's prescription for a good night's rest—

——ter uncti
Transnanto Tiberim, somno quibus est opus alto—

even less accomplished swimmers than Lord Byron and Leander might object to it as inadequate. At the *Pons Milvius* however, now the *Ponte Molle*, the breadth increases; and two miles above Rome, the river is nearly twice as broad as it is within the walls. This contraction of the stream within the town will be a sufficient explanation of the destructive inundations which have taken place at various periods.

Some remains of the Sublician Bridge still exist;—and your guide would wish you to believe that this was the scene of Horatius Cocles' gallantry. But in travelling round the antiquities of Rome, there is, I fear, great occasion for scepticism, with respect to the propriety of the names that have been so confidently applied to many of them.

The Temple of Vesta, a pretty modest little building, seems to belong to this doubtful order;—though here, the doubt is, not whether it is *a* temple of Vesta, but *the* temple of Vesta. Its situation on the bank of the river seems to accord with Horace's *Monumenta Vestæ*; and it geography will agree with the *ventum erat ad Vestæ* of the ninth satire, where it is represented as lying in his way from the *Via Sacra* to the gardens of Cæsar, *trans Tiberim*;—nor is Ovid's description at all unsuitable to it;

> Hic locus exiguus qui sustinet atria Vestæ,
> Jam fuit intonsi regia parva Numæ.

In this quarter of the town, you see a part of the *Cloaca Maxima*;—this is one of the most curious and interesting remains of Roman magnificence; and it has given rise to much difference of opinion with respect to the period when these works were constructed. Ferguson has stated some historic doubts in a note to his *Roman Republic*, which are worth attention. "The common sewers were executed at a great expense. It was proposed that they should be of sufficient dimensions to admit a waggon loaded with hay. (Plin. lib. xxxvi. c. 15.) When these common sewers came to be obstructed, under the republic, the censors contracted to pay a thousand talents, or about 193,000 pounds, for clearing and repairing them. (Dionys. Hal. lib. iii. c. 67.) They were again inspected at the accession of Augustus; and clearing their passages is mentioned amongst the great works of Agrippa. He is said to have turned the course of seven rivers into these subterraneous canals, to have made them navigable, and to have actually passed in barges under the streets and buildings of Rome. These works are still supposed to remain; but as they exceed the power and resources of the present city to keep them in repair, they are concealed from the view, except at one or two places. They were, in the midst of the Roman greatness, and still are reckoned among the wonders of the world; and yet they are said to have been the works of the elder Tarquin, a prince whose territory did not extend, in any direction, above sixteen miles; and, on this supposition, they must have been made to accommodate a city that was calculated chiefly for the reception of cattle, herdsmen, and banditti.

"Rude nations sometimes execute works of great magnificence, as fortresses, and temples, for the purposes of superstition or war; but seldom palaces, and still more seldom works of mere convenience and cleanliness, in which, for the most part, they are long defective. It is not unreasonable, therefore, to question the authority of tradition, in respect to this singular monument of antiquity, which exceeds what many well-accommodated cities of modern Europe have undertaken for their own conveniency. And as those works are still entire, and may continue so for thousands of years, it may be suspected that they existed even prior to the settlement of Romulus, and may have been the remains of a more ancient city, on the ruins of which the followers of Romulus settled, as the Arabs now hut or encamp on the ruins of Palmyra and Balbec. Livy owns that the common sewers were not accommodated to the plait of Rome, as it was laid out in his time; they were carried in directions across the streets, and passed under the buildings of the greatest antiquity. This derangement, indeed, he imputes to the hasty rebuilding of the city, after its destruction by the Gauls; but haste, it is probable, would have determined the people to build on their old foundations, or at least not to change them so much as to cross the direction of former streets. When the only remaining accounts of an ancient monument are absurd or incredible, it follows, of course, that the real account of the times in which it was erected is not known."

Such is the note of Ferguson, which is well entitled to consideration; though it is difficult to reconcile the existence of a more ancient city, on the site of the city of Romulus, with the entire silence of history and tradition; unless, indeed, we carry it up to a period so remote, as would throw an awful mystery over the first origin of the Eternal City, connecting it with times, of which there are no more traces than of the Mammoth or the Mastodon.

22d

Caracalla's Baths and Palace. The ruins of this Palace are, next to the Coliseum, the most striking proof that remains of the grandeur of the Roman buildings. It was here that some of the finest pieces of sculpture were discovered; the famous *Torso*, the

Hercules Farnese, the *Flora*, and the group known by the name of the *Toro Farnese*. This enormous pile of ruins has rather the appearance of the remains of a town than of a single palace. From what is left we may form some notion of the form and proportions of the splendid *Cella Solearis*, or the Hall of Sandals, of which we have such a superb description. "*Cellam solearem architecti negant posse ulla inmitatione qua facta est fieri.*" The baths are underground; one of the vaulted rooms remains entire, and sufficiently indicates how the rest were disposed. While the lower orders mixed in the same bath, rooms were provided for more fastidious persons, with bathing vessels of granite, porphyry, and basaltes; of which many are now in the Museum of the Vatican. It is said that three thousand persons might bathe at the same time; and besides the baths, there was everything that could minister to the gratification of the people;—theatres, promenades, gymnasia, libraries, and magnificent porticoes, to protect them from sun and rain;—where philosophers walked, and talked, and taught. Such were the baths, or rather the *Thermæ* of the Romans; for the baths did not include the same superb establishments as the Thermæ, which have been well described as "*Lavacra in modum provinciarum extructa.*"

Caracalla's Circus, as it is called, rests on very doubtful authority. There is a coin of Caracalla's with a circus on the reverse side;—here is a circus that wants an owner;—how easy the inference then, that it must have been Caracalla's! It has suffered so little alteration from time, that the whole shape and extent are as distinct as they could have been 1500 years ago. By the way, the circus of the Romans is any thing but a *circle*. It is a narrow oblong, with rounded ends. Up the middle ran the *spina*, round which the chariots turned;—and it must have required very delicate driving. The length of the circus is 1630 French feet, the breadth 330. The walls of the two *metæ* are still standing;—and the obelisk, which now stands in the Piazza Navona, once stood in the middle of it.

From hence I drove to the *Fountain of Egeria* which is doubtful again; and cannot well be reconciled with the description of

Juvenal, as to its locality. It is, however, a pretty fountain in a
pretty valley; and, if it be the fountain of which Juvenal speaks,
time has at least realized his wish, and the water is now again
inclosed, *viridi margine*, "with a border of eternal green;"—and
the only marble that profanes the native stone, is a headless
statue, but not of the nymph Egeria; for it is evidently of the
male sex, and was probably intended for the god of the stream
which flowed from this spring. I can vouch for the excellence of
the water, of which I took a copious draught.

IV

CHRISTMAS IN ROME

December 23d

A long morning at St. Peter's—of which I have hitherto said nothing, though I have visited it often. All my expectations were answered by the first impression of this sublime temple. It may be true that, on first entering, you are less struck than might be supposed with the immensity of the building. But this, I believe, is entirely the fault of our eyes;—which are, indeed, the "fools of the senses;"—and we are only taught to see, by reason and experience. In St. Peter's, so much attention has been paid to preserve the relative proportions of all the parts, that for some time you do not perceive the largeness of the *scale*. For example, the figures of the Evangelists, which decorate the inside of the cupola, scarcely appear to be larger than life, and yet the pen in St. Mark's hand is six feet long, from which one may calculate their real stature.

The fact is, that nothing is great or little but by comparison; and where no familiar object exists to assist the judgment, the eye readily accustoms itself to any scale.

Gulliver says very naturally, that he lived with the Brobdignagians without being fully sensible of their stupendous size; but that he was most forcibly impressed with it, on his return to England, by the contrast of his own diminutive countrymen. In the same manner it is, when you enter any other church, that you are most struck with the prodigious superiority of St. Peter's, in magnitude and grandeur.

There is, indeed, one exception to the harmony of proportion in the inside of St. Peter's. The statue of the Apostle himself, which was changed from an old Jupiter Capitolinus by a touch of the Pope's wand;—this famous St. Peter is seated in an arm chair, on the right hand of the altar, and is scarcely above the size of life.

It was the contrast afforded by this statue, that first made me fully sensible of the magnitude of every thing else.

It is to be lamented that Michael Angelo's plan was not adhered to, whose intention was, that the figure of the church should have been a Greek cross. The advantage of this form is, that it exhibits the whole structure at one *coup d'œil.* In the Latin cross accompanied with aisles—as is the case in St. Peter's—the effect is frittered away, and instead of one great whole, there are, in fact, four churches under one roof. In spite, however, of all that the last architect has done to spoil it, St. Peter's stands, beyond all comparison, the most magnificent temple ever raised by mortal hands to the worship of the Supreme Being. It is a spectacle that never tires;—you may visit it every day, and always find some thing new to admire. Then, its temperature is delightful;—after starving in the cold and comfortless galleries of the Vatican, it is a luxury indeed to enjoy the mild and genial air in the interior of St. Peter's; and I am told, the church is as pleasantly cool in summer, as it is comfortably warm in winter. The fact is, the walls are so thick, and it is so wholly free from damp, that the air within is not affected by that without; so that, like a well-built cellar, it enjoys an equability of temperature all the year round.

Immediately under the glorious cupola is the tomb of St. Peter, round which a hundred lamps are constantly burning; and above, written in large characters on the frieze in the inside of the cupola, is this obvious, but admirably appropriate, inscription:—

TU ES PETRUS, ET SUPER HANC PETRUM ÆDIFICABO
ECCLESIAM MEAM, ET TIBI DABO CLAVES REGNI CÆLORUM

Underneath is the old church, upon which the present temple has been built; and it is here that the remains of the Apostle are said to have been deposited;—though many learned men have doubted whether St. Peter ever was at Rome at all. Here too you may read, what no person who has not descended into this subterraneous church probably has read;—the histories of the reigns of Charles III., James IV., and Henry IX.—kings of England! for so they are styled, in the royal chronicles engraved on the tombs of the Pretenders; which, brief as they are, contain almost all that is memorable in the histories of most princes;— the date of their births and their deaths. And yet, as if the present tomb were not sufficient to commemorate the last of the Stuarts, Canova is now employed in working a more costly monument, to the memory of Cardinal York—*alias* Henry IX.

As there is one exception to the otherwise excellently arranged proportions in the inside of the church, in the statue of St. Peter, which is insignificantly little; so there is also one on the outside, in the height of the front, which is extravagantly too great. Architecture is so much an art of the square and the rule, that mere uninstructed common sense ought perhaps to have no voice on the subject. But all the world, learned and unlearned, unite in condemning this barbarous front. There is a drawing, in the Vatican, of the façade, as Michael Angelo intended it should be, which resembles closely the portico of the Pantheon. Maderno's frightful attic rises so high, that, to a spectator on the ground, placed at the farther extremity of the piazza of St. Peter's, the auxiliary cupolas are quite lost, and the great cupola itself is scarcely able to appear above its overgrown proportions. St. Peter's must not be judged of from engravings. The rage for embellishing has possessed more or less all the engravers of Rome. Piranesi, who had more taste, had perhaps less fidelity than any of his brethren. They have all endeavoured to correct the defects of Maderno's front, and have represented it as it never can be seen from the ground. So much for Maderno;—whose performances at St. Peter's are thus appreciated by Forsyth:—"At last," says he, "a wretched plasterer came down from Como, to break the sacred unity of the master idea, and him we must execrate for the Latin cross, the aisles, the attic, and the front."

The inscription on the front, which bears the name of Paul V., is conceived in the true papal taste; and, instead of dedicating the church at once to the Supreme Being, consecrates it—*In honorem principis apostolorum.*

Adjoining and disfiguring St. Peter's are the Wart of the Vestry on one side, and the Wen of the Vatican on the other. The Vestry, however diminutive it seems in juxtaposition with such prodigious masses, is in truth itself a vast pile, built at an enormous expense, by Pius V who was possessed with a rage for embellishing, and perpetuating his name by inscriptions. Over the principal entrance is the following:—

> Quad ad Templi Vaticani ornamentum publica vota flagitabant, Pius VI., Pontifex maximus, fecit, &c.

The Italian wits seldom lose an opportunity of venting their satire in epigram, and the following distich was soon found written underneath the inscription:—

> Publica! mentiris;—Non publica vota fuere,
> Sed tumidi ingenii vota fuere tui.

Pius the VIth's passion for recording his own glory, in the constant inscription—*Munificentia Pii Sexti*—was perhaps, more wittily satirized during a season of scarcity, when the *pagnotta* or little roll of two *baiocchi*, answering to our penny roll—which never varies in price, however its size may be affected by the price of corn—had shrunk to a most lamentable littleness. One morning, one of these Lilliputian loaves was found in the hand of Pasquin's statue, with an appended scroll, in large characters—

MUNIFICENTIA PII SEXTI

24th
Another morning at St. Peter's. Nothing can be more grand than the approach to the church. Instead of being cooped up like our own St. Paul's, it forms the back-ground of a noble and spacious amphitheatre formed by a splendid colonnade of a quadruple

range of pillars. In the middle of this amphitheatre stands the Egyptian obelisk, brought to Rome by Caligula. This curious monument of the history of mankind adds great interest to the scene. Caligula brought it from Egypt; and, after purifying it from the abomination of Egyptian superstition dedicated it with this inscription, which still remains:—

> Divo Cæsari Divi Julii F. Augusto
> Ti. Cæsari Divi Augusti F. Augusto
> Sacrum.

But all things in this world seem made for change:—the same obelisk has undergone fresh purifications, to cleanse it from the heathen abominations; and it is now consecrated to Christianity.

The following are the inscriptions on the four sides of its base:—

> Sixtus V. Pont: Max:
> Cruci invictæ
> Obeliscum Vaticanum
> Ab impurâ superstitione
> Expiatum, justius
> Et felicius consecravit
> Anno MDLXXXVI., Pont. II.
> Ecce Crux Domini
> Fugite
> Partes adversæ
> Vicit Leo
> De tribu Juda.

> Sixtus V. Pont: Max:
> Obeliscum Vaticanum
> Dîs gentium
> Impio cultu dicatum
> Ad apostolorum limina
> Operoso labore transtulit
> Anno MDLXXXVI., Pont. II.
> Christus vincit
> Christus regnat
> Christus imperat
> Christus ab omni malo
> Plebem suam
> Defendat.

The fountains are magnificent. Christina, Queen of Sweden, thought they were made to play in honour of her visit, and begged they might cease;—at least so says the guide—but this is the kind of story which is told of every royal head down to *Prince Le Boo*; who, when he first entered London, thought it was lighted up as a particular compliment to him.

In giving the comparative admeasurements of St. Peter's and St. Paul's, Eustace seems to have been resolved, at all events, to exalt the superiority of the Catholic church above her heretical daughter. I know not from whence he took his dimensions; but they do not accord with those on the cupola of St. Peter's; which are given in every measure of Europe. The St. Paul's mark too on the pavement in the inside of the church—where the lengths of the principal cathedrals in Europe are distinguished—ought to have shown him at once how much he was mistaken, in giving to St. Peter's 200 feet more in length than St. Paul's.

Eustace's dimensions are as follow—where he seems to have comprised the walls and portico of St. Peter's, and taken only the clear inside length of St. Paul's:—

St. Peter's		St. Paul's
Feet		Feet
700	Length	500
500	Transept	250
440	Height	340
90	Breadth of the Nave	60
154	Height of the Nave	120

Now the admeasurement of St. Peter's, taken from the record of the cupola, is very different; and the dimensions of St. Paul's, as given in the descriptions of that church, still less agree with Eustace.

The account taken from these sources will stand thus:—

St. Peter's		St. Paul's.
Feet.		Feet.
673	Extreme length	510
444	Trancept	282
448	Height to the top of the Cross outside	404
88	Breadth of the Nave, 40; with the aisles	107
146	Height of the Nave	100

Such things are of little importance; but when one finds the admeasurement of the "*accurate Eustace*" quoted and followed by succeeding travellers, it is time to ascertain whether he be accurate, or not; though this may not be so easily done with respect to St. Peter's; for it is remarkable that scarcely any two books agree in the statement of its dimensions.

I was surprised to find on the bronze gates of the church, amongst the *bas-relief* representations of scriptural subjects, my old friends, the Eagle and Ganymede, and a very spirited, though not over-decent, group of Leda and her Swan.

Some traces of the old heathen superstitions are indeed constantly peeping out from under their Catholic disguises. I believe it is Warburton who says, that to see variety in human nature, one must go farther than Europe—the tour of which resembles the entertainment given to Pompey. There were many dishes, and a seeming variety, but when he examined them closely, he found them all made out of one hog;—nothing but *pork*—differently disguised. I believe the remark might be extended farther. Human nature seems alike in all ages and countries. "We cannot so inoculate our old stock, but we shall relish of it." If anything could have improved the tree, one would have supposed it must have borne better fruit by being grafted with Christianity; but, in many particulars—at least as far as Italy is concerned—all the change produced has been a mere change of name. For instance, amongst the antiquities of Rome, you are shown the house, or, as it is called, the *Temple of Romulus*;—which you are told was built round the very house in which he lived, and has been fortified and repaired ever since. Need we go farther to seek for the prototype of the tale of Loretto?—though, in this instance, it must be confessed that the moderns have bettered the instruction. "What is the modern worshipping of saints and images, but a revival of the old adoration paid to heroes and demigods;—or what the Nuns, with their vows of celibacy, but a new edition of the Vestal Virgins?—*auctiores* certainly, but whether *emendatiores* or no—I will not undertake to determine. Wherever we turn indeed, "all is old, and nothing new." What are the tales we hear of images of the

Virgin falling from Heaven, but a repetition of the old fable of the *Palladium*; which the ancients assure us was derived from the same celestial manufactory? Instead of tutelary gods—we find guardian angels;—and the *canonization* of a saint, is but another term for the *apotheosis* of a hero. The processions[1] are closely copied from ancient patterns; and the lustral water and the incense of the Heathen Temple remain, without any alteration, in the holy water and the censer of the Catholic Church.

It was the spirit of imitation, seeking to continue the Pontifex of the temple, in the Priest of the church, which perhaps led to the doctrine of transubstantiation, and the daily *sacrifice* of the mass—a ceremony which seems to be copied from the victims and blood-offerings of the heathen ritual, and little consistent with that religion which was founded upon the abolition of all sacrifices—by the offering up of the great Atonement, as a full and complete expiation—once for all—for the sins of the whole world. Again;— the mysterious ceremonial of Isis seems to have been revived in the indecent emblems, presented by women, as votive offerings at the shrine of *S. Cosmo*: nay, some would trace the Pope himself, with his triple-crown on his head, and the keys of heaven and hell in his pocket—to our old acquaiatance Cerberus, with his three heads, who kept guard as the custos of Tartarus and Elysium.

Be this as it may—the pun of Swift is completely realized. The very same piece of brass, which the old Romans adored, now, with a new head on its shoulders—like an old friend with a new face—is worshipped with equal devotion by the modern Italians; and *Jupiter* appears again, with as little change of name as of materials, in the character of the *Jew Peter.* And, as if they wished to make the resemblance as perfect as possible, they have, in imitation of the

> *Centum aras* posuit, *vigilemque* sacraverat *ignem*

of his pagan prototype, surrounded the tomb of the Apostle with a hundred ever-burning lights. It is really surprising to see with what apparent fervour of devotion all ranks, and ages, and sexes, kneel to, and kiss the toe of, this brazen image.[2] They rub it against their foreheads, and press it against their lips, with the most reverential piety. I have sat by the hour to see the crowds of people, who flock in to perform this ceremony—for their turn to kiss;—and yet the Catholic would laugh at the pious Mussulman, who performs a pilgrimage to Mecca, to wash the holy pavement and kiss the black stone of the Caaba;—which, like his own St. Peter, is also a relic of heathenism.—Alas poor human nature!—The Catholic laughs at the Mussulman, we do not scruple to laugh at the Catholic—the Deist laughs at us—and the Atheist laughs at all. What is truth? We must *wait* for an answer. But though all must *wait the great teacher Death* to decide between them, let *us* repose our hopes and fears, with humble confidence, in the promises of Christianity— not as it appears disfigured and disguised at Rome—but as it is written and recorded in that sacred volume, which, in the words of Locke, has "God for its author, salvation for its end, and *truth* without any mixture of error for its matter."

25th

Christmas-day. A grand ceremony in the church of *S. Maria Maggiore*;—where mass was performed before the pope and the cardinals. The night preceding this day of Christian rejoicing is passed in the exercises of religion. Everything is in motion;— processions of priests, and pilgrims, and women fill the streets;— the world of fashion follows in the same track;—while the peasantry from the country, arrayed in their holiday clothing, which, among the women particularly, is very showy and splendid, with much of scarlet and gold, flock into Rome; and the churches, brilliantly lighted up, are crowded to excess during the whole of the night.

It may perhaps be doubted, whether these midnight meetings are not often perverted to less holy purposes;—but, the great majority of those who attend seem to be animated by a sincere and enthusiastic spirit of devotion. It is difficult for a Protestant so far to overcome the prejudices of his education, as not to feel a sentiment of disgust at the theatrical representations which are got up to commemorate the Nativity. Some show of the kind is prepared at all the churches, and the people flock from one to the other, to gaze, admire, and leave their Christmas offerings. The most popular and attractive *spectacle* is at the Aracæli church;— for the *Bambino* there is the production of a miracle, and is said to have been dropped from heaven. Part of the church is fitted up like a theatre, with canvass scenes, canvass clouds, and canvass figures of the Virgin—the shepherds—the wise men—the ox and the ass;—all carefully painted with due attention to stage effect. The miraculous *Bambino*, splendidly accoutred, is placed in the centre of the stage, which is brilliantly illuminated, and offerings of fruit and nosegays appear in great profusion.

This disposition to represent every thing heavenly by sensible images, is the leading feature of the Romish religion; and the Roman Catholics would have us believe, that the distinction between the sign and the thing signified is never lost sight of. This, I fear, is only true of the enlightened few;—between whom, to whatever sect or religion they may belong, there is but little real difference of opinion. For, even amongst the old heathens, the *initiated* were taught the existence of one Almighty Spirit, though this doctrine was considered too sublime for the vulgar; whose grosser feelings were thought to require the interposition of some visible object of adoration. The Roman Catholic priests seem to take the same view of human nature at present.

26th

The Baths of Dioclesian. This vast pile of building, situated on the Quirinal Hill, has not been buried by the same accumulation of rubbish that has overwhelmed most of the ancient remains. The whole of this establishment must have occupied a space of at least 400 yards square. All the rest of the baths have been entirely dismantled of their magnificent columns and splendid marbles; but the great hall of these—the *Pinacotheca*, as it was called—has been converted into a church by Michael Angelo; and the superb granite columns, each hewn out of a single block, forty-three feet in height, still remain as they stood in the days of Dioclesian;

supporting the ancient entablature, which is very rich, and in the highest preservation.

This magnificent hall is now the church of *S. Maria degli Angeli*;—the work of Michael Angelo. The form of the church is the Greek cross; so much more favourable than the Latin, for displaying at one *coup d'œil* all the grandeur of the building. This church shows what St. Peter's would have been, if Michael Angelo's plan had been followed; and it is by far the finest church in Rome—except St. Peter's, which must always be incomparable.

In this church is buried Salvator Rosa.

In my way home I met a funeral ceremony. A crucifix hung with black, followed by a train of priests, with lighted tapers in their hands, beaded the procession. Then came a troop of figures dressed in white robes, with their faces covered with masks of the same materials. The bier followed;—on which lay the corpse of a young woman, arrayed in all the ornaments of dress, with her face exposed, where the bloom of life seemed yet to linger.[3] The members of.different fraternities followed the bier—dressed in the robes of their orders—and all masked. They carried lighted tapers in, their hands, and chanted out prayers in a sort of mumbling recitative. I followed the train to the church, for I had doubts whether the beautiful figure I had seen on the bier was not a figure of wax; but I was soon convinced it was indeed the corpse of a fellow-creature;—cut off in the pride and bloom of youthful maiden beauty. Such is the Italian mode of conducting the last scene of the tragi-comedy of life. As soon as a person dies, the relations leave the house, and fly to bury themselves and their griefs in some other retirement. The care of the funeral devolves on one of the fraternities, which are associated for this purpose in every parish. These are dressed in a sort of domino and hood; which, having holes for the eyes, answers the purpose of a mask, and completely conceals the face. The funeral of the very poorest is thus conducted, with quite as much ceremony as need be. This is perhaps a better system than our own, where the relatives are exhibited as a spectacle to impertinent curiosity, while, from feelings of duty, they follow to the grave the remains of those they loved. But ours is surely an unphilosophical view of the subject. It looks as if we were materialists, and considered the cold clod, as the sole remains of the object of our affection. The Italians reason better, and perhaps feel as much as ourselves when they regard the body—deprived of the soul that animated and the mind that informed it—as no more a part of the departed spirit, than the clothes which it has also left behind.—The ultimate disposal of the body is perhaps conducted here with too much of that spirit which would disregard all claims that this mortal husk can have to our attention. As soon as the funeral service is concluded, the corpse is stripped, and consigned to those who have the care of the interment. There are large vaults, underneath the churches, for the reception of the dead. Those who can afford it, are put into a wooden shell, before they are cast into one of these Golgothas;—but the great mass are tossed in without a rag to cover them. When one of these caverns is full, it is bricked up; and, after fifty years, it is opened again, and the bones are removed to other places, prepared for their reception. So much for the last scene of the drama of life;—with respect to the first act—our own conduct of it is certainly more natural. Here they swathe and swaddle their children, till the poor urchins look like Egyptian mummies. To this frightful custom one may attribute the want of strength and symmetry of the men, which is sufficiently remarkable.

27th

Made a tour of palaces;—splendid and useless. The owners live in a few obscure rooms, and the magnificent galleries are deserted. One of the most superb saloons is at the Colonna Palace.—A fine picture of *St. John preaching in the Wilderness*, by S. Rosa. In another wing is poor *Beatrice Cenci*, by Guido;—taken the night before her execution. It is a charming countenance; of sweetness, innocence, and resignation. Her step-mother hangs near her, by whose counsel, and that of her confessor, she was instigated to prevent an incest, by the "sacrifice" of her father;—but that which she thought a sacrifice, was converted by her enemies into a "murder;"—and she lost her head by the hand of the executioner.

Doria Palace. Large collection of pictures;—*Gaspar Poussin's* green landscapes have no charms for me. The fact seems to be, that the delightful green of nature cannot be represented in a picture. Our own Glover has perhaps made the greatest possible exertions to surmount the difficulty, and give with fidelity the real colours of Nature;—but I believe the beauty of his pictures is in an inverse ratio to their fidelity;—and his failure affords an additional proof, that Nature must be stripped of her green livery, and dressed in the *browns* of the painters, or confined to her own autumnal tints, in order to be transferred to the canvass. *Cain and Abel*, by Salvator;—Rubens' picture of his wife;—a *Magdalen*, by Murillo;—and a superb landscape, by Claude;—are all excellent in their way.

Corsini Palace. Here too is an excellent collection of pictures. An *Ecce Homo*, by Guercino;—*Prometheus* by Salvator Rosa;—*Herodias's daughter*, by Guido;—and *Susannah*, by Domenichino;—are all supereminently good. This last is an exquisite picture; but it is, in fact, one of the nymphs, transplanted from his famous *Chase of Diana*, with the beauties a little heightened and embellished.

Here you see an old senatorial chair, which is a curious sample of antiquity; and resembles closely that low, round-backed chair, with a triangular seat, which we often see occupying a chimney-corner in England.

Close to the Corsini Palace, is *La Farnesina*. Here is the famous *Galatea* of Raphael in fresco;—but the more I see of fresco, the more I am inclined to believe that to paint in fresco is to throw away time and labour. The ceilings are covered with the history of Cupid and Psyche, painted from the designs of Raphael, by his scholars;—and on one of the walls is preserved a spirited sketch of a head in crayons, by Michael Angelo.

Sierra Palace. The collection small but good. A portrait by Raphael;—Titian's Family, by himself;—and *Modesty and Vanity*, by Leonardo da Vinci, are the most striking pictures. Da Vinci seems to have been desperately enamoured of the smile which he has given to *Vanity*;—some traces of which will be found in almost all the female faces that he has painted. I ought not to forget two beautiful Magdalens, by Guido, standing opposite to each other, at full length, in the innermost chamber.

28th.

Another round of palaces. In the *Spada* there are some fine landscapes, by Salvator: but the great curiosity here, is the colossal statue of Pompey; which is said to be the very statue at the base of which—"Great Cæsar fell;"—though the objection to a naked heroic statue, as the representative of a Roman senator, is, perhaps, fatal to its identity;—and then, the holding the globe in his hand, is not in *republican* taste;—this action speaks the language of a *master* of the world, and brings the statue down to the days of the empire. But this does not solve the difficulty; and if we determine that it cannot be Pompey, we shall be again at a loss to find an owner for it amongst the emperors.

Palace of the Pope. The residence of the Pope is on Monte Cavallo;—an immense pile of building; but the apartments of the Pope occupy a very small part of it. The gardens are delicious, with shady evergreen walks, that must be delightful in summer, as affording a complete protection against the sun. The whole circuit of the gardens is at least a mile.

The wing of the palace through which we were shown had been fitted up for the King of Rome;—"*Sic vos non vobis*"—and the furniture does credit to the taste and skill of Roman upholsterers. It is now set apart for the reception of the Emperor of Austria. The pictures are good. The *Annunciation*, by Guido, in the chapel, is in the sweetest style of this sweet painter;—but Guido's Mary, sweet as she is, will never do, after the Mary of Raphael;—and then, the eternal blue mantle in which Guido wraps his females, reminds one of the favourite "sky-blue attitude" of Lady Pentweazle. *A Resurrection*, by Vandyke, affords ample proof that his excellence was not limited to portraits.

In the square before the palace are the marble horses with their attendant figures, which some suppose to be Castor and Pollux;—while others tell you, that the one is a copy from the other, and that it is the representation of Alexander and Bucephalus. When there is so little to fix a story, it is more reasonable to suppose that no story was intended.

If we may believe the inscriptions, which are as old as Constantine, in whose baths these statues were found, they are the work of Phidias and Praxiteles. They are full of spirit and expression;—but are not the men out of proportion? They appear better able to carry the horses, than the horses would be to carry them. The Egyptian obelisk, which is placed between them, was brought hither, at an enormous expense, by Pius VI., from the mausoleum of Augustus; and as this was done at a time when the poor of Rome were suffering very much from distress, the following sentence, taken from Scripture, was placarded underneath the obelisk:

"Di che queste pietre divengano pani."

This was surely *mal-à-propos*; for Pius VI. could not well have adopted a better mode of supplying the poor with bread, than by furnishing them with employment.

Rospigliosi Palace. Here is the famous *Aurora* of Guido. There are no traces to confine the horses to the carriage. Apollo has the reins in one hand, and is laying fast hold of the back of the car with the other; as well he may—to prevent the horses dragging him from his seat.

Barberini Palace. This is the residence of the Ex-King and Queen of Spain, and the Prince of the Peace; whose influence is as omnipotent here, as in the palace of the Escurial. Large collection of pictures. But let the description of one suffice;—*Joseph and Potiphar's wife*. The expression of intense passion on the countenance of the female is wonderful, and every limb is full of meaning;—"there's language in the eye, the cheek, the lip—nay, the foot speaks;"—and such a foot! She has, in her struggles to detain

Joseph, planted one of her naked feet upon his, and the painter has contrived to exhibit, in the voluptuous disorder of her figure, the thrilling sensation communicated by this casual contact.

29th

Amongst the most striking ornaments of Rome, are the fountains;—not only for the architectural designs that embellish them, but for the prodigality of water which they pour out in all parts of the town. The effect of these, in summer, must be delightfully refreshing, from the sensations of coolness which running water always communicates. The fountain of *Trevi* is, perhaps, the most magnificent.—It is here that *Corinne* came, to enjoy her own contemplations by moon-light, when she was suddenly startled by seeing the reflection of *Oswald* in the water. I doubt whether this could have happened;—it is certainly a glorious scene by moon-light—the basin of water is always in a ruffled, troubled state, from the cascades that tumble into it; which prevent it from reflecting any object distinctly.

The design of the fountain of *Acqua Felice* is admirable. Moses is striking the rock in the desert, and the water obeys his wand. The figure of Moses is colossal, and very spirited;—and if ever a colossal statue can be rendered pleasing, it is in some such situation as this.

30th

A morning in the *Pantheon.*—Whoever comes to the Pantheon with expectations excited by engravings will most assuredly be disappointed;—and yet, it is a noble portico, perhaps too grand for the temple to which it leads. This is the most perfect of all the remains of antiquity. Formerly the temple of all the Gods, it has been since dedicated to all the Saints;—and the great and invisible Spirit,—the source of all things—is, perhaps, as little in the contemplation of the modern, as of the ancient worshippers of the Pantheon.

The open sky-light, communicating at once with the glorious firmament, and letting in a portion of the great vault of the heavens, produces a sublime effect. It is as if it were the eye of the Divinity—imparting light and life—and penetrating the most secret thoughts of those that repair to his altar. The Pantheon has been stripped of every thing that. could be taken away, to furnish materials for the embellishment of St. Peter's; but it has been less deformed by what has been subtracted, than by the frightful addition of two ugly towers—the work of Bernini, under the auspices of Urban VIII. It is now made the receptacle of monuments to those who have deserved well of their country, and contributed to sustain the reputation of Italy.[4] Raphael's bust is here, with the epitaph of Cardinal Bembo, of which Pope has availed himself so fully in his Epitaph on Kneller:—

> Ille est hic Raphael timuit quo sospite, vinci
> Rerum magna Parens, et moriente mori.

In my way from the Pantheon, to explore the site of the *Tarpeian Rock*, I passed through the region of the Jews;—who are huddled together in one quarter of the town, and allowed to reside nowhere else. Here, too, they are locked up every night; but—"suffering is the badge of all their tribe." In spite of these strict measures of confinement, which one would suppose must tend still more to isolate the race, I thought the features of these Jews did not exhibit so strongly that peculiar and distinctive physiognomy which is so striking in England, where they have every facility of crossing the breed.

It is not easy to determine the exact site of the Tarpeian Rock;—or, at least, of that part of it from whence criminals were flung;—and, when you have the spot, as nearly as it can be done, you will be more disappointed than by anything else in Rome. Where shall we find any traces of Seneca's description of it? "*Stat moles abscissa in profundum, frequentibus exasperata saxis, quæ aut elidant corpus, aut de integro gravius impellant; inhorrent scopulis enascentibus latera, et immensæ altitudinis aspectus.*" There is absolutely nothing at all of all this—the only precipice that remains is one of about thirty feet, from the point of a wall, where you might leap down, on the dung-mixen in the yard below, without any fear of broken bones.

It is not surprising that the great wreck of old Rome should have so destroyed the features of the Capitoline Hill. Besides, the character of the ground below is completely changed; and the *Campus Martius*, which was at the foot of the Tarpeian Rock—into which the mangled bodies fell—is now, like the rock itself, covered with the modern town.

From hence we drove to the *Catacombs*. These dreary and deserted regions were once filled with thousands of martyrs. The ecclesiastical writers say that 170,000 were buried here; and it is not incredible; for the extent of these caverns is six miles. But the Catacombs are now empty; the bones have been carried all over Christendom, for the edification of the pious;—and there must have been enough, in this mine of martyrs, to furnish relics to the whole world.

31st.

On this last day of the year, there was a grand ceremony at the church of the Jesuits;—to sing out the old year—to offer up thanksgivings for all past blessings—and to solicit a renewal of them in the year to come. The crowd was immense, and the ceremony very impressive. There is a principle of equality in Catholic congregations, more consonant with the spirit of that religion which teaches that God is no respecter of persons, than the practice which prevails in our own church;—where the greatest distinction is made between the accommodations of the rich and the poor. The former are carefully separated from the contamination of the latter, into pews; where everything is provided that luxury can suggest, to render the postures of public worship as little inconvenient as possible. In the Catholic congregations there are no such invidious distinctions;—the rich and the poor kneel down together, on the same marble floor;—as children of the same Parent—to ask the same blessings, from their common Benefactor. All the congregation joined in the chant of thanksgiving, and I was deeply impressed by the touching solemnity of the ceremony. There is always something affecting in a large concourse of people participating in the same emotion; the feeling is heightened, by the contagion of sympathy, and wound up to enthusiasm by the influence of numbers.

And so much for the year 1817. It has been to me, like most of its predecessors—"woven of a mingled yarn;"—much time lost in unavailing hope, and more saddened with the gloom of disappointment. For the Future:—I leave it with humble confidence to the great Disposer of all things, in whose hands are the issues of life and death.

1. Middleton quotes an account of a pagan procession from Apuleius, which, as he says, "might pass quite as well for the description of a popish one." Antistites sacrorum candido linteamine ad—usque vestigia strictim injecti. Deum proferebant insignes exuvias, quorum primus lucernam præmicantem claro porrigebat lumine, &c. Eas amœnus lectissimæ juventutis, veste niveâ prænitens sequebatur chorus, carmen venustum iterantes. Magnus præterea sexus utriusque numerus, lucernis, tædis, cereis.

2. Though the parallel has perhaps been carried quite far enough already, yet I cannot help noticing that for this, too, there is a heathenish precedent: see *Cic. in Verrem.* "Herculis templum est apud Agrigentos, non longe a foro, sane sanctum apud illos et religiosum. Ibi est ex ære simulacrum ipsius Herculis, quo non facile quidquam dixerim me vidisse pulchrius, usque eo, judices, ut rictum ejus ac mentum paullo sit attritius, quod in precibus et gratulationibus non solum id venerari, verum etiam *osculari* solent." The homage paid to the mouth and chin of the Pagan Deity had an excuse which is wanting to the modern *osculation* of the Apostle's toe; for there is certainly nothing in the "christened Jove" of St. Peter's, as piece of sculpture, to palliate the superstition of its votaries.

3. It is a general custom in Italy to paint the faces of the dead; and the ladies seem to agree with Pope's Narcissa:

"One would not, sure, look frightful when one's dead;
    And, Betty, give this cheek a little red!"

4. Most of these have been supplied by the chisel, or the purse of
Canova; whose enthusiasm for the arts, and whose munificent patronage
of younger artists, are too well known to need any praise front me. If I
have presumed to question the supremacy of his merit as a sculptor, it is
impossible not to admire the man.

There seems to be something in the air of Rome that inspires her
artists with a portion of the old Roman feeling. Thorwaldson, on being
applied to by the King of Prussia, to execute some considerable work,
objected that there was at that time in Rome an artist of great merit,
one of his majesty's own subjects,—*Shadoff,* since distinguished by his
Spinning Girl,—who he humbly conceived would be a fitter object for
the King's patronage.

In the same taste, Camuccini purchased for fifty louis, a picture
which a former pupil had brought to him as the first fruits of his pencil;
Camuccini then bade him take his picture to the Pope, knowing that
he could not have afforded to present it unpaid for. The consequence of
the present was, an appointment, and subsequent patronage—in short,
the making of his pupil's fortune.

V

SIGHTSEEING
IN THE NEW YEAR

January 1st, 1818

The new year opened with a dark and dreary morning—foreboding disaster and disappointment;—but, "we defy augury!"

Went to mass in the private chapel of the Pope, in his palace on Monte Cavallo. The most striking trait in the appearance of the venerable Pius VII. is his black hair, wholly unmixed with grey. There is a piety and sincerity in his demeanour that conciliate respect, in spite of the mummery that surrounds him.

But, let the character of the Pope be what it may, the part he is called upon to act must identify him with Lord Peter;—of whom I was reminded incessantly; particularly when the priest, who preached, previously to the delivery of his sermon, prostrated himself at the Pontiff's feet, to kiss the papal slipper.[1]

It would be difficult to imagine such a scene as the Pope's chapel—

> Never I ween
> In any body's recollection,
> Was such a party seen
> For genuflection.

If it were literally represented in a Protestant country, it would be regarded as a burlesque; as far beyond nature, as King Arthur, with his courtiers Doodle and Noodle;—but Noodle and Doodle, with all their bowing and head-shaking, would cease to be ridiculous in the Pope's chapel. Just two such personages were in attendance upon the Pope, during the whole of the ceremony, to arrange the different changes in the order of his petticoats, and to take off and put on his tiara, as the service required; for it would be contrary to all etiquette, that the Pope should do anything for himself; and he cannot even blow his nose without the help of one of his attendant cardinals.

The whole of the conclave were present, each supported by his train-bearer, or tail-twister:—and this office is no sinecure; for on some occasions, the train of Lord knows how many ells, is to be spread out like a peacock's tail, and, at others, it is to be twisted up as close as a cart-horse's; in order that their Eminences may take the corner under their arms, and move about at their pleasure.

Cardinal —— sat amongst the rest—sleek and sly-looking— like a wolf in sheep's clothing. He was conspicuous in the mummery of his part, and so expert in the posture exercise, that he might act as *Flugelman* to the whole corps of cardinals. There was something in his demeanour, which, like an overacted part, excited observation;—a lurking devil in his eye, that seemed to peep out in spite of him.

Pomp and mummery, in a civil or military dress, are fatiguing and ridiculous;—but, when associated with religion, they become disgusting. What a strange idea of the Deity must have first suggested this homage of postures and prostrations. If a Chinese had been present, he might well have concluded that the Pope was the God of this strange worship;—and indeed I doubt whether, on this occasion, the thoughts of many were elevated nearer to heaven, than the *popedom*. But I repeat, that it is impossible not to feel respect for the venerable Pius. The man who is in earnest— especially in religion—can never be an object of ridicule; and far be it from me to judge another man's servant, or condemn the fashion of my neighbour's piety, in whatever shape it may dress itself. But, without ridiculing *piety*, the eccentricities and perversities of human nature have ever been fair game; and I hope we may laugh at each other's absurdities, without giving offence, and with common benefit to all parties.

Consalvi, the Pope's prime minister;—a shrewd, intelligent, well-looking man.—As he passed out of chapel, a well-dressed person in the court-yard threw himself upon his knees before him, and Consalvi, as if he thought the man had some petition to present, advanced towards him, but when he found that his only object was to kiss his hand, he put him aside; being, as it is said, very impatient of all such public demonstrations of homage.

In the evening, we went to a party at Torlonia's, the banker;—or as he now is—the Duke of Bracciano. A suite of rooms was thrown open, in which a mob of people wandered about, without object, or amusement. Such a scene could afford little insight into Italian manners, even if the mob were composed exclusively of Italians—but at present, two-thirds, at least, of the company at every party, are English. Rooms hot;—Music miserable;—as to music, I have heard nothing tolerable, vocal or instrumental, since I left England.

2nd

It is time to record my impressions of the manners, and general appearance of the people;—but I fear I have but little to record. All the world knows that the Italians are a polite and civil people, and universally courteous and obliging to strangers. The education of the men is much neglected; and I believe it would not be difficult to find a Roman prince who could neither read nor write; nor is it surprising, where there are no public objects of ambition to stimulate improvement, that the mere desire of knowledge should be insufficient to counteract the indolence so natural to man. The women are in the grandest style of beauty. The general character of their figure is majestic;—they move about with the inceding tread of Juno. The physiognomy of the Italian woman bears the stamp of the most lively sensibility, and explains her character at a glance. Voluptuousness is written in every feature but it is that serious and enthusiastic expression of passion—the farthest removed from frivolity—which promises as much constancy as ardour; and to which Love is not the capricious trifling gallantry of an hour of idleness—but the serious and sole occupation of life. There is an expression of energy, and sublimity, which bespeaks a firmness of soul, and elevation of purpose, equal to all trials;—but this expression is too often mingled with a look of ferocity, that is very repulsive. Black hair, and black sparkling eyes, with dark olive complexions, are the common characteristics of Italian physiognomy. A *blonde* is a rarity;—the black eye, however, is not always bright and sparkling; it is sometimes set off with the soft melting languishment peculiar to its rival blue, and this, by removing all expression of fierceness, takes away every thing that interferes with the bewitching fascination of an Italian beauty. Much has been said of the laxity of their morals; however this be, there is so much attention paid to external decorum, that the *Ruffiano* is an officer in general use, throughout Italy, to arrange preliminaries, which in other places would not require any intermediate negociation. It is, I believe, from the lying pretensions of these Mercuries, who have the impudence to offer themselves as the bearers of proposals to any woman, of any rank, that erroneous impressions have been received on the subject;—as if it were possible to believe that any woman, above the condition of absolute want, would surrender at discretion to the offers of a stranger. Still, however, the very lies of a Ruffiano must have some foundation; and indeed the existence of such a degrading profession is a sufficient evidence of a lamentable state of society.

3d

Sat an hour in the Sistine Chapel—before Michael Angelo's *Last Judgment.* The choice of the subject shows the nature of his genius, which nothing could daunt. The figure of Christ is sublimely conceived. If Forsyth had called this—*The Apollo of Painting*—the expression would have perhaps been better applied than to the *St. Michael* of Guido, which Smollett describes, with some truth, as exhibiting "the airs of a French dancing master." The frightful calm of despair is admirably expressed in one of the condemned, leaning on his elbow—who is so abstracted in mental suffering as to be utterly unconscious of the demons who are dragging him down to hell. Smollett, whose criticisms are often just, talks of the *confusion* of the picture, and calls it "a mere mob without keeping, subordination, or repose;"—repose in the last judgment!—when the trumpet is sounding—the graves opening—and the dead awakening! I fear the *confusion* was in his mind—especially when, to illustrate the effect which the picture produced upon him, he confounds two things so different—as a number of instruments in a concert—and a number of people talking at the same time. The keeping of the picture is admirable, and all is in subordination to the figure of the Saviour. Nothing can be more sublime than the action of this figure—delivering the dreadful sentence of condemnation—"Depart—ye accursed, into everlasting fire!" By the way; I am obliged to an artist for pointing out to me, what I think would not easily be perceived;—that the Saviour is *sitting down*. The picture has been so much injured, by time and cleaning, that, as the light now falls on it, the figure appears to be standing up. Every body has noticed the solecism of introducing into this picture a personage from the Heathen Mythology;—*Charon* is employed in ferrying over the bodies. Michael Angelo probably followed Dante, without thinking much about the matter:—

> Caron, dimonio, con occhi di bragia,
> Loro accennando, tutte le raccoglie,
> Batte col remo qualunque s'adagia.

The skeletons are *re-fleshing* themselves, which—in the representation at least—has something shocking, if not ridiculous. After all, however,—this famous picture is gone;—it is a ruin;—and what is the ruin of a painting? The soul of beauty may still linger in the remains of architectural ruins, amidst broken entablatures, tottering pillars, and falling arches;—but when the colours of a painting are faded, it is lost for ever;—nothing is left but a remnant of canvass, or a few square feet of mortar. The Last Judgment is fast approaching to this state; though it may still remain for some time, a school of technical excellencies to the artist, who is in pursuit of professional instruction.—If there were no other argument for preferring oil painting to fresco, surely this single circumstance of durability is sufficient to turn the scale;—and yet Michael Angelo said, that oil painting was only fit occupation for boys and women.

It may be sacrilege to say any thing to depreciate the merit of Michael Angelo,—but I suspect his reputation was obtained by the universality of his talents, rather than their separate excellence. He was an original genius, and his great merit seems to be, that he was *the first* to introduce a taste for the grand, and the sublime. He was, as Sir Joshua Reynolds describes him, the exalted father and founder of modern art; but, while he excelled in grandeur of style, and truth of design, he was, surely, too disdainful of the auxiliary ornaments of colouring, which are essential to the perfection of the art. If he is to be judged by his works,—can he be compared to Raphael in painting, or to John of Bologna in sculpture? His *Moses*, which is considered his *chef d'œuvre*, is to me, any thing but sublime. I would propose these doubts to the consideration of those more learned than myself, though with the fear of Quintilian's sentence before my eyes:—"*Modeste tamen, et circumspecto judicio, de tantis viris pronunciandum est, ne, quod plerisque accidit, damnent quæ non intelligunt.*"

Notwithstanding the unbounded and almost extravagant praises which Sir Joshua lavishes in his discourses, on the grand, chaste, severe style of Michael Angelo; it is remarkable that the doctrines he has inculcated by his pen are not supported by his pencil. It may therefore, perhaps, be doubted, whether the doctrines he laid down, were not adopted from *authority*, rather than the real dictates of his own understanding;—for the understanding may become the slave of authority, almost without knowing it;—and the proof of it is, that his own taste and discernment led him to depart from them in practice, and to indulge in all that witchery of colours, and exquisite management of *chiaroscuro*, which constitute so great a part of the charm of his pictures.

In returning through the Pauline Chapel, I was shocked to see a picture to commemorate what the Catholics ought of all others to wish forgotten—the horrible massacre of St. Bartholomew.

4th

Lounged through the *Capitol*;—the work of Michael Angelo, on the site of the ancient *Capitol*. It is opened to the public, as well as the Vatican, on Sundays and Thursdays. It contains an almost inexhaustible mine of antique curiosities. There is a very full and complete collection of imperial busts, which would furnish an amusing study to a physiognomist. The histories of their lives may be read in many of their faces, particularly in those of Nero, Caligula, Caracalla, and Maximin; Germanicus, Vespasian, and Titus. Nature has written these characters too plainly to be mistaken. There are some exceptions. In Julius Cæsar instead of the open generous expression, which the magnanimity and clemency of his character would lead you to expect; you find a narrow contraction of muscles, that would suit the features of a miser; and in Heliogabalus, the swinish temperament which is generally very strongly marked, does not appear.

It will require repeated visits, to examine minutely all the treasures of the Capitol. Perhaps there is nothing more curious or interesting than the maps of old Rome, engraved on stone, which served as the ancient pavement of the Temple of Remus. There is one fragment still extant, which is marked in these maps, just as it now stands, the grand entrance to the Portico of Octavia, now called *la Peschiera*. The front columns, which are Corinthian, and of beautifully white marble, with their entablature and inscription, are entire;—but the filth of a Roman fish-market makes it almost inaccessible. Amongst the statues in the Capitol, I was most struck with a *Cupid* with his Bow—*The Hecuba*—*Cupid and Psyche*—a head of *Alexander*, a bust of *Marcus Aurelius* when a boy,—the famous *Dying Gladiator*—and last, though it should have been placed first and foremost in beauty—the beautiful *Antinous*—who is always hanging down his head as if he felt ashamed of himself—

Sed frons læta parum et dejecto lumina vultu.

This is a charming statue, and considered merely as an exhibition of the beauty of the male figure, superior perhaps to the Apollo itself.

The *Gladiator* is another instance of M. Angelo's great skill in restoring;—he has contributed an arm, a foot, the upper lip, and the tip of the nose. Antiquaries dispute whether this is the representation of a dying warrior, or a dying gladiator;—a question that can only be interesting to antiquaries;—to me it is sufficient that it is a dying *Man*.

The *Palace of the Conservators* forms part of the Capitol. Here is the famous bronze wolf, which has afforded so much discussion to antiquaries, to determine what wolf it is. Those must have better eyes than mine who can discover the marks of lightning, which seem to be necessary to identify it with Cicero's wolf; but, I think, one may safely say that there are the traces of gilding. Two brazen Ducks—for the Roman geese, instead of being expanded into swans, dwindle to the size of widgeons—are also of high antiquity, and appear to be cackling as if the Gauls were again within hearing. A bronze bust of the elder *Brutus* exhibits in the most strongly written characters, the stern inexorable severity of his disposition. Amongst the modern sculpture is a bust of Michael Angelo, by himself. If he were judged by the laws of physiognomy, it would go hard with him;—but some allowance must be made for the accident of his nose, which, they tell you, was flattened by a blow from a rival's mallet. The collection of pictures has not much to boast of. There is a small picture by Salvator of a Sorceress, in his wildest and most romantic style.

Michael Angelo has given us, too, a picture of himself, which does not convey a more favourable idea of his countenance, than is afforded by the bust.

5th

An invitation from Prince Kaunitz;—the Austrian Ambassador. Our valet de place tells us that we owe this to him; he says that when an ambassador gives a fête, his servants distribute tickets to all the valets de place who are in employment, as the readiest way of getting at the strangers who may happen to be at Rome;—and the English in Rome are invited to every thing.

7th
Went to Cardinal Fesch's, who has the best and most extensive collection of pictures in Rome. His chaplain acted as Cicerone. The whole house was thrown open. Madame, Napoleon's mother, inhabits one floor. In the cardinal's bed-room is a splendid bust of Napoleon in porcelain, crowned with a golden chaplet of laurel. Here, too, is the cream of the collection. A *Magdalen*, by Vandyke, is particularly striking. The Magdalen is generally a voluptuous woman, whose "loose hair and lifted eye" express just enough of grief to make her beauties more interesting;—but in this of Vandyke, there is the most affecting contrition, and the eyes are red with weeping.

St. Peter in the high-priest's kitchen, by *Honthorst*, or, as the Italians call him, from an inability to grapple with such a cacophonous name, *Gerardo della Notte*, is a splendid specimen of the skill of the Dutch school in the management of light and shadow. The flaring light of the torches has all the effect of reality. The whole collection amounts to 1300 pictures—far too many for a single morning. It is rich in the works of Rubens; and if Rubens' powers of conception, and skill in execution, had been combined with *taste*, he would have deserved one of the highest pedestals in the temple of painting;—but he cannot get out of Holland; all his figures, particularly the females, savour strongly of a Dutch kitchen.

Here is a superb assortment of Dutch pieces;—and if painting consisted alone of high finishing and exactness of execution, the Dutch would deserve to be exalted above all their rivals;—but painting is as much an art of the mind, as of the hand, and the poetical qualifications are of quite as much importance as the mechanical. There is just enough of Guido and Carlo Dolci. The pictures of the first have been termed the *honey*, and those of the last may perhaps be called the *treacle* of painting.—Too much saccharine is always cloying.

8th

Descended into the Mamertine prisons; which consist at present of two small dungeons. This prison was built by *Ancus Martius*;— "*Carcer ad terrorem increscentis audaciæ, mediâ urbe, imminens foro, ædificatur.*" The subterraneous part was added by Servius Tullius; and thence called *Tullianum*. It was here, in these condemned cells, that we learn from Sallust, the Catiline conspirators were confined and executed.

Nothing can show the difference between the ancient and modern systems of government more strongly, than the limited size of this prison, compared with the innumerable jails that now abound in every quarter of Europe;—and yet this was the only prison in old Rome:—

> ——Sub regibus atque tribunis
> Viderunt uno contentam carcere Romam.

A habeas corpus bill becomes, indeed, an object of importance, when the prisons of a kingdom contain accommodations for thousands of its inhabitants. St. Peter and St. Paul were confined in the same dungeon where Lentulus had been before them; at least, so your guide will tell you—and how can you refuse to believe him, when he shows you the remains of two miracles to confirm his testimony? St. Peter, it seems, knocked his head against the wall, and instead of the usual consequence—bruising his head—he indented the wall; and in the solid rock you now see a tolerable impression of his features. Again—during his confinement, many converts came to be baptized, and Peter, being in want of water, caused a fountain to spring up in the centre of the dungeon—which still remains.

In the evening we went to the Italian comedy, which was so tiresome that we could not endure more than one scene. We drove afterwards to the opera. The theatre large and handsome;—

six tiers of boxes. The seats in the pit are numbered, and divided off separately with elbows;—so that you may take any one of them in the morning, and secure it for the whole evening. Some plan of this kind would surely be a great improvement in our own theatres. The dancing was bad, and the singing worse. A set of burlesque dancers amused us afterwards, by aping the *pirouettes* of the others. The dancing of the stage gives but too much foundation for such caricatures. It is daily becoming less elegant, as the difficult is substituted for the graceful. What can be more disgusting than to see the human figure twirling round with the legs at right angles? In such an attitude, "Man delights not me nor woman neither." All postures, to be graceful, should be easy and natural, and what can be more unnatural than this?

9th

Went for the third time to Canova's *Studio*; who has, perhaps, attained a reputation beyond his merits. There is much grace in his works, but the effect is too often spoiled by an affected prettiness, or a theatrical display. There is a finical fashionable air about his female figures; and his men are all attitudinarians. He is too fond of borrowing from the ancients. This is to be lamented, for it does not seem to be necessary for him to borrow; and his best works perhaps are those in which he has borrowed least; as the *Hercules and Lichas*, *Dædalus and Icarus*, which he finished at 18, the *Cupid and Psyche*, and the *Venus and Adonis*.

But you can too often trace every limb and feature to its corresponding prototype in the antique. This is pitiful. It is no excuse to say that all the beautiful attitudes have been forestalled, and that repetition is necessary. There certainly is nothing new under the sun; but invention is displayed in a new *arrangement* of the same materials; and the human figure may be varied, in its attitudes and contours, *ad infinitum*.

Chloris awakened is an exquisite performance;—but it is plain that Canova's mind was full of the Hermaphrodite, when he modelled it. The introduction of the Cupid is well imagined, as a sort of excuse for the attitude. It is impossible to look at this recumbent nymph, without admiring the delicate finishing of the sculptor, but one cannot applaud the taste of the design. The expression of the whole is scarcely within the bounds of decency;—for it is the expression, and not the nudity of a statue, "the disposition, and not the exposition of the limbs," upon which this depends; and it is a prostitution of sculpture to make it subservient to the gratification of voluptuousness.

This criticism may however perhaps savour of squeamishness; for while we were admiring the exquisite finishing of Canova's chisel, a young Italian lady with a party joined us, who was thrown into an ecstacy of admiration by the charms of Chloris's figure; and she patted the jutting beauties with delight, exclaiming— while she looked round to us for confirmation of her opinion, —*Bella cosa! Bella cosa! O che bella cosa!*

It is curious to see the progress of a statue, from the rough block of marble, to the last *ad unguem* finish; which is all that is done by the master hand. The previous labour is merely mechanical, and may he done by a common workman from the model of the sculptor.

The *Venus and Adonis* is full of simplicity, grace, and tenderness.

The *Cupid and Psyche* is a charming composition, but Psyche's hair looks as if it had been dressed by a French friseur.

There is much to admire in the group of *The Graces*;—but there is also much of that finical prettiness of which I complain. They are three pretty simpletons—with the *niminy-piminy* airs of a fashionable boarding school; there is *silliness* without *simplicity*; and no two qualities can be more opposite.

Again—there is a trickery and quackery in the finishing of Canova's statues, which is below the dignity of a sculptor. The marble is not left in its natural state—but it must be stained and polished to aid the effect. The other sculptors laugh at this, and well they may;—for these adventitious graces soon fade away, and are beside the purpose of sculpture, whose end was, and is, to represent *form* alone.

10th

With the most lively recollection of Canova, I went this morning to examine the *Studio* of Thorwaldson, a Danish sculptor;—whose works are much more to my fancy. There is a freshness and originality in his designs, guided by the purest taste. What can be more elegant and beautiful than his Basso-Relievo of *Night*? His *Venus victrix* approaches nearer than any modern statue to the Venus de Medicis. There is a *Shepherd* too, which is a delightful specimen of simplicity and nature;—and the charm of these statues is, that while they emulate, they have not borrowed any thing from the works of the ancients.

A bust of Lord Byron—a good likeness.

11th

Removed from the Via degli otto Cantoni to the Piazza Mignanelli. The fatigue of mounting 104 steps after a morning's excursion was intolerable;—to say nothing of the fish-stalls, and the other noises of the Corso; amongst which, I was not a little surprised by a daily morning serenade from the odious squeaking bag-pipe. Who could have expected to meet this instrument so far from Scotland?—And yet it is indigenous in this land of music, that is, in the more southern part of it—in Calabria.

Walked on the Pincian Hill; where the French constructed an excellent promenade. Here all the beauty and fashion of Rome resort, when the weather is fine, to parade, either in their equipages, or on foot, and discuss the gossip and tittle-tattle of the town.

The day was beautiful, and the elastic purity of the air has given me an agreeable foretaste of the charms of an Italian spring. Pauline, the Princess Borghese, was on the walk, with a bevy of admirers; as smart and pretty a little bantam figure as can be imagined. She bears a strong resemblance to her brother Napoleon; and her genius seems also to partake of the same character, and to scorn the restrictions of ordinary rules.

The symmetry of her figure is very striking, and she once sat, if that be the phrase, to Canova; who modelled her statue as a *Venus victrix* lying on a couch. This statue is now at the Borghese palace, but it is kept under lock and key, and cannot be seen without a special order from Pauline herself.

12th

Sudden change in the weather.—Excessive cold.—Thermometer in the shade at 29.—Passed the morning in the Vatican, of which I have as yet said nothing, for the subject is almost inexhaustible. The extent of this vast palace may be collected from the number of rooms contained in it, which are said to amount to eleven thousand.

The library is one of the largest in the world; but a stranger has no time to examine its treasures. Amongst the curiosities they show is the famous treatise on the seven sacraments, in the handwriting of Henry VIII., which that orthodox prince sent to the Pope, with this distich;—

> Anglorum Rex Henricus, Leo Decime, mittit
> Hoc opus, et fidei testem et amicitiæ.

Here also you see many curious relics of Roman furniture, with a sample of their household gods, which are the queerest little things in the world; and if Æneas's were not on a larger scale, he might have carried away a hundred of them—in his pocket.

The galleries of Raphael are so called from the famous fresco ceilings, which were painted by him and his scholars. The whole history of the Bible is depicted on the ceilings of these galleries, beginning with the creation of the world. Such a subject must fail in any hands—for what pencil can delineate the great Spirit? Raphael has done as much as painter could do, but it is impossible for a finite mind to imagine infinity, or give a suitable form to that Being who has neither beginning nor end. It is Montaigne, I believe, who says that if every animal were to draw a picture of the Divinity, each would clothe him in its own figure; and a negro painter would, I presume, certainly give him a black complexion. Such personifications and representations would at once appear to us in the highest degree ridiculous; but perhaps it is only one degree less so, to see him under the figure of an old man, with a long beard, as Raphael has done it, with all his limbs at work, separating the elements with bodily energy. Eustace finds fault with the figure, and points out the inferiority of this corporeal exertion, to the sublime description of Moses. No one will deny that the description of the Almighty *fiat*;—"Let there be light, and there was light"—conveys a more sublime idea to the mind, than the picture of the painter;— but this is not the painter's fault; he cannot speak to the mind by the alphabet. His language is in his brush, and he must *represent*, and not *describe*; and I know not how he could *represent* the action of the creation otherwise than by making the Creator corporeally at work. It would not do to place him in tranquil majesty, with a scroll appended to his mouth, as we see in some old pictures, inscribed with γενεσθω φως, και εγενετο—"Let there be light, and light was." The only fault then is the choice of the subject; and for this Raphael is not answerable. He was ordered to represent the whole scripture history, and the creation was too important a part to be omitted. But let future painters profit by Raphael's failure—and let no one hereafter venture to personify that great first Cause, which "passeth all understanding."

The *Chambers of Raphael* are those which were painted by him in fresco; but these works are sharing the fate of all other frescos; it is grievous to witness the progress of decay for the *School of Athens* deserves to be immortal.

There is now a small collection of oil paintings in the Vatican, composed of those which have been brought back from France: but which have not been restored to the places from whence they were taken. Amongst these are the *St. Jerome* of Domenichino, and the famous *Transfiguration* of Raphael. Of this picture so much has been said, that it is almost impossible to say more.

But I suspect this is a memorable instance of the disposition of mankind to follow the leader, and echo the praise which they do not understand. Painters have expressed more admiration than they felt, and the multitude have followed them without feeling any admiration at all.

The want of *unity* in the action is a fault that must strike every body, and Smollett is for getting rid of this by cutting the painting asunder, and thus making two pictures of it.

The *composition* of the picture—by which I suppose is meant the conception of the subject and the arrangement of the figures—is pointed out by artists as its chief merit;—but this is an excellence rather to be felt by artists than common observers. It is the general effect alone that strikes the latter; and nothing can well be more disgusting than the figure of the *possessed*;—who is, however, rather than the Saviour, the prominent figure of the piece.

The colouring of the upper part of the picture, particularly in the countenance of the Saviour, is very defective; the head of Jesus has here none of that peculiar expression of benevolence, and more than human virtue, which are to be found in other pictures of him.

The *figure* however is beautifully managed—conveying the impression of that supernatural lightness which we associate with the idea of a "glorified body;"—but it is impossible to extend this admiration to the opera-dancing attitudes of Moses and Elias.

13th

Saw Camuccini's paintings—a living artist. The death of Virginia, the labour of fifteen years, painted for Lord Bristol, is a splendid picture. The modern artists of Italy, however, though in general excellent draftsmen, delight too much in glaring colours, and strong contrasts of light and shadow; and their style of painting seems better calculated for the tea-board than the canvass.

Went in the evening with a large party, amongst whom was Thorwaldson, to see the Vatican by torch-light. This is absolutely necessary, if you wish to appreciate justly the merit of the statues. Many of them were found in baths, where light was not admitted. They were created therefore for torch-light as their proper element; and the variety of light and shade which is thus produced, heightens the effect prodigiously. There is something of the same kind of difference between the statues by day and by torch-light, as between a rehearsal in the morning and the lighted theatre in the evening.

I have endeavoured in vain to admire the Apollo as much as I did the Venus;—and yet, if it were the perfection of the male figure, one ought to admire it more: for sculptors agree that the male figure is the most beautiful subject for their art. But perhaps it is impossible to divest oneself entirely of all sexual associations;—and this may be the secret charm of the Venus.—The ladies, I believe, prefer the Apollo. By the way, I am surprised at the squeamishness which has induced the ruling powers of Florence and Rome to deface the works of antiquity by the addition of a tin fig-leaf, which is fastened by a wire to all the male statues. One would imagine the Society for the Suppression of Vice had an affiliated establishment in Italy. Nothing can be more ridiculously prudish. That imagination must be depraved past all hope, that can find any prurient gratification in the cold chaste nakedness of an ancient marble. It is the fig-leaf alone that suggests any idea of indecency, and the effect of it is to spoil the statue. I was complaining loudly of this barbarous addition, when an Italian lady of the party assented to my criticism, and whispered in my ear—that I must come again in the *Autumn*. This taste has however become so fixed, that Canova now cuts a fig-leaf out of the original block, and it thus becomes an integral part of the statue.

It is pity that Canova's works are placed in the Vatican. The Perseus might have attracted admiration while the Apollo was at Paris—but Apollo is come back;—and who could ever tolerate a copy by the side of the original?

His Boxers have more spirit and originality;—but is not Damoxenus's posture wrong? Ought he not to have his left leg foremost? As he stands, his lunge is already made, whereas he is only preparing to lunge; but I am confusing the terms of fencing with those of boxing—and I leave this question to the decision of *the fancy*.

14th

The more I see of the antique statues, the more I am struck with the nature and simplicity which constitute their great charm. I have cited many instances, and it would be easy to add more;—for example, Posidippus and Menander sit in their arm-chairs, as they might be supposed to have done in their own studies, without losing an atom of force or expression by this repose. Ease is the consummation of art—"the last refinement of labour"—πολλης πειρας το τελευταιον επιγεννημα.

Canova, on the contrary, seems to have studied too much in the school of Michael Angelo. His muscles are all in action. His figures are struck out, as if they were conscious of the presence of spectators. There is always something in their attitude and expression, which there would not be if it were not for this consciousness;—just as it happens to second-rate actors, who are unable to preserve the simplicity of nature on the stage, but do every thing as if they were aware that an assembly of spectators were looking at them. The statue of Phocion, one of the greatest, because one of the best men of antiquity, is a charming instance of that quiet modesty and simplicity of attitude, so appropriate to his character.

The head of Jupiter, and the noble statue of Nerva, in the round saloon, struck me much. Jove's head looks as if its nod might make Olympus tremble. Sublime divine majesty beams in every feature. By the way, it is impossible not to be struck with the strong likeness between the countenance of the *mild Jupiter—the Jupiter Optimus Maximus* of the Romans—and that of Christ, as it is represented by the great majority of Italian painters; whose pictures are so like one another that they seem to have been copied from some common original. It was, perhaps, this *beau ideal* of the Greeks which furnished them with the idea of their Christ;—and indeed, it would not be easy for the imagination of any painter to put together a set of features better adapted to the subject.

While Jupiter looks the king of the gods, Nerva, with a laurel chaplet on his brow, realizes all one's ideas of what the emperor of *men* ought to be. If the statue of Nerva were not so admirable that it would amount to high treason to remove it, this would clearly be the place for the Apollo. He is very ill-placed where he is, cooped up as it were in a pen. For as the size is above the standard of life, it should he seen from a distance;—but this is impossible in the solitary cell where he is now confined.

The group of the Laocoon has no charms for me;—and I am not at all more disposed to admire it, because Pliny tells us that it was cut out of a single piece of marble. This may render it a greater *curiosity*—but nothing more. Laocoon's sons, too, are not boys, but little men; and there is something unhappy in the materials of which the group is composed, which have all the appearance of painted wood. Yet we collect from Pliny that this was considered as superior to any work of art, in sculpture or painting[2].

As we find that these sculptors lived as early as the year of Rome 320, it is probable that Virgil took his description from this group; and indeed he has hit off the expression of the statue exactly, in his comparison of the cries of Laocoon to the bellowing of a bull—

> Clamores simul horrendos ad sidera tollit:
> Quales mugitus, fugit quum saucius aram
> Taurus—

The ancients were as perfect in their representation of animals as of men; and there are the most delightful specimens of this kind in the chambers of animals. But it would be endless, and indeed hopeless, to attempt a description of the contents of the Vatican. Sculpture and painting, strictly speaking, do not perhaps admit of description. The ideas of beauty received by one sense can hardly be transmitted by another. A man may give the exact proportions of the Venus de Medicis, with the projections of the nose and chin;—but all this, which is literally *description,* can never impart a single idea of the grace and dignity diffused over that divine statue—and if he mention that grace, he describes his own sensations rather than the figure. He who could, by his description, place before the eyes of his reader the *effect* produced by the Venus;—who could convey by words, the manly, resigned, patient suffering of the dying Gladiator, conscious that he is breathing his last;—or that melancholy and terrible gloom which attended the destruction of all things, as exhibited in the *Deluge* of Poussin—with the heart-rending despair of the Husband and Father, who sees his wife perishing, and his child exposed to inevitable death;—who could show him the glowing tints of sunset, or the moonbeams glistening on the scarcely-rippling ocean, as created by the pencil of Vernet;—the man, I say, who could excite sensations similar to those which have been produced by these masters of the sublime and the beautiful, would cease to *describe*;—he would be their equal in a different line;—he would be himself—a poet.

1. Eustace endeavours to furnish at once a reason and an excuse for this strange ceremonial, by explaining, that it is to the *Cross*, embroidered on the slipper, that this homage is really paid. But we are naturally led to inquire, what business the Cross has in such a situation.

The indefatigable Middleton, who traces up every popish custom to some heathen original, contends that this observance was copied from the example of Caligula; who, according to Seneca, introduced this Persian fashion; and, to the indignation of all Rome, *presented his foot to be kissed;—"absoluto et gratias agenti porrexit osculandum sinistrum pedem."* The excuse which Caligula's friends made for him is curious enough; and, though not quite so good as Eustace's, is perhaps not very unlike it: *"Qui excusant, negant id insolentiæ causâ factum; aiunt socculum auratum, imo aureum, margaritis distinctum ostendere eum voluisse."* Senec. de Benef. 1. 2. 12.

2. *Sicut in Laocoonte, qui est in Titi imperatoris domo, opus, omnibus et picuræ et statuariæ artis, anteferendum; ex uno lapide, eum et liberos draconumque mirabiles nexus, do consilii sententia, fecere summi artifices Agesander, et Polydorus, et Athenodorus Rhodii.*

VI

FESTIVAL
AND CARNIVAL

Jan. 15th

It is curious to observe how Pagan and Christian Rome are every where blended and incorporated; and how adroitly the papal capital has invested itself with the pomp of the Gentile city. Besides the *Pantheon*, once dedicated to *All Saints*, and since called *S. Maria ad Martyres*, the *Curia of Pompey* has been converted into the church of *S. Andrea della Valle*; the *Temple of Isis* has been dedicated to *S. Marcello*; and the splendid columns of *Trajan* and *Marcus Aurelius* now support the statues of *St. Peter* and *St. Paul*.

I looked on, this morning, at a curious religious exercise. Adjoining the church of *S. Giovanni Laterano*, is a chapel, to which you ascend by *the sacred staircase*, which is said to have been brought from Pilate's house in Jerusalem, and is believed to be the very staircase which Christ ascended when he was carried to judgment. It would be considered sacrilegious to mount this staircase by any other than a genuflecting progression; and this has been thought so meritorious an act, that there was some danger of the marble steps being worn away by the knees of the pious; so that now, an external covering of wood has been added, which may be renewed as occasion requires. The ascent is no easy task, as I can vouch from the experience of three or four steps, which I achieved myself. There is, of course, another way down; for it would amount to an act of martyrdom to descend in the same manner.

16th

I was arrested in my way through the Campo Vaccino this morning by an extraordinary sight. There was a large herd of about a hundred pigs, and I arrived just as three men were commencing the work of death. Each had a stiletto in his hand, and they despatched the whole herd in a few minutes.

The stab was made near the left leg, and seemed to go directly to the heart, for the animal fell without a groan or a struggle. This appears to be a less cruel, and is certainly a more quiet mode than our own; where the peace of a whole parish is disturbed by the uproar occasioned by the murder of a single pig.

It is to be hoped that the stiletto may soon be confined to this use; and indeed the practice of stabbing is becoming every day more rare. The French, by depriving the people of their knives, did much to put an end to this horrible custom; and the abridgment that has been made in the indulgence of sanctuaries, to which an assassin used to fly, and laugh at the officers of justice, will do more towards abolishing it altogether.

The administration of Cardinal Consalvi is calculated to do all that an honest, wise, and liberal-minded minister can do, to correct the evils of a bad constitution. But in endeavouring to work for the public good, he is exposed to constant opposition from the collision of private interests.

Last year there was a scoundrel in the post-office, who committed wholesale depredations upon the letters, and all the world complained of the loss of remittances. This fellow was however protected by a powerful opposition Cardinal, and it seemed that he could only be got rid of from the post-office, by the promise of an appointment of equal value in some other department.

Nothing can show in a stronger light the weakness of the government, than the regular system of robbers, established in open defiance of it, who push their attacks within eighteen miles of the Pope's palace. Scarcely a month has passed since a most outrageous attempt was made to seize Lucien Buonaparte, at his own villa at Frascati. He had the good fortune to make his escape through a secret and subterraneous door, but the robbers carried off a poor painter to the mountains, who was staying in the house, supposing him to be Lucien. It was with some difficulty, and after three days' detention, that the painter convinced them at last, by giving specimens of his art, that he was really no prince; and they were not a little mortified at the discovery of their mistake: for their custom is to demand an *ad valorem* ransom, and the price of the painter was nothing in comparison with what they would have exacted for the Prince of Canino himself.

All endeavours to put down this barefaced system have failed. The military have been employed, but it seems the robbers can afford to pay them higher for being quiet, than the government can for being active.

Much is expected from the present governor of Rome;—but what can be done by a single man, where the great mass is corrupt? When public spirit is extinct, and the people feel no interest in the preservation of the government, there is no longer any security for the fidelity of agents, or the execution of orders.

17th

Festival of St. Anthony; who interpreted literally the injunction of the Scripture—"Go ye into all the world, and preach the Gospel to every creature;"—and who, according to the legend, like another Orpheus, charmed the beasts of the desert by his eloquence. On this day there was a general blessing of horses. A priest stands at the door of the church, and with a long brush, dipped in a consecrated vessel, scatters the holy water upon the horses as they are driven up to receive the benediction. All the equipages of the nobility, splendidly caparisoned with ribbons, were assembled to participate in the ceremony. The best defence of such a ceremony will be found in the benefit likely to result to the objects of it, from its teaching that comprehensive charity, which includes even the inferior creatures in the great circle of Christian benevolence. There is something that takes a delightful hold on the imagination, in the simple creed of the untutored Indian,

> Who thinks, admitted to that equal sky,
> His faithful dog shall bear him company.

Without attempting, however, to raise the mysterious veil which is drawn over the lot of the lower animals in the scale of creation, it is difficult not to sympathize with any doctrines that inculcate kind and humane feelings towards them.

The indolence of the Romans is a common theme of remark, but I doubt whether it be well founded. Something must be allowed them on the score of their climate, the natural effect of which is to produce listlessness and languor. Still more should be added on account of their government, in the spirit of which there is no encouragement given to individual industry, by the diffusion of equal rights. The barrenness of the Campagna has been attributed to this national indolence, which will not be at the pains of cultivating it. But I believe it would be more correct to say—not that the Campagna is barren, because it is not cultivated—but, that it is not cultivated, because it is barren. The Roman soldiers, before the time of Hannibal, in comparing their own country with that of the Capuans, argued thus:—"*An æquum esse dedititios suos illa fertilitate atque amænitate perfrui; se, militando fessos in pestilenti atque arida circa urbem solo luctari?*" Liv. lib. 7. c. 38.

In many particulars the modern Romans evince no want of ingenuity or industry. In the delicate and laborious workmanship of Mosaic; in engraving in all its branches and in the elegant manufacture of cameos out of oriental shell, they are very industrious. The demand for articles of this kind is constant, and as foreigners are the principal customers, I take it for granted that the profits are considerable, and that they flow directly into the pockets of the manufacturer. This is all that is necessary to promote industry; namely, that there should be a demand for the productions of a man's labour, and that he shall have a security for the enjoyment of the fruits of his work.

The Italians are admirable drivers, and go far beyond our whip-club. I have seen eight horses in hand trot up the Corso; and have heard of twelve, arranged in three rows of four a-breast. Their rule of the road is directly the reverse of ours; they take the right hand in meeting, and the left in passing;—and if two persons are in an open carriage, or on a coach-box together, he who drives will, in defiance of the eternal fitness of things, sit on the *near side*.

18th

A grand fête in St. Peter's. The Pope was borne into the church on the shoulders of men, seated in his chair of state, making continually, as he passed along, the sign of the cross in the air with the two fore-fingers of his right hand. Two pole-bearers, with splendid fans of ostrich feathers fixed on the top of their poles, preceded him, and reminded me of the chief mourner of Otaheite. The red flowing robes of the cardinals are much more splendid and becoming than the sovereign white satin of the Pope; which, bespangled as it is with gold, has a dingy and dirty appearance, at a distance. The Guard Noble, or Pope's Body Guard, the very privates of which are composed of the nobility of Rome, mustered in the church in full uniform, and kept the ground. They did not take off their hats, and the only part they took in the worship was to kneel down at the word of command, in adoration of the Host, when the bell announced the completion of the miracle of transubstantiation.[1]

A strange attendance this, for the successor of St. Peter—the apostle of the Prince of Peace!—but I doubt whether the apostles, if they could return to this world, would be able to recognise their own religion, swelled out and swaddled as it is in the Papal Pontificals.

It is common to hear of the attraction and fascination of the Catholic ceremonials;—for my part, I think mass a more tiresome business than a Quakers' meeting.

There is something very unsocial in the whole transaction. The priest turns his back to the people, and mumbles the prayers to himself. There seems to be no community of worship, except in the general genuflection at the elevation of the Host. The people seem to have no functions to perform, but to look on at a spectacle, which is to me the most fatiguing office in the world.

The vespers, of which music forms the principal art, are more attractive; though one cannot listen to the chants of these "warbling wethers," without feelings of indignation at the system which sanctions such a school of music; but perhaps a government of celibacy may affect to believe the deprivation of virility a loss of small importance.

19th
Passed away the morning in the Capitol. This modern building is not worthy to crown the summit of the *Capitoli immobile saxum*, as the Romans in the pride of their national vanity delighted to call it. But what is now become of their eternal empire, with the fables of *Juventus*, and *Terminus*, which were to them sacred articles of faith?—"The wind hath passed over it and it is gone!"—This devoted attachment to their country is perhaps the only amiable feature in the national character of the Romans. With what spirit it breaks out in the invocation of Horace:—

> Alme Sol corru nitido diem qui
> Promis et celas, aliusque et idem
> Nasceris; possis nihil urbe Roma
>   Viscere majus!

though in these very lines there is a sufficient indication of that jealous hostility towards all other nations, with which this love of their own country was combined.

It may be very amusing to read their history, now that we are out of the reach of that grasping and insatiable ambition, which must have rendered them deservedly hateful to their contemporaries.

But, Heaven be thanked, the bonds of Roman dominion are broken; and it is to be hoped, that any future attempt to revive their plans of universal conquest may be as unsuccessful as the late imitation of them by the French, whose jacobinical watch-word, of "War to the Palace and Peace to the Cottage," was closely copied—though more insidiously worded from the favourite maxim of the Romans—

Parcere subjectis, et debellare superbos

This line of their favourite poet contains a complete exposition of the spirit of their foreign policy; a truly domineering and tyrannical spirit—which could not be at rest, while there was any other people on the face of the globe that claimed the rights of national independence.

In the square of the Capitol is the famous equestrian statue of Marcus Aurelius. The Horse is very spirited, and Michael Angelo's address to it, *Cammina!* is still quoted.

Went in the evening to the Princess Prossedi's. A select ball.— Lucien Buonaparte and his brother Louis, with their respective families, were present.

20th

This morning the Princess's servant called for a fee. This is the custom of Italy, and where-ever you make a visit, the domestics call the next day to levy a tax upon you.

Called on the Princess Prossedi;—an amiable and interesting woman. She is the eldest daughter of Lucien Buonaparte by a former wife; and it was she who refused to be the wife of Ferdinand of Spain. This match was proposed to her when she was on a visit to the Emperor's court, during the disgrace and exile of her father; but, though she was alone, and subjected to the solicitations of the whole court and at last assailed by the menaces of Napoleon himself, she had the firmness and courage to adhere to her resolution. Her answer to an inquiry, whether she did not feel afraid of the consequences of irritating her uncle by a refusal, will explain her character; *O que non! on craint peu celui qu'on n'estime pas.*

The Buonaparte family muster strongly at Rome. *Madame Mère* is said to be immensely rich; Louis has bought a large tract on the Palatine Hill and Lucien has a spacious palace in the Via Condotti. Whatever his political sins may have been, his domestic life is irreproachable. He lives in the bosom of his family, all the branches of which assemble in the evening at his house, which is open also to strangers who have been properly introduced to him.

His wife must once have been a most beautiful woman, and she still retains all that fascination of manner, which is the best part of beauty.

21st

The first day of the Carnival;—or rather the first of the last eight days of the Carnival, which are the paroxysm of the fun and the folly of this season of rejoicing. But, as eight consecutive days of festivities might be too fatiguing, occasional resting days intervene, to give time for the spirits to rally;—and then, when the season of indulgence is over, Lent and fasting begin. This is wisely contrived, for after an excess of feasting, fasting succeeds as a relief, rather than a privation. Whatever Lent may be to the many, it is no light matter to the strict Catholics. The present Pope, who is most exemplary in all religious observances, keeps it with the most rigid abstemiousness.

The usual exhibition has not been given this morning in the Piazza del Popolo. It is customary that an execution should take place on this day, as an edifying prelude to the gaieties of the Carnival, but there is no criminal ready for the guillotine.

22nd

Second day of the Carnival. The Corso is the grand scene of foolery. Here, two lines of carriages, filled with grotesque figures in masks, drive up and down; while the middle of the street is thronged with a multitude of masqueraders. I have seen little fun, and no humour—except in a few English maskers. All that Corinne says of the skill and vivacity of the Italians in supporting characters of masquerade, I suspect to be greatly exaggerated.

I doubt whether a May-day in England be not quite as amusing as the Carnival. All that the people do, is to pelt each other with sugar-plums, as they are called, though they are really made of lime. When a stoppage takes place amongst the carriages, which is frequently the case, those that are alongside of one another might be compared to two ships in an engagement—such is the fury of the fire. One can bear being pelted by the natives, for they throw these missiles lightly and playfully—but the English pelt with all the vice and violence of school-boys, and there was an eye nearly lost in the battle of this morning.

The conclusion of the day's entertainment is the horse-race. There is a discharge of cannon as a signal for the carriages to quit the Corso. The street is soon cleared, and the horses are brought out. It is really surprising to see their eagerness and emulation; indeed they seem to enjoy the scene as much as the spectators. To-day, one of them, in its impatience to start, broke from its keeper, leaped the barrier, and set off alone. Five started afterwards, and, for the first two hundred yards, they seemed to run against one another with thorough good-will; but being without riders, they find out long before they get to the end of the Corso, which is a mile long, that their speed is entirely optional. Many of them, therefore, take it very quietly; the greatest fool runs fastest, and wins the race.

Every sort of stimulant is applied to supply the want of a rider. Little bells are tied about them, and a sort of self-acting spur is contrived, by suspending a barbed weight to a string, which, in its vibrations, occasioned by the motion of the horse, strikes constantly against his flanks. The people encourage them by shouts from all sides; but the most efficacious and the most cruel of the means employed, is the application of a squib of gunpowder to the poor animal's tail; or a piece of lighted touch-paper to some raw part of his hide.

In the evening a masked ball; where I in vain endeavoured to find any thing like the well-supported characters which we occasionally see at a masquerade in England. There were, in fact, no characters at all; nothing but a mob of masks and dominos.

23rd

A day's rest from the Carnival.—Drove to the Borghese villa.— The gardens and pleasure-grounds are on a larger scale, and in a better taste, than I have yet seen in Italy. The trees in the shrubberies are allowed to grow as nature prompts them, without being clipped and cut into all sorts of grotesque figures.

The villa is deserted not only by its owners, but by the famous statues—the Household Gods—which it once possessed. Casts now occupy the pedestals of the original marbles, which were sold by the Prince Borghese to Napoleon, and still remain in the gallery of the Louvre.

We went in the evening to one of the Theatres to hear an *Improvvisatrice*. She was a young and pretty girl of seventeen. The subjects had been written by the audience on slips of paper, and put into an urn, to be drawn out as occasion required. She recited three poems. The subject of the first was, the *Sacrifice of Iphigenia*;—the next, the *Cestus of Venus*;—and the last, *Sappho presents a wreath of flowers to Phaon*, was rendered more difficult by supplying her with the final words of each stanza, which she was to fill up with sense and rhymes. The final words, which were given by the audience, were all to end in *ore*;—some one suggested *sartore*—as a puzzling word for the conclusion of the last stanza; and if one might judge from the laughter and applause of the audience, for I confess I could not follow her, she brought it in with a very ingenious turn.

In the intervals between the poems, she called upon the audience indiscriminately for a word, as the subject of a stanza, which she immediately recited, making every line rhyme with the word proposed. She was seldom at a loss for a moment; and when she did hesitate, she got out of her difficulties most triumphantly. *Drudo* was the word that seemed to puzzle her most; at least she made an attempt to evade it; but it was pressed upon her by the audience.

Upon the whole, it was a wonderful performance; for though I could not catch all she said, one might judge of the merit of such a performance by the *effect* produced upon the audience. Besides, though words may add a great deal, they are not absolutely necessary to the expression of sentiment; the language of gestures, and features, and tones, is universal, and by the aid of these, it was easy to follow the story of Iphigenia perfectly.

After the subject of a poem was proposed, she walked about the stage for about ten minutes, and then burst out with all the seeming fervour of inspiration, chanting her stanzas in a recitative tone, accompanied by music.

Her enunciation and action were a little too vehement for an English taste, and conveyed an idea of vulgarity; but of this it is impossible to judge without knowing more of the national standard of good-breeding.

24th

Of the Palace and Baths of Titus, there are still many interesting remains. It was in the time of Raphael that the group of Laocoon was discovered here, and that several subterraneous chambers were opened, containing very beautiful specimens of painted ceilings, in excellent preservation. Raphael is said to have borrowed all he could from these paintings, for his own designs in the Vatican, and then to have filled up the ruins again. This story is in every body's mouth, but that Raphael, whose character appears in other particulars the essence of candour and ingenuousness, should have been actuated by such feelings of petty professional jealousy, is very improbable. If no care was taken to maintain the communication with the ruins, time and accident would soon do that which is imputed to Raphael. However this may be, it is certain that they were not again excavated till the year 1776; and it is to the French that we owe the interesting discoveries which have been made since that time. They set about the work in good earnest, and they have furnished ample materials for forming a judgment of the nature and extent of these imperial establishments. The colours on the ceilings are, in some instances, as fresh as if they had been painted yesterday; and the whole subject of the picture is often very intelligible; as is the case in the amours of Mars and Sylvia. There is a painting on the end-wall of one of the passages, representing a continuation of the passage, which shows that the Romans were not so ignorant of linear perspective as it has been supposed. In another passage, leading to the baths, which was excavated by the French, and which, as it would seem, had never before been explored since the original wreck which buried it in ruins, was found this scrawl, which has all the appearance of being ancient, and which—as it is under the veil of a learned language—I shall venture to transcribe:

DVODECIM DEOS ET DIANAM ET JOVEM OPTVMVM
MAXVMVM HABEAT IRATOS QVIS QVIS HIC
MINXERIT AVI CACARIT.

The baths seem to have been fitted up with the greatest magnificence. There are traces of Mosaic pavement; and there was a coating of marble carried about ten feet high, probably to prevent the painted walls from being injured by the splashing of the water.

In one of the rooms, the bath itself remains;—it is a circular basin of about twenty-four feet in diameter.

Here too they show what is said to be a part of the House of Mecænas. It is a curious specimen of the perfection of Roman brick-work, in complete preservation; the pointing of which is as perfect as if it had been just finished by the mason, and I doubt whether any modern workmanship, of the same materials, would bear a comparison with it. The bricks are differently shaped from our own, and do not exceed two inches in thickness.

The third day of the Carnival.—Went to see the horses come in, which was a very tame business. All the rivalry is in the start.—The reverse of an English horse-race.—*There* the start is nothing, and the contest is reserved for the goal.

25th

Another respite from the Carnival.—Drove at midnight to see the Coliseum by moonlight;—but what can I say of the Coliseum? It must be *seen*; to describe it I should have thought impossible—if I had not read Manfred. To see it aright, as the Poet of the North tells us of the fair Melrose, one must "Go visit it by the pale moonlight." The stillness of night—the whispering echoes—the moonlight shadows—and the awful grandeur of the impending ruins, form a scene of romantic sublimity, such as Byron alone can describe as it deserves. His description is the very thing itself;—but what cannot he do on such a subject, the touch of whose pen, like the wand of Moses, can produce waters even from the barren rock!

A man should go *alone* to enjoy, in full perfection, all the enchantment of this moonlight scene; and if it do not excite in him emotions that he never felt before—let him hasten home— eat his supper—say his prayers—and thank Heaven that he has not one single grain of romance or enthusiasm, in his whole composition.

If he be fond of moralizing—the Papal sentinels, that now mount guard here—the Cross, which has been set up, in the centre of the amphitheatre, to *protect* these imperial remains from further spoliation—in the very spot, where the Disciples of that despised Cross were most cruelly persecuted—and the inscription which it bears—*Baciando La S. Croce si acquistano duecento giorni di indulgenza*—will furnish him with ample materials for reflection.

27th

Fifth day of the Carnival. Tiresome repetition of the same foolery. It may be, however, that I find it dull, because I am dull myself, for the Italians seem to enjoy it vastly.

Escaped from the noisy crowd of the Corso, to the silent solitude of the Coliseum; where you can scarcely believe that you are within five minutes' walk of such a scene of uproar. Considering the depredations which have for so many ages been committed upon this pile, it is wonderful that so much remains. It is certain that Paul II. built the palace of St. Mark—Cardinal Ricario the Chancery—and Paul III. the Farnese palace—with materials from this mine. The Barberini palace is also said to have been derived from the same stock;—"*et quod non fecerunt Barbari, fecere Barberini.*" I believe, however, that this conceit is the only authority for the fact;—and truth has been often sacrificed to a conceit.

At last, to prevent further depredations, it was consecrated. The present Pope is doing much to prevent dilapidation; but, like his predecessors, he seems to have little reliance on the memory of mankind, for he defaces all his works with an inscription; though it is conceived in a more modest taste than former inscriptions, and instead of *Munificentia*—he is content with—*Cura Pii* VII.

Much has been written on the subject of the holes which are scattered all over the building; but I think it is plain that they were made to extract the metal, used to fasten the stones together. In many of these holes, some small fragments of lead and iron are still remaining.

It must have been a noble sight, to behold this vast Amphitheatre filled with spectators. The very lowest computation allows that it would contain eighty thousand.

There was an awning to protect them from the sun and the rain; and that capricious tyrant, Caligula, is described by Suetonius as venting his spleen by ordering this canopy to be withdrawn:— "*Giadiatorio munere, reductis interdum flagrantissimo Sole veils, emitti quenquam vetabat.*"

The order and arrangement of the seats are still distinguishable, and nothing can be more admirably contrived than the vomitories, for facilitating the ingress and egress of all classes to and from their respective seats, without disorder or confusion. There was probably an upper gallery for the multitude, of which there are now no remains.

Between the arches numbered xxxviii and xxxix, there is one, which is not only without any number at all, but is also deficient in the entablature; whence it is concluded, that this was the entrance to the passage which led to the palace of Titus, by which the Emperor had his private approach to the amphitheatre.

Excavation has also discovered the subterranean passage, by which the Emperors had a secret communication with the palace of the Palatine; and it was here that Commodus was attacked by the conspirators.

It was probably the sight of the Coliseum, the wonder of ancient Rome, as St. Peter's is of the modern city, that struck Poggio with the admiration he so well describes in his work *De Varietate Fortunæ*:—"*Præsenti vero, mirum dictu, nihil imminuit, vere major fuit Roma, majoresque sunt reliquiæ quam rebar. Jam non orbem ab hâc urbe domitam, sed tam sero domitam, miror.*" By the way, Gibbon attributes these words to Petrarch; but if they be his, Poggio has adopted them without acknowledgment.

It is indeed a glorious ruin, and one may sympathize with the superstitious enthusiasm, that believed "*Quamdiu stabit Colyseus stabit et Roma; quando cadet Colyseus, cadet Roma; quando cadet Roma, cadet et mundus.*"

28th

Sixth day of the Carnival. Sat an hour in the Borghese palace, before the charming Sibyl of Domenichino, which is one of the very sweetest pictures in the world. Afterwards to the Piazza Navona, the site of the ancient *Circus Agonalis*; which, by an easy transition through *Agona* and *Nagona*, has become *Navona*. Near here is the ancient statue which has been called after the Tailor Pasquin, who lived near the place where it was discovered; and who, besides indulging himself in satirical raillery against all the world, has had the honour of giving his name to all subsequent effusions of the same kind. The floating capital of wit may be estimated by the squibs and epigrams which are still occasionally affixed to this statue.[2]

29th

Seventh day of the Carnival. The horses started with more animation than ever. The instant they were off, one of the booths opposite to us fell in with a tremendous crash. There was something awfully terrific in the general scream of many hundreds of people, who all sunk down in one heap of confusion. No lives lost. The extent of the mischief was a few broken limbs. What a strange thing is luck—as we call it; but, do we not all too often

Call God's best providence a lucky hit!

I had wished to take my place on this booth, and was with difficulty persuaded by my companion to prefer the opposite one.

Masked ball in the evening at the *Téatro Aliberti*. I am quite amazed at the dulness of this sort of entertainment, in a country where the people are so distinguished for liveliness and wit in their common conversation. You would suppose, from the animation of feature, and vehemence of gesticulation between two men in the street, that they were discussing some question of vital interest; but, upon inquiry, you find they have been talking of the weather, or some such matter. At these balls there is little talking;—perhaps some more serious business may be going on;—for this is the great season of intrigue. Men and women assume the dresses and the characters of each other. The mask enables the lady to speak her mind freely; and whatever her fancy may be, if she fail of success, it is not through any backwardness on her part. The mask does away all distinctions of rank, as well as of sex, and the liberty and equality of the carnival seem to have a close affinity with the license of the *Saturnalia*—or *High Life below Stairs*—of the ancient Romans.

30th and 31st
English November weather. Cold rain. Confined to the house.

Feb. 1
Passed the morning in the Vatican. There is an alabaster urn in the gallery of vases, which was found in the Mausoleum of Augustus, and is supposed to have contained his ashes. The busts

of Cato and Portia, if indeed they have been rightly so called, are interesting portraits;—but we have been so accustomed to associate Kemble's noble physiognomy with our idea of Cato, that it is difficult not to feel a little disappointment at the first sight of this bust, which has not that strongly-marked cast of features which we call Roman. The moral expression, however, is that of the severe, inflexible integrity, the *esse quam videri*, which Sallust describes in his beautiful contrast between Cato and Cæsar

Attended vespers at St. Peter's,—the favourite lounge of the English ladies on Sunday evening.

In the morning they attend the English church, which is now established with an éclat that scandalizes all orthodox Catholics. The English presumed so far upon their favour with the Pope, as to make an application to Consalvi, to authorize the institution of a place of worship, according to the rites of the Church of England. The Cardinal's answer might have been anticipated: "I cannot authorize what would be directly in opposition to the principles of our religion and the laws of the state, but the government will not interfere with any thing you do quietly amongst yourselves as long as it is done with propriety." The English church has accordingly been set up, and boasts a very numerous congregation. The door is thronged with as many carriages as a new fancy chapel in London; but though the Pope and Cardinal Consalvi seem inclined to let the English do any thing, the multitude regard this permission as a sin and an abomination.

Our fair countrywomen not content with celebrating the rites of an heretical church under the very nose of the Pope, go in the evening and jostle the Catholics out of their own chapel in St. Peter's. This attendance might at first have been attributed to devotional feelings but as soon as the music is over, the ladies make their courtesy, and leave the priests to finish their prayers by themselves, while they parade up and down the Cathedral; which then becomes the fashionable promenade.

After vespers, on Sundays all the equipages in Rome are to be found in the Corso, which then answers to our own Hyde Park;

and perhaps there are few places in the world where so many splendid equipages are to be seen as at Rome—in the number and appearance of the horses, and in the rich liveries of the trains of domestics, and running foootmen.

2nd

Holy-day. Grand ceremony of the Pope blessing the candles;—hence, Candlemas-day. After the blessing, each Catholic received his candle, and there was a procession from the church. The second of February is a gloomy day in Rome; it has a black mark in the calendar, and is memorable in the history of national calamities.—Ball at Lady N's—It was intended to commence at nine o'clock, but out of deference to the Catholic guests, it was postponed till midnight, that no infringement might be committed upon the Holy-day.

The English ladies have metamorphosed Rome into a watering-place.—One or other of them is "*at home*" every evening, and there are balls twice a week. The number of English, at present in Rome, is estimated at about 2,000, and it is said that the influx of wealth occasioned by their residence has so increased the supply of money, as to produce some abatement in the rate of interest. We are in high favour—and Inglese is a passport everywhere. The Pope seems to be one of the few sovereigns in Europe who retain any sense of *gratitude* for the good offices of England. The difference of sentiment, in the Roman and Neapolitan courts, towards us, was illustrated in the most marked manner, by their respective treatment of the naval officers who were sent by Lord Exmouth with the Italian slaves, redeemed at Algiers.

The partiality of the Pope to the English excites the jealousy of the natives; and perhaps with some reason. At all ceremonies and spectacles, the guard allow the English to pass over that line which is impassable to the Italians; and I have, more than once, heard a native plead *Inglese*, as a passport to follow me. Seats are prepared for the ladies, of which they are not backward in availing themselves, and I have almost expected on some occasions, to see them elbow the Pope out of his own Chair of State.

3rd

Shrove Tuesday;—the last day and winding up of the Carnival. It was formerly the custom to carry a funeral procession of dead Harlequin, on this expiration of the Carnival. This, however, is now discontinued; but at the conclusion of the horse-race on this day, every body carries a taper, and the great fun seems to consist in lighting your taper at your neighbour's candle, and then blowing out his flame;—a practical joke, with which we may often trace an obvious analogy in the serious pastimes of Politics and Literature.

So much for the Carnival of Rome; of which one has heard tales of wonder, from the days of our nursery;—and, indeed, it is only fit for the nursery. Nothing can be imagined more childish, and there is very little mixture of wit or humour to make the childishness amusing.

4th

Ash Wednesday. Ceremony in the Pope's chapel,—Sprinkling of ashes on the heads of the Cardinals.—Mass as usual.—I have declined being presented to his Holiness, thinking, with the Duke of Hamilton, that when the kissing of the toe is left out, the ceremony is deprived of all its amusement.

The Pope receives strangers, by six at a time, in his own private apartment, in the plain dress of his order, without any pomp or state. The Italians in general dislike perfumes, and the Pope has a particular antipathy to musk. On the last presentation, one of the company was highly scented with this odour, and Pius was constrained to dismiss the party almost immediately.

5th

My health grows worse and worse! Constant irritation.—Day without rest—night without sleep;—at least sleep without repose, and rest without recreation.

If life, with health and wealth, and all "appliances and means to boot," be nothing but vanity and vexation of spirit, what is it, alas! when deprived of all these embellishments?

6th

Beautiful day.—The sun shines upon every thing but me.—My spirits are as dark as November; but *levius fit patientia*! Went to the Borghese Palace, to see and admire again Domenichino's *Sibyl.* —His *Chase of Diana* too is a superb picture.—Raphael's *Deposition from the Cross* has too much of his first manner in the execution,—though it is a noble work in conception and design. Here is a fine collection of Titians;—but, with all their glowing beauties, I doubt whether the Venetian painters ever gave us more than the *bodies*—either of women or of men.

7th and 8th

Very unwell;—but Democritus was a wiser man than Heraclitus. Those are the wisest, and the happiest, who can pass through life as a play; who—without making a farce of it, and turning every thing into ridicule—or running into the opposite extreme of tragedy—consider the whole period, from the cradle to the coffin, as a well-bred comedy;—and maintain a cheerful smile to the very last scene. For what is happiness, but a Will-o'-the wisp, a delusion;—a terra incognita—in pursuit of which thousands are tempted out of the harbour of tranquillity, to be tossed about, the sport of the winds of passion, and the waves of disappointment to be wrecked, perhaps at last on the rocks of despair;—unless they be provided with the sheet-anchor of religion—the only anchor that will hold in all weathers. This is a very stupid allegory, but it was preached to me this morning by a beautiful piece of sculpture, in the *studio* of Maximilian Laboureur. A female figure of Hope has laid aside her anchor, and is feeding a monstrous chimera. The care and solicitude of Hope, in tending this frightful creature, are most happily expressed; and the general effect is so touching, that it illustrates Shakspeare's phrase of *Sermons in stones* with great felicity.

1. Middleton confesses, that, in this instance at least, he cannot find a parallel in any part of the Pagan worship. The credulity of the ancients, great as it was, revolted at a doctrine like this, which was thought too gross even for Egyptian idolatry: "*Ecquem tam amentem esse putas, qui illud, quo vescatur, Deum credat esse?*" Cic. de Nat. Deor. 3.

2. A man called Cæsar lately married a girl of the name of Roma—both common names in Rome. They lived in the Piazza Navona, close to Pasquin's statue, where was found next morning the following advice:

Cave, Cæsar, ne tua Roma
respublica fiat!

The man replied the next day;

Cæsar imperat!

But his antagonist immediately rejoined;

Ergo coronabitur.

Upon the late entry of the Emperor of Austria into Rome, the following squib appeared on Pasquin's statue:—

Gaudium urbis, filetus provinciarum, risus mundi.

VII

NAPLES

9th

When the mind is full of fret and fever, the best remedy is to put the body in motion, which, by establishing an equilibrium between the two, may, perhaps, restore something like tranquillity to the whole system. It was with this hope that I left Rome, before day-break on my way to Naples—as fast as four wheels and sixteen legs could carry me;—and there is nothing like the rattling of wheels to scare away blue devils. The road is excellent; and the posting, however defective it may be in the appearance and appointments of the horses, is in point of celerity equal to that on the best-regulated road in England.

The Pontine Marshes, of which one has heard such dreadful accounts, appeared to me to differ but little from many parts of Cambridgeshire; though the livid aspect of the miserable inhabitants of this region is a shocking proof of its unwholesomeness. The short, but pathetic reply made to an inquiring traveller is well known.—"How do you manage to live here?" said he, to a group of these animated spectres—"We die!"—The excellent road which runs through these marshes for twenty-five miles, in a direct line, as straight as an arrow, was the work of the late Pope Pius VI., for which he will receive the thanks of every traveller; but this, like most of his other undertakings, exposed him to the satire of his contemporaries, and it became a proverb, when talking of sums expended in extravagance, to say, "—sono andate alle paludi Pontine."

Early in the evening, we reached Terracina—the ancient *Anxur* of the Romans. Its situation is strikingly beautiful, at the foot of the Apennines, and on the shore of the Mediterranean; and it is backed, as Horace has accurately described, "*saxis late candentibus.*" We were induced to halt here, by the representations that were made to us of the dangers of travelling after dark. It seems, we are now in the stronghold of the robbers, where they commit the most barefaced outrages.

The man who had no money in his pocket might formerly dismiss all fear of robbers;—but in these days, an empty purse is no longer a security. These modern desperadoes carry then away even from their homes, for the sake of the ransom which they think they may extort for their liberation. We are told that two men were lately kidnapped from this neighbourhood, and taken up into the mountains. The friends of the one sent up nearly the sum that was demanded;—the other had no friends to redeem him. The robbers settled the affair, in the true spirit of that cold-blooded savage disposition that has leisure to be sportive in its cruelty. They sent the first man back without his ears; detaining these as a set off against the deficiency in the ransom;—and the other poor fellow was returned in *eight pieces*!—So much for Italian government. An edict has been lately issued against ransoms, as operating to encourage kidnapping. This may be an excellent law for the public; but it would require the patriotism of Regulus, in an individual falling into the hands of these marauders, to consider the public interest in preference to his own.

10th

Soon after quitting Terracina, we entered the Neapolitan territory, where the road begins to wind among the Apennines; and, for many miles, it is one continued pass through a wild and rugged country. It seems intended by nature for the region of robbers. The government of Naples has adopted the most vigorous measures for the protection of travellers. Small parties of soldiers are encamped, at half a mile's distance from each other, during the whole line of road, from Terracina to Capua. But, *quis custodiet ipsos custodes*?—it is said that the soldiers themselves, after dark, lay aside their military dress, and act as banditti. The richness and luxuriance of the country between Terracina and Naples are very striking. Hedges of laurustinus, olives, and vineyards;—orange and lemon groves covered with fruit;—myrtle, fig, and palm-trees, give a new and softer character to the landscape.

The orange-tree adds richness to the prospect, but its form is too *clumpy*—round and regular—to be picturesque.

The inhabitants seem to increase in misery, in proportion to the improving mildness of the climate and fertility of the soil. I have never seen such shocking objects of human wretchedness, as in this smiling land of corn, wine, and oil. At Fondi especially, the poor naked creatures seemed absolutely in a state of starvation, and scrambled eagerly for the orange-peel which fell from our carriage. Surrounded by these squalid spectres, we might almost have fancied ourselves already arrived at the confines of *Orcus*; and that we had actually before our eyes the "*terribiles visu Fornæ*" with which the poet has invested its entrance:

> *Luctus*, et ultrices posuêreo cubilia Curæ,
> Pallentesque habitant *Morbi*, tritisquei Senectus;
> Et *Metus*, et malesuada *Fames*, et turpis *Egestas*.

Most of these might have been painted to the life from the ghastly group around us; and indeed, with the exception of "*Labos*," there is scarcely a personage in the passage alluded to, that might not find an adequate representative at Fondi. This very absence, indeed, of *Industry* goes far to account for the presence of the rest; for though the greater part of this misery may be attributed to the faults of the government, yet some little seems to flow from the very blessings of a fine climate and rich soil—for nothing will supply the want of industry.

At Fondi we have a specimen of the old Appian way, and are jolted on the very pavement that Horace travelled over in his journey to Brundusium. There is, too, in the Bureau of the

Custom-House, just such a jack-in-office as Horace ridicules on the same occasion.

The extortions of the various Custom-Houses are the most flagrant impositions; and I have always resisted them with success, when, from an unwillingness to submit to injustice, I have been foolish enough to encounter the inconvenience of maintaining the rights of travellers: but, I believe, it is a wiser plan to get rid of all trouble by a small gratuity; for though they have no right to make you pay any thing, they may detain and search you, if they please, and an exemption from such delays is cheaply bought by the sacrifice of a few pauls.

In consequence of a detention of two hours at Capua, which all travellers must reckon upon, we did not reach Naples till after dark.

11th

First view of the bay of Naples,—of which the windows of our lodging command a fine prospect.

The weather is beautiful, and as warm as a June day in England. We sit at breakfast, without a fire, on a marble floor—with the casements open, enjoying the mild fresh breeze from the sea. The first view of Vesuvius disappoints expectation. You would not know that it was a burning mountain if you were not told so; the smoke has only the appearance of that light passing cloud, which is so often seen hanging on the brow of a hill. Drove after breakfast to the *Campo di Marte*; where to my great surprise, I found myself transported ten years backwards, into the middle of old schoolfellows.

There was a regular double-wicket cricket match going on;—Eton against the world;—and the world was beaten in one innings! This disposition to carry the amusements of their own country along with them is a striking characteristic of the English. One of them imports a pack of hounds from England to Rome, and hunts regularly during the season, to the great astonishment of the natives.—At Florence, they establish races on the Cascine, after the English manner, and ride their own horses, with the caps and jackets of English jockeys;—and, every where, they make themselves independent of the natives, and rather provide entertainment for themselves, than seek it from the same sources with the people amongst whom they may happen to be. What should we say in London, if the Turks, or the Persians, or the Russians, or the French, were to make Hyde Park the scene of their national pastimes? It is this exclusively national spirit, and the undisguised contempt for all other people, that the English are so accustomed to express in their manner and conduct, which have made us so generally unpopular on the continent. Our hauteur is the subject of universal complaint—and the complaint seems but too well founded.

The view of Naples, from the hill immediately above it, forms a magnificent *coup d'œil*. It combines all the features of the grand and the splendid;—the town—the Bay—Vesuvius. It would be complete, if the sea part of it were more enlivened with shipping.

12th

Oh this land of zephyrs! Yesterday was as warm as July;—to-day we are shivering, with a bleak easterly wind, and an English black frost. I find we are come to Naples too soon. It would have been quite time enough three months hence. Naples is one of the worst climates in Europe for complaints of the chest; and the winter is much colder here than at Rome, notwithstanding the latitude. Whatever we may think of sea air in England, the effect is very different here. The sea-breeze in Devonshire is mild and soft,—here it is keen and piercing; and, as it sets in regularly at noon, I doubt whether Naples can ever be oppressively hot, even in summer.

We are lodged in the house of a Bishop;—by which term must not be understood, a personage bearing the slightest resemblance to the dignified character we mean by it in England, but a little dirty-looking chocolate-coloured creature, with no single pretension to the appearance of a gentleman. We occupy the whole of his house, except one bed-room, in which *Monsignore* lives like a snail in his shell. He will chatter for two hours, to extract a few carlini from our pockets; and his great occupation and pleasure consist in scolding his servants;—but some excuse may be made for this, as it is a duty which may seem to devolve upon him from the law of celibacy.

13th, 14th, and 15th
Confined to the house;—the little Bishop endeavours to amuse the hours of my confinement, by exhibiting all his episcopal trappings, which he has done with the sort of fiddle-faddle vanity, with which an old maid of three-score would display the court of her youth. Nothing would please him but I must try on his mitres, while he stood by giggling and skipping, as if it had been the best joke in the world. He tells me that he was in attendance upon the Pope during his captivity in France; and was a witness of the scene between Napoleon and his Holiness, at which it has been erroneously stated that Napoleon, in the heat of anger, was brutal enough to strike him.

The Bishop describes it as an altercation; in which Napoleon exhausted all his efforts in endeavouring to overcome the Pope's objections to signing the treaty, which he, Napoleon, had dictated. The Pope remained firm, declaring that he could sign no treaty but in his own palace at Rome. Irritated by this inflexible opposition, Napoleon burst out with a *sacre Dieu!* at being thwarted *par un petit Prêtre*, and with ruffian violence, forgetting what was due to the age and character of the venerable Pius, he did, according to the Bishop's account, lay hold of the Pope's garments:—but without striking him.

The little Bishop, it seems, had a great curiosity to see England, and begged hard of Napoleon for permission to make a visit to London for a few weeks: Napoleon, however, would never consent; but used to pull him playfully by the ear, and tell him, that he would be corrupted, and converted, in our Island of Heretics.

16th
Sunshine again—Delightful lounging day. The noise of Naples is enough to drive a nervous man mad. It would be difficult to

imagine the eternal bustle and worry of the streets;—the people bawling and roaring at each other in all directions; beggars soliciting your charity with one hand, while they pick your pocket of your handkerchief with the other;—and the carriages cutting their way through the crowd, with which the streets are thronged, with a fearful rapidity. It requires the patience of Job to carry on any dealings with the people, who are a most unconscionable set; every bargain is a battle, and it seems to be an established rule, to ask, on all occasions, three times as much as is just. An Englishman cannot show himself without being immediately surrounded by a troop of clamorous applicants, as ravenous as birds of prey about a carcass;—all anxious to have their share of the carrion.

The Toledo is the principal street in Naples; and a very splendid and showy street it is. The shops are gay and gaudy, and "the tide of human existence" flows with almost as much volume, and a great deal more noise than at Charing-Cross; but I think it cannot be compared with the solid and substantial magnificence of the Corso at Rome. This street is the very paradise of pick-pockets; I detected a ragged urchin this morning in the act of extracting my handkerchief, but he looked up into my face with such an arch, though piteous expression, that my resentment was disarmed, and he made his retreat under a volley of *eccellenzas*, which he showered upon me with a grateful profusion.

Upon arriving at Naples after a residence in Rome, one is immediately struck with the inferiority of taste displayed in the architectural ornaments of the town.

After Rome, every thing at Naples looks poor and paltry;— show and glitter seem to be the great objects of admiration;—and every thing, as Forsyth says, is gilded, from the cupolas of the churches to the pill of the apothecary.

17th

The rate of living is much the same at Naples as at Rome. The ordinary price of lodgings, sufficient for the accommodation of two persons, is forty dollars a month—about eight pounds

English. Our dinner is supplied from the kitchen of a neighbouring archbishop, by his lordship's cook, at eight *carlini* per head;—the *carlino* being about four-pence English.

The wines of Naples are remarkably good, if care be taken to get them genuine, which is easily done where so many people make their own wine;—but beware of the adulterations of the wine *trade*! The *lacryma Christi* is not the rare precious *liqueur*, which it has been sometimes de scribed, but a strong-bodied generous wine, which is made in great quantities. The vineyards that supply this liquor are situated at the foot of Vesuvius. It appears to be very well calculated for the English taste, and it is said to bear the voyage without injury. The cost of a pipe, with all the expense of importing it to England, duty and freight included, would not amount to more than 80*l*; and Mr. Grandorges, the host of the *Albergo del Sole*, and the proprietor of a magazine of all sorts of English goods, tells me that he has already sent many pipes to London.

All sorts of English manufactures are to be found at the above-mentioned magazine, which can only be accounted for by the partiality of the English to the productions of their own country; for the importation duty to the Neapolitan government is no less than 60 per cent.

The Neapolitans seem to like us as little as the Portuguese, and the temper of the government is constantly breaking out in little spiteful exertions of power directed against English subjects.

18th

Excursion to *Pompeii*. The remains of this town afford a truly interesting spectacle. It is like a resurrection from the dead;—the progress of time and decay is arrested, and you are admitted to the temples, the theatres, and the domestic privacy of a people who have ceased to exist for seventeen centuries. Nothing is wanting but the inhabitants. Still, a morning's walk through the solemn silent streets of Pompeii, will give you a livelier idea of their modes of life, than all the books in the world. They seem, like the French of the present day, to have existed only *in public*.

Their theatres, temples, basilicas, forums, are on the most splendid scale, but in their private dwellings we discover little or no attention to *comfort*. The houses in general have a small court, round which the rooms are built, which are rather cells than rooms; the greater part are without windows, receiving light only from the door.

There are no chimneys;—the smoke of the kitchen, which is usually low and dark, must have found its way through a hole in the ceiling. The doors are so low, that you are obliged to stoop to pass through them. There are some traces of mosaic flooring, and the stucco paintings, with which all the walls are covered, are but little injured; and upon being wetted, they appear as fresh as ever. Brown, red, yellow, and blue, are the prevailing colours. It is pity that the contents of the houses could not have been allowed to remain in the state in which they were found;—but this would have been impossible. Travellers are the greatest thieves in the world. As it is, they will tear down, without scruple, the whole side of a room, to cut out a favourable specimen of the stucco painting. If it were not for this pilfering propensity, we might have seen every thing as it really was left at the time of this great calamity; even to the skeleton, which was found with a purse of gold in its hand, trying to run away from the impending destruction and exhibiting "the ruling passion strong in death" in the last object of its anxiety. In the stocks of the guard-room, which were used as a military punishment, the skeletons of four soldiers were found sitting; but these poor fellows have now been released from their ignominious situation, and the stocks, with every thing else that was moveable, have be placed in the Museum; the bones being consigned to their parent clay.

Pompeii therefore exhibits nothing but bare walls, and the walls are without roofs; for these have been broken in by the weight of the shower of ashes and pumice stones, that caused the destruction of the town.

The Amphitheatre is very perfect, as indeed are the other two theatres, intended for dramatic representations; though it is evident that they had sustained some injury from the earthquake, which, as we learn from Tacitus, had already much damaged this devoted town, before its final destruction by the eruption of Vesuvius:

> *Et motu terræ celebre Campaniæ oppidum Pompeii, magna*
> *ex parte proruit.* Tacitus, Ann. xv. c. 22.

The paintings on the walls of the Amphitheatre represent the combats of gladiators and wild beasts, the dens of which remain just as they were seventeen hundred years ago.

The two theatres for dramatic entertainments are as close together as our own Drury Lane and Covent Garden. The larger one, which might have contained five thousand persons, like the amphitheatres, had no roof; but was open to the light of day. The stage is very much circumscribed—there is no depth; and there are consequently no side scenes: the form and appearance are like that of our own theatres, when the drop-scene is down, and forms the extent of the stage. In this back scene of the Roman stage, which, instead of canvass, is composed of unchangeable brick and marble, are three doors; and there are two others on the sides, answering to our own stage-doors. It seems that it was the theatrical etiquette, that the *premiers rôles* should have their exits and entrances through the doors of the back scene, and the inferior ones through those on the sides.

The little theatre is in better preservation than the other; and it is supposed that this was intended for musical entertainments.

The Temple of Isis has suffered little injury. The statues, indeed, have been taken away; but you see the very altar on which the victims were offered; and you may now ascend without ceremony the private stairs which led to the *sanctum sanctorum* of the Goddess, where those mysterious rites were celebrated, the nature of which may be shrewdly guessed from the curiosities discovered there, which are now to be seen in the *Museo Borbonico*. In a niche, on the outside of the temple, was a statue of

Harpocrates—the God of Silence—who was most appropriately placed here; but

> Foul deeds will rise,
> Though all the earth o'erwhelm them, to men's eyes.

The streets are very narrow; the marks of wheels on the pavement show that carriages were in use; but there must have been some regulation to prevent their meeting each other; for one carriage would have occupied the whole of the street, except the narrow *trottoir*, raised on each side for foot passengers, for whose accommodation there are also raised stepping-stones, in order to cross from one side to the other. The distance between the wheel-tracks is four feet three inches.

There is often an emblem over the door of a house, that determines the profession of its former owner.—The word "*Salve*" on one, seems to denote that it was an inn, as we have, in our own days, the sign of "*The Salutation*." In the outer brick-work of another is carved an emblem, which shocks the refinement of modern taste; but which has been an object even of religious adoration, in many countries, probably as a symbol of creative power. The same device is found on the stucco of the inner court of another house, with this intimation—*Hic habitat Felicitas*—a sufficient explanation of the character of its inhabitants.

Many of the paintings on the walls are very elegant in the taste and design, and they often assist us in ascertaining the uses for which the different rooms were intended. For example;—in the baths,[1] we find Tritons, and Naiads; in the bed-chambers, Morpheus scatters his poppies; and in the eating-room, a sacrifice to Esculapius teaches us, that we should eat, to live;—and not live, to eat. In one of these rooms are the remains of a *triclinium*.

A baker's shop is as plainly indicated as if the loaves were now at his window. There is a mill for the grinding of corn, and the oven for baking; and the surgeon and the druggist have also been traced, by the quality of the articles found in their respective dwellings.

But the most complete specimen that we have of an ancient residence, is the villa which has been discovered at a small distance without the gate. It is on a more splendid scale than any of the houses in the town itself, and it has been preserved with scarcely any injury.

Some have imagined that this was the *Pompeianum*—the Pompeian Villa of Cicero. Be this as it may—it must have belonged to a man of taste. Situated on a sloping bank, the front entrance opens, as it were, into the first floor; below which, on the garden side, into which the house looks—for the door is the only aperture on the road-side—is a ground floor, with spacious arcades and open rooms, all facing the garden;—and above are the sleeping rooms. The walls and ceilings of this villa are ornamented with paintings of very elegant design, all which have a relation to the uses of the apartments in which they are placed. In the middle of the garden there is a reservoir of water, surrounded by columns, and the ancient well still remains. Though we have many specimens of Roman glass, in their drinking vessels, it has been doubted whether they were acquainted with the use of it for windows. Swinburne, however, in describing Pompeii, says "in the window of a bed-chamber some panes of glass are still remaining." This would seem to decide the question;—but they remain no longer. The host was fond of conviviality, if we may judge from the dimensions of his cellar, which extends under the whole of the house and the arcades also; and many of the *amphoræ* remain, in which the wine was stowed. It was here that the skeletons of seven and twenty poor wretches were found, who took refuge in this place from the fiery shower that would have killed them at once, to suffer the lingering torments of being starved to death.

It was in one of the Porticos, leading to the outward entrance, that the skeleton, supposed to be that of the master of the house, was found; with a key in one hand, and a purse of gold in the other.

So much for Pompeii:—I lingered amongst its ruins till the close of evening; and have seldom passed a day with feelings of interest so strongly excited, or with impressions of the transient nature of all human possessions so strongly enforced, as by the solemn solitudes of this resuscitated town.[2]

19th

Passed the morning in the *Museo Borbonico*;—a magnificent establishment, containing rich collections of statues, pictures, and books. Here too are deposited the greater part of the curiosities found at Herculaneum and Pompeii, which were formerly at Portici. When the King was obliged to fly from Naples to Sicily, he took with him, from Portici, every thing that could be easily packed up; these articles have now been brought back, and are arranged in the *Museo Borbonico*.

Here you see—"the ancient most domestic ornaments"—the furniture—the kitchen utensils—the surgical instruments—the trinkets, &c. &c., of the old Romans.

This collection illustrates Solomon's apophthegm—that there is nothing new under the sun.—There is much that, with a little scouring, would scarcely appear old fashioned at the present dry. This is not surprising in many of the articles, considering that our makers of pottery, and tea-urns, have been long busied in copying from these ancient models. But it is the same with other things; the bits of the bridles, and the steel-yard and scales for weighing, the lamps, the dice, the surgeon's probe, are all very much like our own. We seem to have improved principally upon the Romans, in hardware and cutlery. Their locks and keys, scissors and needles, are very clumsy articles; and their seals, rings, and necklaces, look as if they had been made at the blacksmith's forge. The toilets of the ladies, too, were not so elegantly furnished with knick-knacks in those days;—we have specimens of the whole arrangement of their dressing-tables, even to their little crystal boxes of essences and cosmetics. Their combs would scarcely compare with those which we use in our stables; and there is nothing that would be fit for a modern lady's dressing-case. We find nothing like knives and forks.

The weight of the steel-yard is generally the head of an Emperor. There is a sun-dial—the gnomon of which is the hinder part of a pig, with the tail sticking up, to cast the shadow. The *tesseræ* or tickets of admission to the theatres, are of ivory; and I remarked one with the name of the poet Æschylus written on it in Greek characters. The apparatus of the kitchen may be studied in all its details, through every variety of urn, kettle, and saucepan. The armoury presents to us the very helmets, and breast-plates, and swords, with which the Romans gained the empire of the world; in a word, every thing here excites the liveliest interest, even to the tops, and play-things, which prove the antiquity of our own school-boy amusements; but in these, as in other matters, the poverty of human invention is strikingly displayed;—for, whether we ride upon sticks or play at odd and even, we find that we are only copying the pastimes of children who were wont two thousand years ago—

Ludere par impar, equitare in arundine longâ.

Among the pictures, there is an old woman selling Cupids to a young female, behind whom stands a sort of duenna, in the attitude of advice and caution. The old retailer of loves holds a fluttering Cupid by the wings, and has another in her cage.

Many articles, even of food, are to be seen, preserved in a charcoal state. There is a loaf of bread on which the baker's name is still visible.

It is easy to recognise the different fruits and vegetables, corn, rice, figs, almonds, walnuts, beans, lentils, &c. They show you also the necklace and bracelets of gold, belonging to the female whose remains, together with the incrustation of ashes which overwhelmed her—and which, hardened by time, still retain the impression of her bosom—are preserved at Portici.

In a small room in the Museum are collected those curiosities, which, interesting as they are, as throwing light upon the manners of ancient times, are justly offensive to modern delicacy. The most extraordinary of these are, the ornaments and decorations of the Temple of Isis, some of which will scarcely bear a detailed description.[3]

Amongst these, there is a priapic goblet; from the mouth of which it is plain that the votaries must have quaffed the wine.

20th

The weather is beyond measure severe and trying:—with a hot sun, there is a winter wind of the most piercing bitterness. A pulmonary invalid had better avoid Naples at any time, but certainly during the winter, unless he wish to illustrate the proverb, "*Vedi Napoli e po' mori.*" It is not easy for such an invalid, if his case is notorious, to get lodgings; or at least he will, on that account, be asked a *much higher price* for them; for consumption is here considered to be contagious, and in case of death, the whole of the furniture in the occupation of the deceased is burnt, and his rooms are fumigated and white-washed.

Drove to *Capo di Monte*, a palace of the King, in the environs of the town—Palaces, however, are the most tiresome things in the world, for one is just like another—all glitter and tinsel. Here are some of the best works of *Camuccini*. There was one that pleased me much, representing Pericles, Socrates, and Alcibiades, brought by Aspasia to admire the works of Phidias. This has all the fidelity of an historical picture, for the faces have been closely copied from the antique marbles.

21st

Again to the *Museo*. The library is said to contain 150,000 volumes, and it seems to be well furnished with the literature of all nations. Permission is easily obtained here, as at the British Museum, to enjoy the privilege of reading. Amongst the curious manuscripts, I was shown the *Aminta* of Tasso, in his own hand-writing—which, by the way, was a vile scrawl.

In another quarter, is a large collection of Etruscan vases, in which the elegance of the form shames the badness of the painting. It is strange that a people, who seem to have had an intuitive tact for the elegant and the beautiful, in the form and shape of their vessels, should have had so little taste in the art of design.

In the collection of pictures there is much that is curious, and much that is beautiful. In the former class, are the specimens of the first essays of the first founders of the art of painting in Italy. It is curious to trace its progress through the different stages of improvements till it was at last brought to perfection in the age of Raphael.

In the same class, is an original picture of *Columbus*, by Parmeggianino and a portrait of *Philip the Second* of Spain, which looks the narrow cold-blooded tyrant, that he was in reality.

And, lastly, here is the original sketch of the *Last Judgment*, by Michael Angelo, from which he afterwards painted his great picture. It has been coloured by a later hand.—It ought to be hung up in the Sistine chapel, as a key to make the fresco intelligible; for much is here seen distinctly, that is quite faded in the large picture. For instance, time has done for Cardinal Biagio, what he in vain asked of the Pope; and it is only in this sketch that the bitter resentment of the painter is recorded, which placed him amongst the damned, in the gripe of a malignant dæmon—who is dragging him down to the bottomless pit, in a manner at once the most ferocious and degrading.

In the latter class, there are many that deserve enumeration. Two *Holy Families* by Raphael, are full of the almost heavenly graces with which he, above all other painters, has embellished the subject

There are two landscapes;—and a wild witch on a wilder heath, in the very wildest style of Salvator Rosa.

Titian's *Danæ* is all that is lovely and luscious; and there are some charming pictures of Corregio;—but, I believe, this collection altogether detained me less than it deserved; for, after feasting the imagination, in the galleries of Florence and Rome, with the contemplation of the very finest efforts of the pencil, it requires excellence to stimulate the languid attention, and satisfy the increasing fastidiousness of the taste. This is a cruel deduction from the pleasure which is expected to be derived from familiarity with excellence, and improvement in knowledge; so that, after all it may be doubted whether we grow happier, as we grow wiser;

and, perhaps, those who are at the most pains to see the best that is to be seen—to read the best that is to be read—and to hear the best that is to be heard—are only labouring to exhaust the sources of innocent gratification, and incapacitating themselves from future enjoyment, by approaching nearer to that condition which has been so truly described as a state of

> Painful pre-eminence yourself to view,
> Above life's weakness, and its comforts too!

22d

Yesterday we had December's wind; to-day we have November's rain; and such is the climate of Naples.

Dined with an Italian family, to whom I brought letters of recommendation from Rome. This was the first occasion that I have had of seeing an Italian dress dinner;—but there was scarcely any thing strange to excite remark. The luxury of the rich is nearly the same throughout Europe. Some trifling particularities struck me, though I think the deviations from our own customs were all improvements. There was no formal top and bottom to the table, which was round, and the host could not be determined from his place. All the dishes were removed from the table as they were wanted, carved by a servant at the sideboard and handed round. Each person was provided with a bottle of wine, and a bottle of water, as with a plate, and knife and fork. There was no asking to drink wine, nor drinking of healths; no inviting people to eat, nor carving for them. All these duties devolved on the domestics; and the conversation, which, in England, as long as dinner lasts, is often confined to the business of eating, with all its important auxiliaries of sauces and seasonings, took its free course, unchecked by any interruptions arising out of the business in hand. This is surely the perfection of comfort—to be able to eat and drink what you please without exciting attention or remark;— and I cannot but think it would be a great improvement upon our troublesome fashion of *passing the bottle*, to substitute the Italian mode of placing a separate decanter to each person.

Economy, in a country where wine is so dear as in England, can be the only objection; for, though I have heard some persons argue that the pleasure of drinking is increased by a common participation in the very same bottle; such a notion can scarcely be founded in reason, unless it is allowed that this pleasure is still more exquisitely enjoyed in the tap room, where each man partakes of the same mug, without even the intervention of glasses. For my part, I am for extending the privilege of Idomeneus's cup to every guest:

> πλεῖον δέπας αἰεὶ
> Ἕσηχ᾽, ὥσπερ ἐμοὶ, πίεειν, ὅτε θύμος ἀνώγοι.
>
> Iliad, iv. 262

But an invitation to dinner is a rare occurrence in Italy; for dinner is not here, generally speaking, the social feast of elaborate enjoyment, which we are accustomed to make it in England—occupying a considerable portion of the day, and constituting the principal object of meeting—but a slovenly meal, despatched in haste, and in dishabille; and it is for this reason that an Englishman is rarely invited, except on extraordinary occasions, to partake of it.

In the evening, to a conversazione, at the archbishop of Tarento's;—one of the finest and most respectable-looking old men I ever saw. The intercourse of society is perhaps managed better abroad than in England. The system of being at home in the evening, to those persons with whom you are desirous of associating, without the formality of sending a special invitation, facilitates that pleasant and easy society, which enlivens, without at all destroying, the retirement of domestic life;—and it is carried on with no greater expense than a few additional cups of coffee, or glasses of lemonade. How much more rational is such a friendly intercourse, than the formal morning visits, or the heartless evening routs, of our own country!

23d

Again to the *Museo*.—Examined the ingenious machinery
employed to unroll the manuscripts found at Herculaneum. These
are reduced to a state of tinder, but the writing is still legible.
From the specimen that I saw, it seemed necessary, however, to
supply at least a fifth, by conjecture. Curiosity is kept alive till the
last, for the name of the author is inscribed on the beginning of
the manuscript, and this of course cannot appear till the whole
roll is unravelled. The collection of statues is very extensive, but I
must repeat, of the statues, what I have said of the pictures. After
the Tribune—the Capitol—and the Vatican—what remains to be
seen in sculpture?—and yet the *Venus callipyge* is a most beautiful
creature;—but how shall we excuse her attitude?

The famous *Farnese Hercules* may be calculated to please an
anatomist, but certainly no one else. This is the work of Glycon,
and is perhaps the allusion of Horace, in his first epistle, where
he mentions the "*invicti membra Glyconis*;"—a passage that does
not seem to be satisfactorily explained.

The Flora is generally admired; but a colossal statue is seldom a
pleasing object, and never when it represents a woman. Gigantic
proportions are absolutely inconsistent with female loveliness.

24th to 28th

Confined to the house with a cough;—the effect of the bitter
wind that has been blowing upon us from the mountains.—The
Lord deliver us from another winter at Naples!—Our episcopal
landlord turns out a very caitiff. The last occupier of our
lodgings—a young Englishman, who was confined to his bed by
illness—had occasion to send a bill to his banker's to be cashed;
on which errand he employed the servant of Monsignore. As
it has been imputed to Italian bankers that they sometimes
miscount dollars, he took the precaution to examine immediately
the contents of his bag. Finding that there was a deficiency of
twenty dollars, he summoned the servant, and being unable to
get any explanation, he was preparing a note to the banker to
institute an inquiry, when the man confessed that his master had

stopped him, upon his return, and taken twenty dollars out of the bag;—trusting, as it seems, to the proverbial carelessness of our countrymen. If a bishop will do this, what might we not expect from the poorer classes of society? and yet I must confess I have never met with any such dishonesty in the lower orders, except amongst the pick-pockets in the *Strada Toledo*.

In an arbitrary government like that of Naples, a stranger is surprised by the freedom of speech which prevails on political subjects. The people seem full of discontent. In the coffee-houses, restaurateurs, nay, even in the streets, you hear the most bitter invectives against the government, and tirades against the royal family.

One would imagine, from such general complainings, that the government was in danger—but all seems to evaporate in talk; and indeed Gen. Church (an Englishman) at the head of a body of 5000 foreign troops, is engaged in stopping the mouths of the more determined reformers; which may probably explain the secret of the stability of the present system.

It must be owned that the people have some grounds for complaint; for the King has not only retained all the imposts which Murat, under the pressure of war, found it necessary to levy, but he has also revived many of the ways and means of the old regime. The property-tax alone amounts to twenty-five per cent; and there is a sort of excise, by which every roll that is eaten by the beggar in the streets, is made to contribute a portion to the government purse.

The military, both horse and foot, make a very respectable appearance. To the eye, they are as fine soldiers as any in Europe; and the grenadiers of the King's guard, dressed in the uniform of our own guards, might be admired even in Hyde Park. But it appears that they do not like fighting. The Austrian general Nugent married a Neapolitan princess and is now commander in chief of that very army which, under Murat, ran away from him like a flock of sheep.

It is the fashion to consider soldiers as mere machines, and to maintain that discipline will make soldiers of any men whatever. This may be true as a general rule;—but may not a slavish submission to a despotic government for a long period of years, and confirmed habits of effiminate indolence, on the part of any people, produce an hereditary taint in their blood—gradually making what was *habit* in the parent, *constitution* in the offspring—and so deteriorate the breed, that no immediate management or discipline shall be able to endue such a race with the qualities necessary to constitute a soldier? If this maxim need illustration, I would appeal to the conduct of the Neapolitan army in Murat's last campaign.

1. In one of the baths, which probably belonged to a female, is a pretty and well-preserved fresco of the story of Actæon.

2. Romanelli's's hint is worth attention, who recommends travellers to enter Pompeii by the way of the tombs, that so the interest may be kept alive by reserving the more important objects until the last.

3. The *phallic* ornament, worn round the necks of the ladies, as a charm against sterility, appears in every variety of material,—gold, silver, and coral; and invention seems to have been racked, to represent it in every variety of shape.

Sometimes it is a snail peeping out of its shell; sometimes, a Cupid astride is crowning it with a chaplet; and sometimes it terminates in some frightful reptile, that turns round with an expression of rage; illustrating perhaps the passage of Horace: "*mea cum conferbuit ira*" What can demonstrate more clearly, the coarseness and corruption of ancient taste? unless it be the monstrous conjunctions, consecrated by their abominable superstition, which are still more shocking evidences of the depravity of their imaginations. There is an example of these, in a piece of sculpture, dug up at Herculaneum, now in this museum, which exhibits great powers of expression and execution; but it had better have remained buried under the ruins of Herculaneum.

VIII

ROMAN AND
MODERN SIGHTS

March 1st

The summer sun of to-day brings me again out of my hiding-place.—Explored the Grotto of Posilipo; and the tomb of Virgil—as it is called; though there is little doubt that the poet was buried on the other side of the bay. On a marble slab which is inserted in the rock opposite the entrance of the sepulchre, is the following inscription:—

QUI CINERES? TVMVLI HÆC VESTIGIA ˙ CONDITVR OLIM
ILLE HOC QVI CECINIT PASCVA RVRA DVCES ˙
CAN ˙ REG ˙ M.D.LXIIII

Eustace, in his account, gives us Virgil's own couplet of *Mantua me genuit*, &c., but the real inscription is as I have transcribed it. How this came to be substituted for Virgil's, may be difficult to explain;—but being there, it is more difficult to understand why Eustace should give an inscription that does not exist, when the true one was staring him in the face.[1]

This tomb ought to yield a good revenue to the proprietor. The English pilgrims are the most numerous. A bay-tree once grew out of the top of it; but the keeper told me that the English had pulled off the leaves, as long as any remained; in the same spirit, I suppose, which induced the ladies in England to pull the hairs out of the tail of Platoff's horse. It has been since cut up altogether, and not a root is left to mark the spot.

Beautiful drive along the coast, on the *Sirada Nuova*. This road was the work of Murat, who has done a vast deal to improve and embellish Naples. It was he who enlarged and laid out the *Villa Reale*, in the English style of shrubbery, which forms a delightful promenade between the Chiaja and the sea.

In the centre of this walk is the group of Dirce, commonly called the Toro Farnese. Pliny tells us it was cut out of a single block—

> *Zethus et Amphion, ac Dirce, et Taurus, vinculumque ex eodem lapide, Rhodo advecta, opera Apollonii et Taurisci.*

But the integrity of the original block has been much invaded; for, the head and arms of Dirce—the head and arms of Antiope—the whole of Amphion and Zethus, except the bodies and one leg—and the legs and rope of the bull—are modern.

2nd

Excursion to *Pozzuoli* and *Baiæ* where all is fairy ground.—Here you may wander about, with Virgil and Horace in your hand, and moralize over the changes that time has produced. How are the mighty fallen!—Here the great ones of the earth retired, from the noise and smoke of Rome, to their voluptuous villas. Baiæ was the Brighton, the Cheltenham—or, perhaps, with more propriety, the Bath of Rome;—for it was a winter retreat. The rage for building was carried to an extent that made it necessary to encroach upon the sea:

> Contracta pisces æquora sentiunt,
> Jactis in altum molibus. Huc frequens
> Cæmenta demittit redemptor.

But their *redemptors* built with more solid materials than our modern builders, whose structures will never endure to afford the remnant of a ruin, seventeen hundred years hence, to our curious posterity, as a sample of the style of building of their ancestors.

One might fancy that Horace had been gifted with a prophetic sight of the changes that have taken place when he wrote

> Debemur morti nos, nostraque; sive receptus
> Terrâ Neptunus, classes Aquilonibus arcet,
> Regis opus—

Who can recognise, in the present appearance of the *Lucrine* Lake, any vestiges of the superb description of Virgil?

> An memorem portus, Lucrinoque addita claustra:
> Atque indignatum magnis stridoribus æquor,
> Julia qua ponto longe sonat unda refuso,
> Tyrrhenusque fretis immittitur æstus Avernis?

But it is thus that the fashion of this world passeth away. The lovely *Lucrine*—the scene of imperial *Regatas*—is now a mere morass—or at most a fenny fish-pond. It was curtailed of its fair proportions, and indeed almost filled up, by the monstrous birth of the *Monte Nuovo*—the offspring of a volcano—which burst out in 1538 with a fearful eruption of flames and fire; the ashes of which, after being shot up into the air to an immense height, in their descent formed this prodigious mountain of cinders.

Avernus has no longer any thing diabolical about it. The axe of Agrippa, by levelling the woods that enveloped it in impenetrable gloom, and mysterious dread, long ago deprived the lake of all its terrors. Silius Italicus describes the change which had already taken place in his time:—

> Ille, olim populis dictum Styga, nomine verso,
> Stagna inter celebrem nunc mitia monstrat Avernum.

Popular superstition might well fix upon such a spot, situated in the midst of volcanoes, and supposed to be of unfathomable depth, as the mouth of hell: Homer probably followed the real belief of his time, in sending Ulysses thither;—and Virgil followed Homer. But if Italy has furnished the hells of the poet, it has also supplied them with the scenery of Elysium. Milton seems to have culled the flowers of his delicious garden of Eden, from the soft and sublime scenery of Tuscany; and the charming retreats in the neighbourhood of Avernus were probably the prototypes of Virgil's habitations of the blessed; though he could scarcely intend to fix the geographical position of his *Elysium*, which, by the concluding words, seems evidently transferred to another world,—"*Solemque suum sua sidera norunt.*"

From hence we made a pilgrimage to *Torre di Patria*—the ancient *Liternum*;—the retreat and the tomb of Scipio. The word "*Patria*" is still legible on the wall of a watch-tower, which, you are told, is all that remains of the angry epitaph which he dictated himself:—"*Ingrata Patria, neque enim mea ossa habebis.*" It is evident, however, that this tower is of modern construction, and therefore, the inscription on it only affords evidence of the tradition that this was the place of Scipio's interment. And this tradition is at least as old as Pliny, who tell us there was a notion, that a dragon watched over the manes of Scipio, in a cavern at Liternum.—*Plin. Nat. Hist.* lib. xvi. cap. 44.

Such traditions have usually some foundation in truth. But it is extraordinary that the memory of so great a man should not have outlived his grave long enough to enable history to record where he was buried. All that we gain from Livy however on this point, rests on the same vague tradition:—"*Silentium deinde de Africano fuit. Vitam Literni egit, sine desiderio urbis. Morientem rure eo ipso loco sepeliri se jussisse ferunt, monumentumque ibi ædificari, ne funus sibi in ingrata patria fierit*" A heap of stones is all that remains of the ruins of *Liternum*!

We hurried rapidly over the ruins of *Pozzuoli*, in our way home. A peasant showed us a tomb containing three *Sarcophagi*, which he had lately discovered in his vineyard. He complained bitterly that the King had sent a party of soldiers to remove one of these to his *Museo*, without giving him any remuneration. Further excavation might lead to the discovery of curious remains of antiquity; but who excavate on such terms? The bones in the *Sarcophagi* were in perfect preservation.

Solfatara is well worth seeing.—Murat carried on sulphur works here, for his domestic manufacture of gunpowder.—Three pounds of stone yield one pound of sulphur. *Solfatara* is the crater of an extinguished volcano—it is a fearful spot; the smoke now bursts out in many places;—the whole area is hollow;—and the ground vibrates when you stamp with your foot. Water is found at the depth of thirty feet.

Alum works are also carried on here. Earth and water are put into a large earthen vessel, which is sunk up to the brim in the soil, the heat of which causes the water to boil, and as this evaporates, the alum is deposited in a crystallized state on the sides of the vessel.

It is from the waters of *Solfatara*, that the baths of *Pozzuoli* are supplied; which are said to be very efficacious in cutaneous and rheumatic disorders.

3d

The weather continuing fine, we drove to the lake of *Agnano*; situated in a delightfully retired valley, surrounded by hills. On the border of this lake is the *Grotta de Cane*. Travellers have made a great display of sensibility in their strictures upon the spectacle exhibited here; but, to all appearance, the dog did not care much about it. It may be said with truth of him, that he is *used to it*; for he dies many times a day, and he went to the place of execution wagging his tail.

He became insensible in two minutes;—but upon being laid on the grass, he revived from his trance in a few seconds, without the process of immersion in the lake, which is generally mentioned as necessary to his recovery. From the voracity with which he bolted down a loaf of bread which I bought for him, the vapour does not appear to injure the animal functions.

Addison seems to have been very particular in his experiments upon the vapour of this cavern. He found that a pistol would not take fire in it; but, upon laying a train of gunpowder, and igniting it beyond the sphere of the vapour, he found, "that it could not intercept the train of fire when it had once begun flashing, nor hinder it from running to the very end." He subjected a dog to a second trial in order to ascertain whether he was longer in expiring the first than the second time:—and he found there was no sensible difference. A viper bore it *nine minutes* the first time he put it in, and ten minutes the second:—and he attributes the prolonged duration of the second trial to the large provision of air that the viper laid in after his first death, upon which stock he supposes it to have existed a minute longer, the second time.

4th

Read the *Italian* in a French translation; and afterwards explored the church of *S. Nicolo*, where Mrs. Radcliffe has laid the scene of that admirable interview between the Marchesa and Schedoni, at Vespers; during which they plot the death of Ellena. I went afterwards to the church *S. Severo*, where there are some statues of great celebrity. One represents a female covered with a veil, which is most happily executed in marble, and has all the effects of transparency. This new effect of sculpture was the invention and the work of *Corradini*, a Venetian.

There is another statue of the same kind, in the same church, by the same workman;—a dead Christ—covered with the same marble imitation of a thin gauze veil, which appears as if it were moist with the cold damp of death.

There is also a statue of a figure in a net, the celebrated work of *Queirolo*, a Genoese; which is a model of pains and patience. It is cut out of a single block: yet the net has many folds, and scarcely touches the statue.

5th

Explored the scenery of the *Italian*. Went to vespers at the church of *Spirito Santo*; but the places themselves are as different from Mrs. Radcliffe's romantic description, as the fat unmeaning faces of the present monks are from the sublime portrait of her stern and terrible Schedoni. But it is ever thus. Life is only tolerable in a romance, where all that is common-place and disgusting is kept out of sight;—for what is the reality but, as Mr. Shandy says, to shift about from side to side, and from sorrow to sorrow—to button up one vexation, only to unbutton another!

6th
Seized with an acute pain in the side.

9th
Decided pleurisy—summoned an English surgeon to my assistance. High fever—Copious bleeding.—Owe my life, under Heaven, to the lancet; whose repeated application was necessary to relieve me from the intolerable distress under which I had been gasping for some days. I find pleurisy is the *endemic* of Naples.

14th
Ægri Somnia—If a man be tired of the slow lingering progress of consumption, let him repair to Naples; and the *dénoument* will be much more rapid. The *sirocco* wind, which has been blowing for six days, continues with the same violence.

The effects of this south-east blast, fraught with all the plagues of the deserts of Africa, are immediately felt in that leaden oppressive dejection of spirits, which is the most intolerable of diseases. This must surely be the "*plumbeus Auster*" of Horace.

Neapolitan gossips.—It seems there is a great dispute at present between the Pope and the King of Naples. His Holiness claims feudal superiority over the kingdom, as a fief of the popedom; and, indeed, it would appear, that he has always exercised the right of investiture to every sovereign of Naples, since the foundation of the monarchy by Roger the Norman.

Murat, who in the days of his prosperity laughed at the papal pretensions, after the downfall of Napoleon, thought it prudent to make his submission to his Holiness, and was about to obtain the papal investiture.

It is incontestable, that a certain tribute has always been paid annually by the King to the Pope. The Pope receives this as an acknowledgment of his feudal superiority; the King would fain consider it as a charitable contribution of Peter's Pence. The question is still left open, and here the matter rests.

In another branch of the dispute, the King has gained his point, and established his claim to appoint his own Bishops;—subject to the papal confirmation.

The King of Naples is the oldest *reigning* sovereign in Europe, having ascended the throne in 1759. Though a devotee in religion, he is so fond of field-sports that he cannot give up the pleasures of the *chasse* for a single day; and he has actually obtained a dispensation from the Pope to permit him to shoot on Sundays! It must be remembered, however, in his excuse, that he is seventy and odd years old, and has therefore no time to lose.

15th

Convalescence.—Crawled to the Archbishop of Tarento's—Small collection of pictures;—three by Murillo excellent.

First day of Passion week.—There is a strange mixture of straining and swallowing in the observance of Lent here. The opera and the theatres have been open; but the ballet has been suppressed. Dancing, it would seem, is more unholy than singing or gambling; for the gaming-hell, under the same roof with the opera, and under the sanction of government has been allowed to go on without interruption—

Noctes atque dies patet atri Janua Ditis.[2]

This is a very large establishment; it hold its daily session in a house in the Corso; and adjourns in the evening to a splendid suite of rooms in the upper part of the opera house. The Neapolitans are devoted to play, and they pursue it with a fatal energy, that hurries many of them to the last stage of the road to ruin.—The relaxation of morals, as you advance towards the south, is very striking.—I am afraid to believe all that I hear of the licentiousness of Naples; but I see enough to make me think nothing impossible.

The plain-speaking of the Neapolitan Ladies is truly surprising;—they call every thing by its right name without any circumlocution;—and in the relation of a story, whatever be the character of the incidents, there is nothing left to be collected by inference, but the facts are broadly and plainly told, with the most circumstantial details.

16th

The gaming-table is permitted to go on even during the present week; and the only restraint imposed upon this den of destruction is a short interdict, from Thursday next to Sunday; when the doors will be re-opened. Strange infatuation! that men should thus devotedly pursue a fancied good by means which—occupying all their time and absorbing all their interest—must take away the power of profiting by its acquisition:—

—et propter *nummos, nummorum* perdere causas—

for it almost universally happens, that the *means* at last become the *end*; money being seldom, I believe, the object of any but the selfish, calculating gamester. The true children of play are delighted with the pursuit, and care as little for the object, as the sportsman does for the fox.—They find, in the vicissitudes of play, that strong excitement of the soul, which furnishes a constant succession of deep and agitating emotions. There are minds so unhappily constituted; that, to them, the innocent and peaceful pleasures of tranquil security are as insipid and disgusting, as milk and water would be to the lover of brandy. *Ennui* is too light a term for that heaviness of spirit, and weariness of soul, which find all the uses of the world stale, flat, and unprofitable. The stagnant puddle of existence then must be stirred and freshened, by the torrent, tempest, and whirlwind of the passions; and this stimulant is sought in the dangers of war, the fever of ambition, or the hopes and fears of love. But love, and war, and ambition, are not within the reach of all;—while the gaming-table is ever at hand. The passion for play is universal, and seems to have its root in the very heart of man;—no rank, or age, or sex, is exempt from its influence. The silken baron of civilization, and the naked savage of the desert, show how nearly they are related, in the common eagerness with which they fly to gaming, for relief from the same *tædium vitæ*, the same oppressive void of occupation, which is of all voids, that which nature—at least human nature—abhors the most.

I was a witness, this morning, of the effect of the procession of the Host upon these orgies. At the sound of the bell the groom-porter suspended the work of dealing;—and there was a half-solemn, half-sneering pause, till the bell was out of hearing. All England would exclaim against the government that could be accessary to the corruption of the morals of its subjects, by the encouragement of gaming-tables, for the sake of the revenues derived from such unhallowed practices; but there are too many of us, who cannot, because they will not, see, that evils of the same kind—though it is to be hoped in a less degree—are produced by our own system of state lotteries.

17th.

At this pious season, the strangest dramatic representations are prepared for the edification of the people.—There is no disputing about taste;—if a man, in London, were to get up a puppet-show, to represent the ministry, passion, crucifixion, and ascension of the Saviour, he would probably receive an intimation, the next day, from the Attorney-general, and have to defend himself against a charge of blasphemy. All this however I saw this morning for three half-pence, very fairly represented in a theatre on the quay, by puppets of three feet high, to a crowded and admiring audience. The opposition theatre held out the temptation of a grand spectacle—representing Lord Exmouth's exploits at Algiers; but I ought to record, that the sacred piece seemed to be the most attractive.

The quay of Naples affords a scene, such as I think can scarcely be equalled in the world. Tom Fool is there in all his glory—with such a motley train at his heels, and with such a chorus of noise and nonsense—wit and waggery—fun and foolery—all around him; that, however a man may be disgusted at first, the effect in the end is like that of Munden's face in a stupid farce—where that admirable actor condescends to buffoonery, to save the author of his piece; you are constrained to laugh in spite of yourself.

18th

Spring has once more returned in good earnest. Visited the *Albergo dei Poveri*; a sort of Foundling Hospital, and House of Industry. Here we saw 1500 men and boys; and about as many women and girls. From whence we drove to the *Campo Santo*—the great *Golgotha* of Naples. It is situated on a rising ground behind the town, about a mile and a half from the gate. Within its walls are 365 caverns; one is opened every day for the reception of the dead, the great mass of whom, as soon as the rites of religion have been performed, are brought here for sepulture. There were fifteen cast in, while we were there; men, women, and children—without a rag to cover them; literally fulfilling the words of scripture:—"As he came forth out of his mother's womb, naked shall he return, to go as he came!" I looked down into this frightful charnel-house;—it was a shocking sight—a mass of blood and garbage;—for many of the bodies had been opened at the hospitals. Cockroaches, and other reptiles, were crawling about in all their glory. "We fat all creatures else to fat us, and we fat ourselves for maggots: that's the end!"

We made the sexton of this dreary abode, who, by the way, had been employed in this daily work for eleven years, open the stone of the next day's grave, which had been sealed up for a year. The flesh was entirely gone; for, in such a fermenting mass, the work of corruption must go on swimmingly. Quick-lime is added to hasten the process, and nothing seemed to remain but a dry heap of bones and skulls. What must be the feelings of those, who can suffer the remains of a Friend, a Sister, a Mother, or a Wife, to be thus disposed of? Indifferent as I feel to the posthumous fate of my own remains, Heaven grant that I may at least rest and rot *alone*;— without being mixed up in so horrible a human hash as this!

There were some women saying *Ave Marias*, within the square, for the departed souls of their friends; but our arrival took them from this pious work, and set them upon some calculations—connected with us, and our carriage, and the number of it—to direct them in the selection of lucky numbers in the lottery, upon their return to Naples!

19th

The king waited upon a company of beggars at their meal; and afterwards washed their feet. This day is observed with the greatest solemnity. No carriages have been allowed to move about the streets. All the higher classes have put on mourning, and the soldiers have paraded, with arms reversed, and muffled drums. In the evening, the king, attended by his whole court, walked in procession, bareheaded, through the Toledo; visiting the churches in his route, and kneeling before the images of the Virgin, who, on this occasion, is dressed in deep mourning.

20th

Good Friday.—Continuation of the mourning of yesterday.—It must be confessed that there is much more of religious observance in Catholic, than in Protestant countries. Then comes the question, to what extent is it wholesome to encourage these outward observances? If too much importance be given to them, there is danger that religion will stop there, and degenerate into a mere homage of rites and ceremonies, in the place of that homage of our hearts and lives, which the Christian religion requires of us. And this is the objection which we make against the Catholics. Again, if there be no attention paid to forms, there is danger that the substance may be lost sight of: and that a religion without any rites, will soon become no religion at all; and this, I apprehend, is the objection that the Catholics make against the Protestants. Both sides agree that some ceremonial is necessary, and it is only a question of degree between them after all. In determining this question of degree, it is not easy to lay down a rule that would be universally applicable, for it must vary with the different characters and habits of different nations; and perhaps climate would not be without its influence, in regulating the standard of propriety. For example, the natives of the south seem to have an intuitive love of show and spectacle, which forms a strong contrast with the plain and simple habitudes of the northern nations. And this consideration ought perhaps to have made me more tolerant in my remarks on Catholic ceremonies abroad;—for I believe that they may be less characteristic of the religion itself, than of the taste of the people.

21st
The Paschal Lamb, which I have observed in many of the houses, as a sort of pet during Lent, appears no more. The knife is at work for tomorrow's feast.

Drove to *Portici*.—The museum consists principally of specimens of the paintings found at Pompeii. These remains are very interesting, as illustrative of the state of the art amongst the Romans; but it would be ridiculous to take the paintings on the walls of the houses of a provincial town as the standard of their skill.

It is fair to suppose, that the taste of the ancients was as refined and fastidious in painting, as in the sister art of sculpture; and that the praises which they have lavished upon Zeuxis and Apelles, would have been supported by their works, if these works had come down to us.

All traces of these great masters are lost; but, we know some of the most admired pieces of the latter were brought by Augustus to Rome; and Pliny's descriptions, which do remain, seem to demonstrate that they must have been executed in a much higher style of finishing, and with a technical knowledge, that will in vain be sought in the painted walls of Herculaneum and Pompeii. Many of these, however, are designed with great taste, grace, and feeling; and, if we suppose that the works of Zeuxis and Apelles were as superior to these, as the *Last Judgment*, and the *School of Athens*, are to the painted walls of a modern Italian room, we shall probably not form too high an estimate of the excellence of the great masters of ancient art. One of the most elegant figures in this museum, is the picture of a female, with a pencil and tablets in her hand, which they call Sappho. The story of the picture is often plain, as in that of Orestes, Pylades, and Iphigenia, in the temple of Diana. Thus, too, we cannot mistake the representation of a schoolmaster's room, where an unhappy culprit is horsed on the back of one of his fellows—precisely as the same discipline is administered in many parts of England at present.

We have also a specimen of their taste in caricature. A little delicate chariot, that might have been made by the fairies' coachmaker, is drawn by a parrot, and driven by a grasshopper. This is said to be a satirical representation of Nero's absurd pretensions as a Singer and a Driver; for Suetonius tells us he made his debut on the Neapolitan theatre:—"*Et prodiit Neapoli primum: ibidem sæpius et per complures cantavit dies.*"

We adjourned afterwards to the royal palace, which was fitted up by Murat. Every thing remains in the state he left it, except that the family pictures of himself, and his wife, and her two brothers, Napoleon and Joseph, have been taken down from their high places, and thrust into a garret, "amongst the common lumber." He is represented in a fancy dress, which is almost ridiculously fantastic, with ear-rings in his ears, but, though a fine handsome man, I doubt whether he has not a little the air of Tom Errand in Beau Clincher's clothes. Madame Murat's room and adjoining bath are strikingly elegant and luxurious. In her dressing-room is a small library; in which I observed that the majority of the books were translations of English authors;—Gibbon, Fielding, Hume, Thomson, Coxe's House of Austria, Mrs. Radcliffe, and a long train of novels. In Joachim's room, almost every article of furniture is ornamented with the head of his favourite Henry IV.—the royal model which he is said to have proposed to himself—but he was not fortunate enough to meet with a *Sully* for his minister; and he lived to learn that the "divinity which used to hedge a King," was to be no protection to him, though he had won a crown by his valour, and worn it with the consent and acknowledgement of all Europe. That man must have the feelings of humanity strangely perverted by political enmities, who can read the story of his ignominious death without pity.

The leading feature in his character seems to have been, that gallant generous bravery so becoming a soldier, which he displayed on all occasions. In his very last retreat, he is said to have risked his life, to save the son of one of his nobility, who wanted the courage to do it himself. They were crossing the river, under the fire of the Austrians; the horse of the young man was wounded, and his situation appeared hopeless. Joachim, moved by the distress of the father, plunged into the stream, and brought the son in safety to the bank, where the father had remained a helpless spectator of the whole transaction. But peace be to his ashes.—I am no advocate for the scum, to which the fermentation of the French Revolution has given such undue elevation; but there are always exceptions;—and Joachim, however he might be tainted with the original sin of the school in which he was bred, had deserved too well of mankind, by his own conduct in power, not to merit more compassion than he found, in the hour of his adversity.

In the gardens of Portici is a Fort, built to teach the present King the art of fortification, during his childhood; and in the upper apartment is a curious mechanical table, which is made to furnish a dinner, without the attendance of domestics.

In the centre of the table is a trap-door. The dinner is sent up by pullies from the kitchen below. Each person has six bell-handles attached to his place, which ring in the kitchen, inscribed with the articles most in request at dinner. These are hoisted up by invisible agents, something after the fashion of the entertainment in *Beauty and the Beast*; or to compare it with something less romantic, and nearer home, Mr. O.'s establishment at Lanark, where dinner is served up by steam! A double chain, arranged like the ropes of a draw-well, sends up the dinner on one side, and carries down the dirty plates, &c. on the other.

22nd

Easter Sunday.—Grand holiday.—A feast at Portici, which reminded me of Greenwich fair.—The dress of the peasantry

gaudy and glittering;—crimson satin gowns, covered with
tinsel.

Excursion to Vesuvius.—My surgeon warned me against this
ascent, but I was resolved to go. To leave Naples, without seeing
Vesuvius, would be worse than to die at Naples, after seeing
Vesuvius. The ascent was laborious enough, but no part of the
labour fell upon my shoulders. When we arrived at the foot of the
perpendicular steep, where it was necessary to leave our mules,
while my companions toiled up on foot, I got into an easy arm-
chair, and was carried on the shoulders of eight stout fellows, to
my own great astonishment, and to the greater amusement of my
friends, who expected every moment to see us all roll over together.
I certainly should not have thought the thing practicable, if I had
not tried it; for the ascent is as steep as it is well possible to be; the
surface however is rugged; and this enabled the men to keep their
footing. It was not the pleasantest ride in the world; for without
pretending to any extraordinary sensibility, there is something
disagreeable in overcoming difficulties by the sweat of other men's
brows, even if they are well paid for it. The men, however, seemed
to enjoy it exceedingly.

When you arrive at the top, it is an awful sight, more like the
infernal regions, than anything that human imagination could
suggest. As you approach the great crater, the crust upon which
you tread becomes so hot, that you cannot stand long on the
same place—your progress is literally "*per ignes suppositos cineri
doloso;*"—if you push your stick an inch below the surface, it
takes fire, and you may light paper by thrusting it into any of
the cracks of the crust. The craters of the late eruption were still
vomiting forth flames and smoke, and when we threw down
large stones into these fiery mouths, one might have thought they
were replying to Lear's imprecation—"*Rumble thy belly full!—Spit
fire!*"—Altogether, it was a most sublime and impressive scene,
and may be classed amongst the very few things in the world that
do not disappoint expectation.

The look down, into the great crater at the summit, is frightfully
grand; and when you turn away from the contemplation of this

fearful abyss, you are presented with the most forcible contrast, in the rich and luxuriant prospect of Naples, and the surrounding country; where all is soft and smiling as far as the eye can see.

In our way home we explored Herculaneum; which scarcely repays the labour. This town is filled up with lava, and with a cement caused by the large mixture of water, with the shower of earth and ashes that destroyed it; and it is choked up, as completely as if molten lead had been poured into it. Here, therefore, the work of excavation was so laborious, that all which could be done has been to cut a few passages. Besides, it is forty feet below the surface, and another town is now built over it; so that you grope about under ground by torch light, and see nothing.

Pompeii, on the contrary, was destroyed by a shower of cinders, in which there was a much less quantity of water. It lay, for centuries, only twelve feet below the surface; and these cinders being easily removed, the town has been again restored to the light of day.

In the evening the Theatre of S. Carlo re-opened with a new opera, and a splendid ballet.

23rd

The finest-looking men in Naples are the *Lazzaroni*; the lowest class in the order of society; answering to the Lazzi in the old Saxon:division of classes in our own island: "*Dividebantur antiqui Saxones in tres ordines; Edilingos, Filingos, et Laszzos; hoc est, nobiles, ingenuos, serviles. Rest antiquæ appellationis commemoratio. Ignavos enim* lazie *hodie decimus.*"—(Spelman.)

But, if Lazzaroni be at all connected with laziness, the term has little application to the bearers of burdens in Naples; unless it be explained in the same manner as *lucus à non lucendo*. If they are fond of sprawling in the sun, they are enjoying the holiday of repose which they have earned by their own industry; and which they have a right to dispose of according to their own taste. There is an amphibious class of these fellows, who seem to live in the water. I have stood watching a boat for hours, which I had at first imagined was adrift without an owner; to which one of these fishermen would occasionally mount out of the water with an oyster, and then, down he went again, in search of another.

They appear to be a merry joyous race, with a keen relish for drollery, and endued with a power of feature, that is shown in the richest exhibitions of comic grimace. Swinburne says well, that Hogarth ought to have visited Naples, to have beheld the "*sublime of caricature*."

I know few sights more ludicrous, than that which may be enjoyed by treating a Lazzarone to as many yards of *macaroni* as he can contrive to slide down his throat without breaking its continuity.

Their dexterity is almost equal to that of the Indian Jugglers, and much more entertaining.

24th

In ascending the scale of society, we do not find progressive improvement in information, as we mount to the top.

The ignorance of the higher classes has long been proverbial. Murat had instituted a female school of education, on a large scale, which was well attended by the principal families in Naples; and a taste for knowledge was beginning to spread very rapidly;— but Murat is dead! The most thriving profession is the law;—and almost every tenth man is a lawyer.

25th

Went in the evening to the *Teatro Nuova*, where Italian tragedies and comedies are performed; and which is attended, particularly by the younger classes of the Neapolitans, as a school of pronunciation, and a lesson in language. Nothing can be more barbarous than the Neapolitan dialect. There was but little of *vis comica* in the performance; and indeed the piece was a suspicious, lacrymose, white-handkerchief business, translated from a sentimental German comedy.

The rustic, who seems to be the same—at least in the stage representation of the character—all the world over, was well done, and reminded me of Emery.

26th

Intended excursion to Paestum. Prevented by a fresh attack of pleurisy. Perhaps there is no great cause for regret; for, however fine the ruins may be, there is no story of the olden time to make them particularly interesting. If ruins are sought out as mere objects to please the eye, I doubt if there be any thing in Italy that could be put in comparison with Tintern Abbey. But it is the deeds that have been done, and the men that did them—the Scipios, and the Catos, and the Brutuses—that invest the ruins of Rome with their great charm and interest. Independently of these recollections, there is perhaps nothing to be seen in Italy so *beautiful* as the light, elegant, and graceful ruins of a Gothic Abbey.

This associating principle seems to operate, and give an interest, even to places where the adventures which make them memorable are notoriously fictitious; for to no other cause can I attribute the pains I have taken to identify the scenery of *the Italian*; and I experienced serious disappointment at being unable to find the ruined archway in which Vivaldi was intercepted by the mysterious monk, in his visits to the villa of Signora Bianca;—which had probably never any existence except in the imagination of Mrs. Radcliffe.

The vicissitudes of the weather here are beyond every thing I have ever felt. During Easter week, it was intensely hot. On the 28th of March, Vesuvius was covered with snow, and the four succeeding days have been as cold and comfortless as wind, sleet, and hail, could make them.

April 2nd

Convalescence. Visited the opera for the first time. Of all the stupid things in the world, a serious opera is perhaps the most stupid, and the opera of to-night formed no exception to this observation. The theatre is, I believe, the largest in Europe, and it is certainly too large for the singers, whose voices sound like penny trumpets on Salisbury Plain.[3]

The pit contained 674 elbowed seats, in 19 rows; and there is standing room for at least 150 persons.

The ballet of *Gengis Khan* was splendidly got up. The dancing was admirable, for though excellence must necessarily be confined to a few, all were good. These spectacles are better managed here than in England. I am afraid there is always something lumpish and awkward in the general effect of our *corps de ballet*; but here the groups are so picturesque, their motions so graceful, there is such a general expertness in the most complicated movements of the dance, and such a lightness and perpetual motion in all the figures, that the whole spectacle has the effect of phantasmagoria.

3rd

The ex-king of Spain arrived, accompanied by his brother the present king of Naples, who had gone to *Mola di Gaeta*, to meet him. It is said that they now met for the first time after a separation of sixty years.

1. Some fatality seems to hang over this inscription, which I have never yet seen printed correctly; and which, indeed, is scarcely worth recording. In correcting the first impression of my work, I was induced to alter the hasty transcript I had made on the spot, in deference to a friend in whose accuracy I had more faith than in my own. It turns out however after all that my original note was correct, and therefore, the true reading is now restored, as well as the punctuation, which might easily escape notice without careful observation. The last line is perhaps not the least important of the three, as serving to fix the date of this semi-barbarous distich.

2. It ought to be recorded to the honour of the revolutionary government in 1820, that one of their first acts was to suppress those public gaming-tables.

3. It ought to excite little wonder, that there are so few good singers in Italy; for she is unable, from her poverty, to retain those whom she has herself formed. As soon as they become eminent, they are enticed away to foreign countries, and often return to Italy, after years of absence,

enriched with the spoils of half the provinces of Europe. Besides, the Italians of the present day have no taste for the higher kinds of music, for full and grand harmonies,—or for instrumental music in general. If you talk to them of Haydn, Mozart, or Beethoven, they shrug up their shoulders, and tell you—*"E Musica, Tedesca,—non ci abbiamo gusto"* Cherubini, their only really great composer, might perhaps be cited as an exception, but he is in fact a most striking confirmation of their want of taste; for his works are almost unknown, and he seems to be himself aware of the inability of his countrymen to appreciate his merits, by residing at a distance, and composing for foreign theatres. What the Italians like, is an easy flowing melody, *unencumbered*, as they would call it, with too much harmony. Whatever *Corinne* may say to the contrary, they seem to have little or no relish for impassioned music. Take an example of the taste of the times from the Opera of to-night—*Armida*—the composition of their favourite Rossini. His operas are always easy and flowing;—abounding in prettinesses and melting cadenzas, but he never reaches, nor apparently does he attempt to reach, the sustained and elevated character which distinguishes the music of Mozart. But Rossini's works ought not to be too severely criticised; for the continual demand for new music is greater than any fertility of head could supply. The Italians never like to go back;—without referring so far as their own great Corelli—Cimarosa, Paisiello, and others of equally recent date, are already become antiquated; and as Rossini is almost their only composer, he is obliged to write an opera in the interval of a few weeks, between the bringing out of the last, and its being laid on the shelf.

It is a sad tantalizing thing to hear music in Italy which you may wish to carry away with you; for they have no printed music!—This alone is sufficient to indicate the low state of the art. From Naples to Milan, I believe, there is no such artist as an Engraver of Music, and you never see a Music shop. You must therefore go without it, or employ a Copier, whose trade is regulated by the most approved cheating rules. He charges you according to the quantity of paper written on, and therefore takes care not to write too closely.

IX

FROM ROME
TO FLORENCE

April 5th.
Left Naples in a fit of spleen and disgust at the continued inclemency of the weather, and slept at Capua; where we found none of those seducing luxuries which enervated the soldiers of Hannibal.

6th.
This day's journey brought us to Velletri. It was nearly dark when we left Terracina to pass over the Pontine Marshes. During the last stage, our postilion was constantly stopping, upon some pretence of the harness wanting repairs; at other times he pleaded that his horses were knocked up, and could not go beyond a foot's pace, on which occasion he would set up a loud song. All this was so like the common prologue to a robbery scene in romance, that we suspected the fellow must be a confederate with the banditti. At last we lost all patience—my companion produced his pistols, and swore that the next time he relaxed from a trot, he would blow out his brains. This seemed to have its effect, and we rattled on to Velletri without clearing up the mystery.

7th.
Reached Rome to breakfast.—Went to bed in a high fever.—Summoned a Roman surgeon to open a vein, which he did very tolerably; but their practice is much more timid than our own, for as soon as he had taken a large thimbleful of blood, he was for binding up the arm again, and protested, in the most urgent

manner, against the madness of my proceeding when he saw me determined to lose ten ounces.

11th.

Emerged from the confinement of a sick room, to enjoy again the genial air of Rome. How delightful is the calm tranquillity of this fallen capital, after the din and clatter of Naples! There is something so soft and balmy, in the air, that I feel every mouthful revive and invigorate me;—and it is now as warm as midsummer in England.

Went to the church of *S. Maria del Popolo*, where there is a great curiosity in sculpture;—a statue by Raphael. It is Jonas, in the moment of his deliverance from the jaws of the great Leviathan of the Deep. The. figure is beautifully elegant, and displays the same delicate skill in outline, for which Raphael is so distinguished in his pictures. It is doubted whether Lorenzetto. executed this statue from Raphael's design, or whether it received the finishing strokes from Raphael himself. As no other works of Lorenzetto display the same powers, it is fair to suppose the latter; and indeed there is a masterly touch in the expression, that seems in itself sufficient to decide the question.

12th.

Passed the morning in the *Studio* of Canova and Thorwaldson. —Confirmed in my former opinions of their respective merits.— A statue of *Washington*, for the United States, just moulded by Canova;—in which there is the same want of repose and simplicity, that is so often observable in his works. Thorwaldson had just finished the model of a *Mercury*, putting Argus to sleep with his pipe; a figure of exquisite grace, archness, and spirit—the veritable son of Maia.

Some traces of antiquity are continually meeting you in your walks through Rome; for instance, the white robes of the modern Italian Butchers which, considering their occupation, are strikingly neat—seem to be the cast off dresses of the priests who performed the act of sacrifice.

13th.

An execution in the Piazza del Popolo. The culprit was a "Fellow with a horrid face," who had murdered his father. The murder was detected in a singular manner, affording an extraordinary instance of the sagacity and faithful attachment of the dog to his master. The disappearance of the deceased had given rise to inquiry, and the officers of police went to his cottage, where, on examining his son, they learned that his father had gone out to work as usual, a few days before, and had not been seen since. As the officers were continuing their search in the neighbourhood, their attention was excited by observing a dog lying in a lone place; who seemed to endeavour to attract their notice, by scratching on some newly-turned earth. Their curiosity was excited, by something peculiar in his action and manner, to examine the spot where they found the body. It would seem that the dog must have been an unobserved witness of his master's murder, and had not forsaken his grave. On returning to the cottage with the body, the son was so struck with the discovery made by the officers by means which he could not divine, that, concluding it must have been by supernatural intimation, he made a full confession of his guilt;—that he had beaten out his father's brains with a mallet, at the instigation of his mother; that he had dragged him to this by-place, and there buried him. The mother was condemned to imprisonment for life;—the son to the guillotine. He kept us waiting from ten o'clock till almost three; for the execution is delayed till the culprit is brought to a due state of penitence.

At last the bell rang, the Host was brought from a neighbouring church that he might receive the last sacrament; and soon afterwards the criminal was led out. *Inglese* was a passport on this as on other occasions. The guards that formed in a square round the guillotine, made way for me to pass; and I was introduced, almost against my will, close to the scaffold.

A crucifix and a black banner, with death's heads upon it, were borne before the culprit who advanced between two priests. He mounted the scaffold with a firm step, and did not once flinch till he stooped to put his head into the groove prepared to receive it.

This is the trying minute; the rest is the affair of less than a moment. It appears to be the best of all modes of inflicting the punishment of death; combining the greatest impression on the spectator, with the least possible suffering to the victim. It is so rapid, that I should doubt whether there were any suffering; but from the expression of the countenance when the executioner held up the head, I am inclined to believe that sense and consciousness may remain for a few seconds after the head is off. The eyes seemed to retain speculation for a moment or two, and there was a look in the ghastly stare with which they glared upon the crowd, which implied that the head was aware of its ignominious situation. And indeed there is nothing improbable in this supposition; for in all injuries of the spine whereby a communication with the sensorium is cut off, it is the parts below the injury which are deprived of sensation, while those above retain their sensibility. And so, in the ease of decapitation, the nerves of the face and eyes may for a short time continue to convey impressions to the brain, in spite of the separation from the trunk.

14th.

Ægina Marbles;—these belong to an earlier age of sculpture than that of Phidias, and are curious specimens of the infancy of the art amongst the Greeks.

The symmetry is very defective; and there is a sort of sardonic smile in the expression of all the faces that is unintelligible, without knowing the history of the group.

Amongst the amusements of the people there is nothing more striking than the energy and interest which they exhibit in the common game of *Morra*.

This game is played by two persons; they both hold out their right hands, with the fingers extended; then, each contracts or shuts one, or as many of his fingers as he pleases; calling out at the same time the number which he guesses will be the whole amount of his own and his adversary's contracted fingers; this they both do, at the same moment, and very rapidly. Whichever guesses rightly, scores one, which is done by holding out one finger of the left hand;—the game may be five or ten, or more, at pleasure.

The vivacity with which they pursue this game is extraordinary. As may be supposed, from the nature of the game, it often creates disputes and quarrels, and in the days when every man carried his stiletto, these quarrels but too often ended in blood.

15th to *20th.*

There is now scarcely a stranger in Rome. The ceremonies of Easter being over, all the world is gone to Naples; and the best lodgings are now to be had for half the price that would have been asked two months ago.

Accidentally encountered some old friends and school-fellows. What a delightful thing it is to laugh and talk over the almost forgotten days of boyhood; when all was fun and frolic. For a moment, one escapes from the present to the past, and becomes a boy over again.

22nd.

Excursion to Tivoli.—We rose before the sun, and reached Tivoli to breakfast.—The morning was beautiful—and the morning is the spring of the day, when all nature is fresh and joyous, and man is fresh to enjoy it. It is the custom of the Cicerone to lead you a long round of some miles, to see the *cascatelle*, and other things which are not worth seeing; and I regretted that I had not rather remained the whole morning in the charming environs of the temple of Vesta.

The great cascade is artificial—the work of Bernini; but I prefer much the natural fall which the waters have worked for themselves through the fissures of the rock; which is seen with such admirable effect from the hollow cavern called Grotto of Neptune. A pretty and intricate shrubbery covers the precipice, through which a path has been cut to enable you to descend to this spot; and I have seldom looked upon a scene which unites at once so much of the sublime and the beautiful;—but I will not attempt to describe it. A cascade is one of those things that bids defiance to the pen or the pencil; for the noise and the motion, which constitute, in fact, almost all that is grand and graceful in a real waterfall, are lost in a picture; arid when these are taken away, what remains but an unseemly patch of white paint? If the imagination is to supply the loss, it might as well represent the whole scene.

Horace may well be justified for his partiality to the *præceps Anio et Tiburni lucus.* It is an exquisite spot; and well calculated to suggest the idea of a retreat from the world, with the calm pleasures of a life of rural retirement:

> Tibur Argeo positum colono
> Sit meæ sedes utinam senectæ!
> Sit modus lasso maris, et viarum
>   Militiæque!

It was in the scenery of Tivoli that Claude delighted to study nature; and in most of his landscapes there may be traced some features of the soft and beautiful combinations of the elements of landscape, which the scenery of Tivoli affords in such abundance. But the pictures of Claude represent nature rather as she might be, than as she is. His pictures are poetic nature; nature abstracted from all local defects;—by which I mean, that though all the separate features of his pictures are true to nature, yet that he has compounded them in a manner, to form a general whole such as will never be found existing together in a real landscape. Thus he has done in landscape what the Greek artists have done in sculpture, who, from the separate excellences of different individuals, have combined perfect figures, far superior in grace and beauty to any single living model.

23rd.
Visited the Lunatic Asylum.—I should have been inclined to suppose, in a country where the natives display so much vivacity and energy in the ordinary and healthy state of their minds, that their mad-houses would have exhibited a strange scene of violent

excitement. But I was surprised to find every thing calm and tranquil. There were no raving patients. and only two whom it was necessary to confine, by a slight chain, to the wall of their apartment. I was much struck by the appearance and expression of two unfortunates labouring under the most opposite symptoms.— The one was a captain in the army, who had been driven mad by jealousy.—He was walking up and down a long room, with a quick and agitated step, and, I was told, he had been occupied in the same way for ten years; except during the few hours of sleep. He seemed to be suffering the pains of the damned, as they have been described to proceed from the worm that never dieth. The other was a melancholy maniac, lying in the sun; so utterly lost in vacancy, that I endeavoured in vain to rouse him from his reverie. He had a cast of countenance so cynic, that he might have furnished a painter with an admirable study for a Diogenes.

24th.

The politicians of Rome look to the future with gloomy apprehension. The general opinion seems to be, that the temporal power of the Pope will end with Pius VII.; and that Austria will lay her paw upon the ecclesiastical dominions.

Connected as the House of Austria is with the reigning families of Tuscany and Naples, such an attempt might have little opposition to fear in the rest of Italy; and indeed as to the Papal States, even if there were any *national feeling* to keep them together, which I believe there is not, the people seem too much disposed to rely upon the interposition of miraculous assistance from above, to do any thing for themselves.

When the French were advancing in 1798—how was it that the Papal Government prepared to resist them? By a levy *en masse*? No—but by a procession of three of the most sacred relics in the possession of the church. These relics were—*Il Santo Volto*, a miraculous portrait of the Saviour;—and a *Santa Maria*, a portrait of the Virgin, supposed also to be painted by supernatural agency;—and the *chains* which St. Peter wore in prison, from which the angel liberated him.

This procession was attended by nearly the whole population of Rome, comprehending all ranks and ages and sexes, the greater part of them bare-footed.—Satisfied with this, they remained in a state of in activity, in the hope that Heaven would interpose in their favour, by some miraculous manifestation of its power. Such is ever the effect of superstition, which substitutes rites for duties, and teaches men to build their hopes of divine favour upon any other rather than the only true and rational foundation of such hopes—the faithful and exemplary discharge of their own duties.

The Italians now make a triumphant appeal to the late restoration of the Pope, as a visible interference of Providence, which ought to convince a heretic that it is decreed by the counsels of Heaven, that the Pope shall endure for ever; and they hail this return as an omen and security for the same miraculous assistance in the time to come, forgetting the admirable doctrine of the Trojan patriot,

Εἷς οἰωνὸς ὔριςος; ἄμύνεσθαι περὶ πάτρης!

In the evening went to the theatre.—An Italian comedy, or rather a German play, translated into Italian.—German sentiment seems to please all the world, in spite of its stupidity; else, why do we all pilfer from Kotzebue? Vestris, the great comic actor of Italy, played the part of a valet, with considerable archness and humour; but he is a "tun of man;" and a fat man is fit to act nothing but a fat man;—for perhaps there is no character but Falstaff, of which fat is an essential attribute. But, when I speak slightingly of Vestris, I forget his Tale-bearer in the *Bottega di Café*, and his *Burbero benefico*;—both admirable pieces of acting.

25th.

I looked on this morning at a game at *Pallone*. This is a great improvement upon our *fives*. It is played by parties of a certain number on each side, generally six against six. The pallone is a ball filled with air, about as big as a foot-ball. The players wear a sort of wooden guard, called *Bracciale*, into which the right hand is introduced; this instrument, which is in shape not unlike a muff, reaches half way up to the elbow, and is studded with sharp wooden points. The player, grasping firmly a bar fixed in the inside of the *Bracciale*, to keep it steady, takes the ball before the bound, and *vollies* it, according to the tennis term, with amazing force. The object of the players is to prevent the ball falling within their lines. The weight of the *Bracciale*, placed as it is at the extremity of the arm, must require great muscular strength to support it, during a long game. It is a truly athletic exercise, and though it is said to be the ancient *follis* of the Romans, it must have undergone some alteration;—for the line,

> Folle decet pueros ludere, folle senes

has no application to the modern game of the *Pallone*.

Joined Lucien Buonaparte's domestic circle in the evening.

26th.

Nothing is more perplexing in Italy, than the computation of time. It is pity that the Italians will not reckon their hours in the same manner with their neighbours. The ancient Romans divided the day into twenty-four hours. Twelve of these, from the rising to the setting of the sun, composed their day, and the other twelve, from sunset till sun rise, made up the night. Hence, as the seasons changed, there must have been a proportionate variation in the length of their hours. They had, however, two fixed points; midday and midnight, which they called the sixth hour.

The modern division of the Italians differs from this; they divide the day and night into twenty-four hours, which are all of an equal length, in every season of the year.

Perhaps it may be more simple to reckon twenty-four hours in one series, than by our double series of twelve and twelve.

But the perplexity arises from their not beginning to reckon from some fixed point, that shall not vary; as, for instance, from twelve o'clock at noon—when the sun crosses the meridian every day in the year. The Italians call half an hour after sunset the twenty-fourth hour; and an hour and a half after sunset, the first hour, or one o'clock. Hence the nominal hour of midday constantly changes with the season; in June it is sixteen, and in December nineteen o'clock.

27th.

I ought to say something of the pulpit eloquence of Italy, of which I have heard many specimens both here and at Naples. Lent is least *memoriter*, there must necessarily be many bad preachers— but there are scarcely any drawlers; there is nonsense enough, but not that lifeless, dull monotony of topic, style, and voice, which so often sets our own congregations to sleep. Some of them, particularly at Naples, are very ridiculous, from the vehemence of their gesticulations; and there is always a crucifix in the pulpit, which often leads to the introduction of a dramatic style. There is a practice, too, common to all, which at first is apt to excite a smile. The Preacher pronounces the sacred name without any particular observance, but as often as he has occasion to mention *la santissima Madonna*, he whips off his little scull-cap, with an air that has as much the appearance of *politeness* as of *reverence*. But lest my preaching article should grow into a Sermon, I conclude it abruptly—as most of the Italian Preachers do their sermons —who hurry down the stairs of the pulpit, without doxology, prayer, or blessing.

28th

Visited again and again the relics[1] of "Almighty Rome". At this delightful season you are tempted to pass the whole night in wandering among the ruins, which make a more solemn impression than when lighted up by the "garish eye" of day. I have never encountered any obstruction in these midnight rambles, nor seen any robbers, except the other evening, in the castle of St. Angelo. I had ascended to the roof to enjoy the view, when I observed a party drinking wine on the leads, who very courteously invited me to partake of their good cheer. I found that these fellows were the leaders of a gang of robbers, for whose apprehension a large reward had been offered. As the robbing trade was becoming slack, they hit upon the ingenious expedient of surrendering themselves, in order to obtain it; and it is not a little extraordinary that the Government should have consented to these terms, so that these fellows will, after a confinement of a year in the castle of St. Angelo, be let loose agnin upon society. In the mean time, they seem to live pleasantly enough; the English go and talk to them about the particulars of their robberies, and I am told that one of our countrywomen has made them a handsome present. This is a strange mode of putting down robbers, but, if it were not to see strange things, who would be at the pains of travelling—for, after all, I believe Madame de Stael is right when she calls it a "*triste plaisir*."

29th

Amongst the charms of an Italian evening, I ought to mention the street-singing and serenading. That has happened to music in Italy, which happens to language and style, to poetry and painting, and indeed to every thing else in this world. When a certain point of perfection has been attained, the progress afterwards is in a contrary direction; and a corruption of taste is introduced by the very attempt to pursue improvement beyond that line, which limits all human exertion by the irreversible fiat;—"thus far shalt thou go, and no farther." But though music must be considered as on the decline in Italy, there is, notwithstanding, a general diffusion of musical taste and musical talent, extending to the lowest ranks. I have often set my window open at night to listen to the "dying falls" of a favourite air, distributed into parts, and sung by a party of mechanics returning home from their work, with a degree of skill and science that would not have disgraced professional performers. The serenade is a compliment of gallantry, by no means confined to the rich. It is customary for a lover, even of the lowest class, to haunt the dwelling of his mistress chanting a *rondo*, or roundelay, during the period of his courtship.

One of these swains infested our neighbourhood, and my Italian master[2] caught the words, which were pretty enough; though as he says is generally the case, they are not reducible to the rules of Syntax;—

> Fiori d'argento
> Che per amare a voi
> Ci ho pianto tanto
> Poveri pianti miei
> Gettati al vento.

In saying "that the Italians have no taste for instrumental music in general," I do not mean to assert that they have not individual performers of consummate talent, among whom it would be injustice not to mention the celebrated Paganini.[3] He is a man of eccentric character, and irregular habits. Though generally resident at Turin, he has no fixed engagement; but, as occasion may require, makes a trading voyage through the principal cities of Italy, and can always procure a theatre, upon the condition of equal participation in the receipts. Many stories are told of the means by which he has acquired his astonishing style;—such as his having been imprisoned ten years with no other resource—and the like. But, however this may be, his powers over the violin are most extraordinary.

30th

A grand ceremony at the church of St. John Lateran; at the conclusion of which the Pope, from the balcony, gave his blessing to the people, who were assembled in thousands in the large square below.

As soon as the Pope appeared, there was a discharge of artillery; the bands of military music struck up; and the people sunk on their knees, uncovered. A solemn silence ensued, and the blessing was conferred. All seemed to receive this with reverential awe, and it was impossible not to imbibe a portion of the general feeling.

In my way home I encountered his Holiness's equipage, and had an opportunity of observing the Roman mode of testifying respect to the Sovereign. All ranks take off their hats and fall on their knees, till the carriage has passed. But this is in harmony with the titles which are conferred upon the Pope[4] at his coronation; when the Senior Cardinal puts the tiara on his head, and addresses him in these words: *Accipe Tiaram, tribus coronis ornatam, et scias Patrem te esse Principum et Regum, Rectorem orbis, in terra Vicarium Salvatoris nostri Jesu Christi.*

May 4th

Left Rome at sunrise.—My carriage is a sort of buggy on four wheels, drawn by a single horse.—My bargain with my voiturier is, to be taken to Florence in six days, and to be fed and lodged on the road; for which I am to give him twenty dollars. The pace is tiresome enough at first; for the horse seldom quits his walk, even for an equivocal amble; but if you have no particular object in getting on, you soon become reconciled to this. Besides, it affords ample leisure for surveying the country, and gratifying your curiosity at any particular point, where you wish to deviate from the road; for you may easily overtake your carriage. We halted for the night at *Civita Castellana*—ancient *Veii*[5]—as it is said—and it saves a great deal of trouble to believe every thing that is said. The town is beautifully situated; and old *Soracte*, under the modern disguise of *St. Oreste*, stands up boldly by himself in the middle of the plain, at a short distance from the town.

5th

Left Civita Castellana before daylight, in order to reach Terni in good time.—Nothing can be more beautiful than the views on entering the vale of Terni, through which the road and the river Nera meander. This day's journey was delightful.—It was a May morning, such as you may *read* of in England, in Izaak Walton's description. The scenery is always rich, and sometimes romantic. The features of an Italian landscape are very peculiar.

The bold and the grand are constantly blended with the soft and the beautiful. Thus, amongst the rugged rocks of Terni, the ilex, the cypress, and the fir, with the spring leaves of the other trees of the forest, refresh the eye with every variety of green; while the mountain-ash, the acacia, the laburnum, and the pink-flowered Judas tree—all in full blossom—add a richness, which never belongs to the English landscape. Of the falls of Terni I will only say, that I enjoyed this charming scene, with all the embellishments that a lovely May evening could add to it. The day has its seasons like the year, and evening—rich in every variety of tint—is its autumn, to me the most delightful of all the seasons, whether of the day or the year.

The rays of the setting sun, playing on the light foam of the cascade, created innumerable rainbows; and the thrush, whose note is more grateful to my ear than that of the nightingale herself—though I believe this preference must be traced to the all-powerful principle of association, for I have listened to her song in some of the happiest hours of my life—gave me a concert, in harmony with all around it.

There is, however, always something to disgust in *reality*;—and much of the pleasure of my walk was destroyed by a troop of clamorous beggars, who beset me on every side; and the more money I gave, the more beggars I had. This was villanous;—for if ever there were a walk which "silence" ought to "accompany," and with which she might be "pleased"—it is a still evening's walk in the vale of Terni.

The cascade has been often described; but perhaps no description can give a more lively idea of the impression which the first sight of it makes upon the spectator, than the exclamation of Wilson the painter, overheard by Sir Joshua Reynolds, who happened to be on the spot. Wilson stood for a moment in speechless admiration, and then broke out with "*Well done, Water, by G—!*"

6th

I am more reconciled every day to my mode of travelling.—The weather is beautiful. Thirty-five miles is the average of a day's journey. By starting at sunrise, one-half of this is accomplished by ten o'clock. It is then usual to halt till two, which affords time for a *siesta* during the heat of the day and the remainder of the journey is concluded about seven in the evening. To me, whose object in life seems unhappily confined to the task of killing time—till time shall kill me—no mode of travelling could be better suited; and the day, thus filled up, slips away imperceptibly. But time is a sad antagonist to contend against; kill him as you may, day after day, you find him up again fresh and revived—more pertinacious than Sinbad's old man—to renew the battle with you in the morning. Again—I doubt, all things considered, whether it be not better to travel by yourself, than with a companion. It is true, you may not always please yourself, but you may at least bear with your own ill humour. If you could select the very companion you would wish, it might alter the case; though it seems fated that all travelling companions should fall out;—and history is full of instances, from Paul and Barnabas, down to Walpole and Gray.—So I jog on, contented at least, if not happy, to be alone; though not perhaps without often feeling the truth of Marmontel's observation:

> *Il est triste de voir une belle campagne, sans pouvoir dire à quelqu'un, Voilà une belle campagne!*

Breakfasted at Spoleto—which held out successfully against Hannibal, after the battle of Thrasymene; the inhabitants of which still pride themselves on the prowess of their ancestors, and show the *Porta d'Annibale*. In digging the foundation of a new bridge, the remains of an old Roman bridge have lately been discovered here.

Near Foligno, I encountered a troop of pilgrims, on their way home from Loretto to Naples, dressed in picturesque uniform, and chanting the evening hymn to the Virgin, in very beautiful harmony.

7th

Debated for some time whether I should pursue my route to
Florence; or proceed by way of Loretto and Ancona, to Bologna;
but Our Lady, when put into the scale against the heathen
Goddess of the Tribune, immediately kicked the beam—so
I turned to the left, and continued my way to Perugia. Here
my voiturier contrived to take up another passenger's luggage,
without my perceiving it, and soon after we got out of the
town, he overtook his fare, to whom he assigned a place on the
outside, in spite of my remonstrances; arguing that I had only
taken the inside of the carriage to myself, and that he had the
patronage of the spare seat on the box. The shortest road to
redress would have been to take the law into my own hands; but
the appeal to force is the worst, and therefore should be the last
resort, especially in this case, where the issue was doubtful—for
the odds were two to one. On arriving at Passignano I applied
to the police, and brought my voiturier to his senses.

By-the-by, a written contract, with a voiturier, to be valid,
ought to be signed by two witnesses, and stamped by the
police; but when the merits of the case are plain, a stranger
will generally find redress, in spite of informalities. If, however,
you wish to secure the good behaviour of your voiturier—keep
the command of the purse in your own hands. You must make
occasional advances on the road, but let these always be less
than the fare.

8th

Passignano is a miserable hamlet, on the brink of the lake of
Perugia; and the wretched inhabitants bear witness, by their pallid
appearance, to the pestilent air in which they live.

Near this place is the scene of the memorable battle of
Thrasymene. It requires no lights of generalship to perceive the
egregious error of Flaminius, in marching his army down into
a trap; where Hannibal, by taking possession of the heights,
completely check-mated, or rather, to preserve the analogy of the
game, stale-mated him.

Took my morning rest at *Castiglione Fiorentino*, a beautiful village in the Tuscan dominions. The change in the appearance of the country, or rather of the inhabitants, as you leave the dominions of the Pope, and enter the Grand Duke's territories, is very much in favour of the latter.

In the Papal States all is slovenly and squalid; there seems to be no middle link in the chain of society between the cardinal and the beggar.

In Tuscany, the very cottages are neat and ornamental; and there is in the dress and the appearance of the peasantry something which bespeaks a sense of self-respect, and a taste for comforts, which will never be found where the peasantry is in a state of hopeless vassalage.

It was now the hay-making season, and the women, in their neat picturesque dresses, and tasteful straw-hats, handled their rakes with an elegance of manner that would have suited a scene in Arcadia.

After a long drive through a delightful country, I arrived two hours after dark at Rimaggio. The night was beautiful; the air cool and sweet, and the nightingales singing all round us. A meagre supper.—Mine host said it was the positive order of the government, and that he should be exposed to a fine if he allowed any meat to be dressed in his house on a Friday; so that it was in vain I pleaded my heretical right to eat what I pleased.

The cheapness of living in Italy, and the imposition practised upon travellers, may be collected from the price a voiturier pays for the supper at the table d'hôte, and the lodging of his passengers, which I have ascertained to be four Pauls per head;—something less than two shillings. The common charge to an Englishman travelling post, who does not fare a whit better, is ten Pauls for dinner, and as many more for lodging.

9th

This day's journey carried me through a poorer country than I have yet seen. I conversed a good deal with the peasants, but found them too ignorant to explain much of their own economy.

Their farms seemed to be very small—seldom exceeding thirty acres. There is no such thing as capital amongst them; the landlord finds implements of all kinds, seed, and manure; and divides the produce with the tenant, after the manner of the French *Metayers*. In their mode of cultivation, manual labour appears to bear a much greater proportion to the other means of production than in ours. For certain crops, the ground is broken entirely with the spade. I observed no farm servants, but the peasant's whole family, male and female, mustered in the field. Their fare seemed to be very poor; a mess of *lupini* boiled up in a little broth, and washed down with a very weak sour wine, was the dinner, of which they invited me to partake. In the richer parts of Tuscany, large farms and rich farmers are not uncommon. The breed of cattle is large and fine, and invariably of a grey dove colour. At Incisa, to-day, I saw a calf being led to the slaughter-house; adorned about the head and horns, like a victim in an ancient sacrifice. Other ancient customs still linger in the mountainous parts of this country, where the people still believe and practise the mysteries of augury, a science in which their Etruscan ancestors were so deeply learned. Indeed, it was from them that the Romans derived it:—"*Quo circa benè apud majores nostros Senatus tum, cum florebat Imperium, decrevit, ut de principum filiis sex singulis Etruriæ populis in disciplinam traderentur, ne ars tanta propter tenuitatem hominum, à religionis auctoritate abduceretur, ad mercedem atque quæstum.*"—Cic. de Div. However we may now laugh at such a pretended science, we need not wonder, when we remember to how late a period the belief in witchcraft has continued in our own country, that it was made the subject of a controversy in the age of Cicero, whether there was any real *power of divining* to be collected from the flight of birds; and the supporter of this opinion dedicated his book to Cicero himself.

Two years ago, when the scarcity of provisions was so severely felt throughout Italy, the inhabitants of the Tuscan Apennines, who rely very much upon chestnuts for their support, would have been almost exterminated, from the complete failure of that crop, had they not been persuaded, the year before, into the more general cultivation of the potato. The prejudice against it was so great, that it was only by offering a reward to each peasant, for a certain quantity of his own cultivation, that the government succeeded in the attempt. It is to the credit of the Tuscan character, that numbers, who in the time of famine had felt the benefit and importance of this vegetable, when they produced certificates of their being entitled to the government bounty, declined accepting it; declaring that they no longer wanted bribing into the belief of the great utility of a plant, to which they owed the preservation of their lives.

After a broiling day's journey, I caught a view of fair Florence, from the top of the last hill, with all its domes and towers glittering in the last rays of the setting sun. Thinking the character of my equipage little suited to the magnificence of Schneiderf's hotel, I established myself at the Pelican; a good house, and much better adapted than Schneiderf's to the finances of a man who does not travel *en grand Seigneur*.

1. It is a remarkable circumstance that the whole Palatine Hill is now, with the exception of one small portion, in the possession of the English, of that people whom the Romans used contemptuously to designate as "penitus toto divisos orbe Britannos." Sir W. G. has purchased the Villa Spada with a large tract of garden and vineyard, and almost all the remainder is the property of the English College.

2. I am sure every stranger going to Rome will thank me for pointing out to his notice Signor Armellini; a man whose mind is richly stored with the treasures of ancient and modern literature, end of such pleasing manners, and such variety of information, that the study of a grammar, which is usually an irksome task, becomes, in his hands, an agreeable recreation.

3. I subjoin the spirited description of a friend, whose musical science and acknowledged taste enable him to speak with much more authority than myself. "Paganini's performance bears the stamp of the eccentricity

of his character. As to mechanism, it is quite perfect; his tone and the thrilling intonation of his double stops are electric; his bow moves as if it were part of himself, and endued with life and feeling; his *stacccato* is more strongly marked than I ever knew, and in the smoother passages there is a glassiness, if one may so say, which gives you the notion of the perfection of finish, and the highest refinement of practice. Though, in general, there is an ambition to display his own talents, by an excess of ornament, yet he can, if he will, play with simplicity and pathos, and then his power over the passions is equal to that of any orator or actor."

4. Let me here record the compliment with which the Pope lately received a party of English, upon their presentation to him; "*Ho sempre gran piacere net videre gl' Inglesi, tanto hanno fatto per la causa di tutto il mondo.*"

5. The real Veii has been discovered at *Isolo Barberini* about a mile and a half from *La Storta*, and ten from Rome. This discovery is not a doubtful one, but is authenticated by numerous inscriptions, which, with several marble pillars, fragments of temples, and statues, have been lately found here. What a mean opinion does this give of the prowess of the Romans, who, in so advanced a period of their history, could only subdue a city, situated thus at their Gates, by a lucky stratagem, and after a ten years' siege.

X

VENICE AND BUONAPARTE

May 16th, 1818

After six days of continued travelling, a short season of repose succeeds as an agreeable vicissitude. Let me employ a portion of it in recording my impressions of the moral and political state of the country in which I have been sojourning.

The discontent of the people, particularly in the Papal and Neapolitan states, is loud and open;—for, though the liberty of the press is unknown, they indulge in the fullest freedom of speech in canvassing the conduct of their rulers. There is indeed ample cause for discontent;—the people seems every day more impatient of the civil and ecclesiastical oppressions to which they are subjected; and a revolution is the common topic of conversation. If there were any rational hope of revolution bringing improvement, it would be difficult not to wish for a revolution in Italy.

A revolution, however, to be productive of benefit, ought to be effected by the quiet operation of public opinion—that is, of the virtuous and well-informed part of the public;—and this would be, not revolution, but reform—the best way of preventing a revolution, in the modern sense of that term. But where shall we look, in Italy, for the elements of such a reform? There can be little hope of its *political* amelioration till some improvement has taken place in its *moral* condition. How can anything great or good be expected from a people where the state of society is so depraved as to tolerate the *cavieliere servente* system?—A system which sanctions the public display of apparent, if not real infidelity to the most important and religious engagement of domestic life. And yet, constituted as society is in Italy, this system ought perhaps to excite little surprise. For marriage is here, for the most part, a mere arrangement of convenience; and the parties often meet for the first time at the foot of the altar. An Italian does not expect from such an union the happiness of home, with the whole train of domestic charities which an Englishman associates with the marriage state; the *spes animi credula mutui* is certainly not the hope of an *Italian* husband—and the *Cavaliere* robs him of nothing which he is not quite content to spare.

It is indeed, nine times in ten, to the fault of the husband that the infidelity of the wife is to be ascribed. This is a reflection I have often made to Italian men, who have always seemed disposed to admit the truth of it; but the truth is better attested by the exemplary conduct of those women, whose husbands take upon themselves to perform the offices of affection that are ordinarily left to the *Cavaliere*. An Italian said to me one day, "*Una donna ha sempre bisogno d'appoggiarsi ad un uomo!*"—If she cannot repose her cares and her confidence in the bosom of her husband, is it very surprising that she should seek some other support? Consider the character of the Italian woman. Ardent and impassioned—jealous of admiration—enthusiastic alike in love or in resentment—she is tremblingly alive to the provocations which she has so often to endure from the open neglect and infidelity of the man who has sworn to love and protect her.

The *spretæ injuria formæ* is an insult which has provoked colder constitutions than the Italian to retaliate. What indeed is there to restrain her? A sense of duty? There is no such sense. An Italian woman is accustomed to consider the conjugal duties as strictly reciprocal, and would laugh to scorn, as tame and slavish submission, the meek and gentle spirit which prompted the reply of the "divine Desdemona"—

> "Unkindness may do much;
> And his unkindness may defeat my life,
> But never taint my love."

And while there is so little to restrain, the effect of example is to encourage her to follow the bent of her inclinations; and she is attended by a licensed seducer, privileged to approach her at all hours, and at full liberty to avail himself of all the aid that opportunity and importunity can lend him for the accomplishment of his purpose.

These observations can only be meant to apply to the higher classes of society, to which the *Cavaliere* system is confined; and it must not be supposed, even amongst these, that there are not many examples of domestic virtue and domestic happiness;—or that husbands and wives may not be found in Italy, as in other places, fondly and faithfully attached to each other. Nor is it always a criminal connexion that subsists between a Lady and her *Cavaliere*, though it is generally supposed to be so; but many instances might be cited where it is well known that it is not.

There is indeed a sort of mysticism in the tender passion, as it seems always to have existed in this country, which it is difficult to understand or explain. Platonic love, in the verses of Petrarch, if indeed Petrarch's love were Platonic, glows with a rapturous warmth, which often speaks the very language of a grosser feeling; while the most depraved of all passions has been clothed with a tenderness and delicacy of sentiment and expression, which would seem to belong only to our purest affections. Witness Horace's address to Ligurinus:—

> Sed cur heu Ligurine, cur
> > Manat rara meas lacryma per genas?
> Cur facunda parum decoro
> > Inter verba cadit lingua silentio?

What can be more tender, unless it be Pope's beautiful imitation—

> But why—ah! tell me—ah! too dear!
> Steals down my cheek th'involuntary tear?

Why words so flowing, thoughts so free,
Stop or turn nonsense at one glance of thee?

But to return;—the *Cavaliere* system must ever remain the great moral blot in the Italian character;—and yet, this system, founded as it is in the violation of all laws and feelings, has its own peculiar regulations, which it would be an unpardonable breach of etiquette to transgress. The Lady must not have children by her Paramour;—at least, the notoriety of such a fact would be attended with the loss of reputation. What can be said of a state of society that can tolerate such things, but—"Reform it altogether."

I am afraid the morals of England will not derive much benefit from familiarizing our countrywomen to hear these connexions talked of, as they constantly are, without censure or surprise. It would be impossible, however, to introduce the system into England as it exists here.

Few Englishmen would be found to bear the yoke that is here imposed on a *Cavaliere*. An Italian, without pursuit or profession, may find in this philandering drudgery a pleasant mode of employing his time; but in England, politics and field-sports would, if no better feelings or principles should oppose its introduction, be in themselves sufficient to interfere with such a system of female supremacy. But though much may be feared from familiarity with vice, I would rather hope that a nearer contemplation of its evil consequences will induce them to cling with closer affection to the moral habits and institutions of their own country, where the value of virtue and fidelity is still felt and appreciated as it ought to be;—and to cultivate with increasing vigilance all those observances, which have been wisely set up as bulwarks to defend and secure the purity of the domestic sanctuary.

I remember Fuller says—"Travel not beyond the Alps. Mr. Ascham did thank God that he was but nine days in Italy; wherein he saw in one city more liberty to sin, than in London he had ever heard of in nine years. That some of our gentry have gone thither and returned thence, without infection, I more praise God than their adventure." If he entertained apprehensions for the "travel-tainted" gentry of his time, we may well feel anxiety for the ladies of our own; feeling, as we must, that it is to the female virtues of England we should look, not only for the happiness of our homes—but also for the support of that national character, which has led to all our national greatness;—for the character of a nation is ever mainly determined by the institutions of domestic life;—and it is to the influence of maternal precept and maternal example upon the mind of childhood, that all the best virtues of manhood may ultimately be traced.

17th

The Venus pleases me more than ever. There is nothing in Rome, or elsewhere, that can be compared with her. There is that mysterious something about her, *quod nequeo monstrare, et sentio tantum*, impressed by the master-touch, which is as inexplicable as the breath of life. It is this incommunicable something, which no copy or cast, however, accurate, is able to catch. I doubt whether the same thing can be observed of the Apollo; whence I am inclined to believe the notion which, it is said, was first started by Flaxman—that the Apollo itself is but a copy. The style of the finishing has certainly not the air of an original work;—it possesses little of that indefinable spirit and freedom, which are the characteristics of those productions in which the author follows only the conceptions of his own mind. The form and disposition of the drapery are said to afford technical evidence of the strongest kind, that the statue must have been originally executed in bronze; and the materials of which the Apollo is composed, which, it seems, are at last determined to be Italian marble, favour the same opinion.

18th

The Tuscan dialect sounds harshly, and almost unintelligibly, after the soft and sonorous cadence of the Roman pronunciation. However pure the *lingua Toscana* may be, the *bocca Romana* seems necessary to give it smoothness. It is delightful to listen to the musical flow of the words, even independently of their sense. Then how pretty are their diminutives! What answer could he invented more soothing to impatient irritability than "*momentino, Signore!*" The Romans however are too apt to fall into a sort of sing-song recitative, while the Tuscans—that is, the lower orders—offend you with a guttural rattle, not unlike the Welsh. There is perhaps no country where the dialects vary more than in the different provinces of Italy. The language of Naples and the Milanese is a sort of Babylonish jargon, little better than gibberish. The origin of the Italian language has long been a subject of discussion. The literati of Florence are fond of tracing it up to Etruscan antiquity. We know that Etruria had a language of its own, distinct from the Latin. This was the language in which the Sibyl was supposed to have delivered her oracles, and in which the augurs interpreted the mysteries of their profession. Livy says, "*Habeo auctores, vulgo tum Romanos pueros, sicut nunc Græcis, ita Etruscis literis erudiri solitos.*" This language is by some supposed to have continued to exist during the whole time of the Romans, as the *sermo vulgaris*—the *patois*—which was in common use amongst the peasantry of the country; while the Latin was confined to the higher classes, and the capital;—to the senate, the forum, the stage, and to literature.

This opinion does not seem entirely destitute of probability. We have living evidence in our own island of the difficulty of changing the language of a people. In France, too, till within the last half century, the southern provinces were almost utterly ignorant of French; and, even at present, the lower classes of the peasantry never speak French, but continue to make use of a *patois* of the old Provençal language.

In like manner it is supposed by many that pure Latin was confined to the capital and to high life; while the ancient Etruscan, which, had an additional support in being consecrated to the service of religion, always maintained its ground as the colloquial *patois* of the greatest part of Italy. Thus, when Rome fell, the polished language of the capital fell with it; but the *patois* of the common people remained, and still remains, in an improved edition, in the language of modern Italy. For, if this be not so, we must suppose, first, that the Etruscan was rooted out by the Latin, and that the Latin has again yielded in its turn to a new tongue. But innovations in language are the slowest of all in working their way; and if the pure Latin of the classics had ever been the colloquial language of the common people, some living evidence of it would surely have been discovered, as we now find the ancient language of the Britons lingering in the fastnesses of Wales and Cornwall;—but no information is handed down to us by which we can ascertain when Latin was the common spoken language of Italy, or at what period it ceased to exist.

Still, however, on the other hand, it is perhaps equally extraordinary that we should meet with no traces of this colloquial *patois* in the writings of the ancients. Some allusion indeed is made by Quintilian to the *sermo militaris*— a dialect in use among the soldiery;—but if the language of the common people was so distinct as it is supposed, it is strange that we do not find more direct mention of it; especially in the plays of Plautus, who with his love of broad humour, might naturally have been expected, after the example of Aristophanes, to have availed himself of such a source of the ridiculous. And when one reads in modern Italian such lines as the following, the parent language seems to stand confessed in the identity of the resemblance:

> In mare irato, in subita procolla
> Invoco te nostra benigna stella.

Or, again,

> Vivo in acerba pena, in mesto orrore,
> Quando te non imploro, in te non spero,
> Purissima Maria, et in sincero
> Te non adoro, et in divino ardore.

These lines however were probably studiously composed in this indiscriminate character; and they might be counterbalanced by examples of early Roman inscriptions, which certainly bear more affinity to the modern Italian than to the Latin;—and this would seem to show that the two languages might have existed and gone on progressively together. After considering therefore all that is urged by opposite writers on this subject, one is reduced to the conclusion of Sir Roger de Coverley, of happy memory,—that much may be said on both sides. Thus much is certain; that at least the guttural accent of Tuscany is as old as Catullus, who has ridiculed it in one of his epigrams:

> *Chommoda* dicebat, si quando commoda vellet
> Dicere, et *hinsidias*, Arrius insidias

19th

An evening at *Fiesole*—which is situated on a commanding eminence, about three miles distant from Florence. The country is now in the highest beauty. Spring is the season for Italy. We have little Spring or Summer in England—except in Thomson's *Seasons*. Climate, if it do not constitute the happiness, is a very important ingredient in the comfort of life. An evening or night, in an Italian villa, at this season of nightingales and moonlight, is a most delicious treat. How could Shakspeare write as he has done, without having been in Italy! Some of his garden scenes breathe the very life of reality. And yet if he had been here, I think he would not have omitted all allusion to the fire-fly, a little flitting insect, that adds much to the charm of the scene. The whole garden is illuminated by myriads of these sparkling lights, sprinkled about with as much profusion as spangles on a lady's gown.

There is something delightfully pleasant in the voluptuous languor which the soft air of an Italian evening occasions;—and then the splendour of an Italian sun-set! I shall never forget the impression made upon me by a particular evening. The sun had just gone down, leaving the whole sky dyed with the richest tints of crimson while the virgin snows of the distant mountains were suffused with blushes of "celestial rosy red;" when, from an opposite quarter of the heavens, there seemed to rise another sun, as large, as bright, and as glowing as that which had just departed. It was the moon at the full;—and the illusion was so complete, that it required some few moments to convince me that I was not in Fairy Land.

But one season is wanting;—there is no interval between day and night; and the "sober livery" of gray twilight is here unknown. Night, however, of which we know little in England, but as it is connected with fire and candle, is now the most charming period of the whole twenty-four hours; and there are no unwholesome dews, no sore-throat-bringing damps, to disturb your enjoyment with fears of to-morrow's consequences.

20th

Left Florence at day-break; travelling as before in a voiturier's carriage; indeed, little would be gained in point of speed by travelling post between this place and Bologna: for the road is so hilly, that you must necessarily be limited to a foot-pace. I was stopped at the custom-house on re-entering the Papal dominions, where they obliged me to pay the full value of a parcel, of Italian books, which I had with me, giving me an order to receive the same again at the frontier custom-house, when I should quit the Pope's dominions. It was explained to me that this was merely intended as a necessary precaution;—for it might be that I was a book-merchant, and wished to sell these books in the Pope's territories, without paying the entrance duties. As there seemed no help for it, I was obliged to comply with the demand; and take the officer's word that the scrap of paper he gave me would reproduce my money at the opposite extremity of his Holiness's territories.

We slept at the half-way house between Florence and Bologna.

21st

Wild romantic road over the Apennines—recalling the descriptions of Mrs Radcliffe in her Romance of Udolpho. Reached Bologna early in the morning. Grand fête of *Corpus Christi*. All the streets were hung with satin, and covered in with splendid awnings, which on this occasion were of more use against the rain than the sun.

One of the most striking ornaments of the town is John of Bologna's bronze Neptune, who presides over a fountain in the great square; but there is a poverty of water, and Neptune seems here out of his element.

22d

The more you travel, the less you will rely upon the descriptions of guides and itineraries. There are no degrees in their descriptions, and all you collect from them, in general, is the ignorance of the compilers. One of these compares the leaning lump of brick at Bologna, which looks like the chimney of a steam-engine blown a little out of the perpendicular, to the graceful and elegant tower of Pisa. Bologna is very rich in paintings;—the works of Guido, collected here, have shown him to me in a new light; and have convinced me that I had not hitherto formed a just estimate of his merit. There is a force and grandeur in some of these, of which the generality of his pictures gives little indication. The *Crucifixion*, and the *Massacre of the Innocents*, are specimens of the highest excellence of composition and execution.[1]

It is necessary to come to Bologna, to appreciate properly the excellence of Guido, Domenichino, and the fraternity of Caracci. The *Persecution of the Albigenses*, by Domenichino—a magnificent picture. A *Madonna*, by Ludovico Caracci—exquisitely elegant;—but then it is the elegance and refinement of a woman of fashion. She is not the Madonna, such as Raphael has represented her, and such as she will ever exist personified in the imagination of him who has seen Raphael's pictures. A *Transfiguration*, by the same painter—an admirable conception of a subject which, with reverence to Raphael be it spoken, does not seem adapted to painting.

The *Cecilia* of Raphael has, I suspect, been retouched, and spoilt, at Paris.

Bologna is a clean and well-built town; though the arcades, which project in front of the houses, give it a heavy appearance. The fish-market is excellently arranged, with streams of water running through it, securing cleanliness.

This is a country famous for the excellence of its frogs, though the French alone hear the reproach of eating them;—if reproach there be in eating a very excellent dish.

The reproach might, perhaps, with more reason be directed against the prejudice that prevents us from availing ourselves of the plentiful provision which nature has put within our reach. But I suppose nothing would induce the lower classes in England to have recourse to such means of subsistence, however wholesome and nutritious.

The fish-market was full of frogs, ready prepared for dressing, and trussed upon skewers; in the manner described in the simile of Ariosto, where he says, that Orlando spitted his enemies upon his spear—like frogs upon a skewer.

After a long morning of picture-gazing and sight-seeing, I contrived to reach Tedo in the evening, on my way to Venice.

23d

Halted at noon at Ferrara—a large dull dilapidated town; which contains nothing to interest or detain you, unless you can derive pleasure from visiting the prison in which Tasso was confined, and expectorating a few imprecations against the tyranny of his oppressor; though, perhaps, after all, the more recent opinion may be better founded—that Alphonso confined the insane poet out of pure good will.

Reached Ponte Lago-scuro early in the evening, the last town of the Papal territory; where I was agreeably surprised by the recovery of my deposit-money, without deduction or difficulty;—and so good bye to the Pope and the Cardinals!—with whom I wish to *part* in charity and good humour; though it is difficult to preserve those feelings towards them, amidst the constant vexations to which one is subjected in *travelling* through their dominions.

Quitted my carriage at Lago-scuro; and crossing the Po—
which is here much like the Thames at Putney—agreed with the
Venetian courier for a place in his boat to Venice. The fare is 17
francs 25 cents; and for this he not only conveys yourself and your
baggage a distance of 80 miles, but also provides a table for you
on the way.

Excellent boat;—the cabin fitted up with a settle on each side
the table, in which a seat was elbowed in for each person.

24th

On mounting the deck this morning at sun-rise, I found we had
glided about forty miles down the stream in the course of the
night, and were at the gate of the lock, where we were to quit
the Po, to enter a canal, which connects this river with the Adige.
From the height of the Po, it was judged unsafe to open the gate
of the lock, for fear of inundating the whole country; so that we
were obliged to wait till the courier from Venice arrived with his
boat on the other side of the gate.

This occasioned a delay of five hours; and when he did come,
we had to shift passengers and baggage on both sides.

We soon got into the Adige; after floating down which for a
few miles, we entered another canal, which brought us into one
of the *lagune* that lead to Venice.

The accommodations of the passage-boat must be greatly
improved since Arthur Young's time, whose description had
almost deterred me from venturing the experiment. Every thing
was well managed; our courier gave us an admirable dinner; and
at sun-set we caught a glimpse of the domes of Venice, rising out
of the sea.

It was midnight before we reached the post-office.

25th

Breakfasted at a cafe in the *Piazza of St. Mark*. After threading a
narrow line of alleys, not half the width of that of Cranbourne,
I came unexpectedly upon this grand square, the first sight
of which is very striking. It would be difficult to compare it

with any thing. It is *unique*; rich, venerable, magnificent. The congregation of all nations, in their various costumes, who lounge under the purple awnings of the cafés—smoking, playing at chess, and quaffing coffee—add much to its embellishment, and are in character with the buildings; where all orders of architecture seem jumbled together. The cathedral certainly belongs to no single one;—it is of a mixed breed, between a Mahometan mosque and a Christian church; but, when it was built, the imaginations of the Venetians were full of Constantinople, and the glorious exploits of Dandolo. The famous horses which he brought in triumph to Venice, as the trophies of his conquest of Constantinople, have again resumed their place over the portal of the cathedral.

In this age of scepticism, it is doubted whether these are indeed the famous horses of Lysippus which have made so much noise in history, connected with the names of Nero, Trajan, and Constantine; and a passage is quoted from the Byzantine Fathers, to prove that they were cast at Chios, so late as the fourth century. However this be, I think they are scarcely worth the trouble that has been taken about them, that is, for any merit they have as representations of horses;—though, if their identity be made out, they are great curiosities, as historical memorials of the rapacity of conquerors, and the instability of fortune. The fashion of *hogging* the mane, ugly as it is, may plead the example of these horses in its favour. They were reinstated in their former place at Venice, with great pomp and ceremony; and the Emperor Francis has recorded, in a golden inscription, the robbery of the French, and his own triumph:

QUATUOR EQUORUM SIGNA A VENETIS BYZANTIO CAPTA, AD TEMP. D. MAR. A. R. S. MCCIV POSITA—QUÆ HOSTILIS CUPIDITAS A. MDCCCIII ABSTULERAT—FRANC. I. IMP. PACIS ORBI DATÆ TROPHÆUM A. MDCCCXV VICTOR REDUXIT.

I rejoice that the horses have been restored, and that France has been made to disgorge all her plunder; but they should not throw stones who live in a house of glass. The French had surely as much right to take them from Venice, as Dandolo had to bring them thither; in both cases, it was but the right of the strongest.

Before the door of the cathedral stand three bare poles, where formerly the flags of Crete, Cyprus, and the Morea, the three vassal kingdoms of the haughty republic, floated in the wind.

26th.

Though there is enough in the historical recollections of Venice to invest it with great interest, yet there is a further and more powerful fascination in its scenery, which is derived from the magic illusions of poetry.

At least, in my own case, I confess that I thought more of Shakspeare and Otway—Othello and Shylock—Pierre and Jaffier—than of Dandolo and all his victories. It is wonderful how *place* aids the effect of poetry. Went over the Ducal Palace, and sat in the seat of the Doge. The hall, where the senate used to assemble, remains in its ancient state. The chamber in which the famous Council of Ten held their meetings was converted by Napoleon into a Court of Cassation.

The hall of the general assembly is now a library, where there are some beautiful remains of ancient sculpture. The rape of Ganymede is an exquisite little morsel, and is thought to be the work of Phidias himself. Leda and her Swan is a *bijou* in the same taste. It is surprising that the French, who knew so well what to steal, should have overlooked two articles that might have been so easily carried away.

The famous lion's mouth is destroyed. The Bridge of Sighs—*il Ponte dei Sospiri*—connects the ducal palace with the state-prison. Criminals were brought through a covered way over this bridge, from their dungeons, to the tribunal of the Council of Ten. Criminal proceedings are still carried on in secret, and I saw to-day a man being conducted back to prison after trial, through the covered passage over the Bridge of Sighs.

It is impossible to walk through these splendid chambers, decorated with pictures commemorating the most brilliant achievements, and the most signal examples of the ancient power and glory of the Venetian republic, without feeling sorrow for its present condition. The only consolation the people seem to feel is something like King Arthur in Tom Thumb, who congratulates himself that he has at least outlived all his neighbours;

> Thus all our pack upon the floor is cast,
> And my sole boast is, that I die the last.

Thus, the Venetians appeal with triumph to their fourteen centuries of power; a longer duration than that enjoyed by any other people on record. Fourteen centuries were indeed a pretty long reign; but, in fact, the republic had ceased to exist before the invasion of the French. Napoleon gave the *coup de grace*, but the life of the commonwealth was already expiring. The government had degenerated into an oligarchical tyranny, of all tyrannies the most detestable; and the people had nothing left to fight for. It is ever thus; for it seems that there is in all governments a tendency to abuse, and it ought perhaps rather to excite surprise that Venice endured so long, than that she fell at last.

The Doge and his Privy Council yielded without a struggle at the first approach of the enemy; and instead of dying "with harness on their back," they betrayed the interests of their country, to make favourable terms for themselves with the conqueror. Junot delivered Buonaparte's threatening letter to the Doge himself in council; thus insulting him to his face by the grossest breach of the laws of the republic. In the last scene of all, the Doge had the baseness to propose, and the Grand Council had the baseness to consent to, a still more disgraceful compliance with the demands of Buonaparte; who insisted, as a preliminary condition to a treaty, that the three State Inquisitors, and the naval commander, who had alone evinced courage to do their duty in the defence of their country, should for this very performance of their duty, be arrested and brought to trial.

A few days afterwards, the Doge and the Council in full assembly, with pusillanimous unanimity, voted their own abdication. Such was the last inglorious act of a republic that had endured for fourteen hundred years—"Oh lame and impotent conclusion!"

Thus fell the Republic of Venice; and when a republic does fall,—she falls like Lucifer, never to rise again. If there had been no hostility on the part of the great ones of the world to the re-establishment of her free government, I believe it would have been impossible to find in Venice that life blood of public spirit, which is necessary to restore animation and energy to the body politic of a commonwealth. A republic indeed cannot be *restored*; it is a constitution that must be claimed, and won, by the spirit and courage of the people themselves; and where these qualities are wanting, a republic would not be maintained if it were restored. It is not every people that is fit to be free; and Machiavel has long ago pronounced, that to make a servile people free is as difficult a task, as to make a free people slaves.

27th.

Established myself at the *Albergo Favretti*, near the grand ducal palace, commanding a fine view of the sea. I should prefer this in all respects to either of the two great hotels, even if it had not many recommendations on the score of economy. I give my landlord seven francs per day; for which I have an excellent room, with breakfast and dinner, both good of their kind. Venice abounds in all sorts of fish;—mullet, thunny, an excellent variety of the sturgeon, and the S. Pietro, or; as it is sometimes called—*Il Janitore*—from which is derived our own corruption of *John Dory*.

A tour amongst churches and palaces; but I am tired of churches as curiosities to be stared at; and having seen St. Peter's, I shall content myself with the maxim of *omne majus continet in se minus*, and be satisfied with my own parish church for the rest of my life.

Venice is rich in the works of her own Titian; his two most celebrated pictures are the *Martyrdom of a St. Peter*—not the apostle—in the church of St. John and St. Paul, and the *Assumption of the Virgin*, in the academy.

Connoisseurs have lavished encomiums upon these productions of Titian in the grand style of composition, but I confess I like him better when he confines himself to "the primrose path of dalliance;" for it is in the representation of the soft and the beautiful, embellished with all the rich and glowing varieties of colour that he seems to follow the bent of his genius, and to paint *con amore*. There are also many splendid works of Paul Veronese, and of Tintoretto.

Visited the Arsenal, where there were accommodations for building six and thirty ships of war, under cover;—but the ships and the commerce of Venice have vanished with its freedom. There is now scarcely a cock-boat in the harbour. The vulgar are taught to believe, that England abstained from exercising her influence in procuring the restoration of the Republic, from feelings of commercial jealousy. Nobody seems to doubt our power to have effected this good work, both in the case of Venice and of Genoa. But, if it really were in our power, it is indeed difficult to account for our supineness. All commercial considerations would have prompted us to further this measure; for, excluded as our manufactures are from the Continental States—at least, as far as the governments can exclude them—it would have been greatly to the advantage of England, that free commercial states should have been established at Venice and Genoa, which would have afforded channels of communication for the introduction of English goods to the whole south of Europe. Austria would willingly, if she could, exclude all English manufactures; but the effect of her rigorous prohibitions is to put that money into the pockets of the custom-house officers, which she would otherwise receive herself, in the shape of duties. The bribery of the custom-house has been reduced to a regular system, and the insurance of the safe arrival of goods at Vienna is negotiated upon an accurate calculation of these expenses.

In the evening I mounted to the top of St. Mark's tower, where Galileo used to hold commerce with the skies. It commands a fine panoramic view of Venice, and shows you all the details of this wonderful town, which rises out of the waters like the ark of the deluge.

The height of the tower is about 330 feet, and when you look down to the busy crowds below, in St. Mark's Place, they look like bees in a hive, or ants in a molehill, crawling about without any apparent object.

28th

The gondolas afford a pleasant lounging mode of moving about Venice. These light sharp-beaked boats glide along with great rapidity. In the middle of them is a sort of tented cabin, covered with a black cloth awning, which gives them a very funereal appearance. This universal black colour was imposed by a sumptuary law of the Republic, to check the extravagant expense in which it had become the fashion to indulge in fitting up these vessels. At night, they carry lanterns attached to the prow and stern, and the effect of these lights, scudding along in all directions, while the vessels that carry them are invisible, is very pleasing.

There are only eight horses in Venice: four are of brass, over the gate of the cathedral; and the other four are alive in Lord Byron's stable. The little island of Lido affords room for a short canter. The Venetian women are superb;—there is some thing peculiarly bewitching in their air and gait: but, I believe, they are but little changed since the time of Iago, and that still

> In Venice they do let Heaven see the pranks
> They dare not show their husbands.

Walked upon the Rialto;—if no more were included under this name than the single arch across the canal, the congregation of merchants before whom Antonio used to rate Shylock must have been a small one;—nor could Pierre well have chosen a worse place for "his evening walk of meditation."

The fact is, however, that the little island which formed the cradle of Venice, where the first church was built by the fugitives from the persecution of Attila, was called Riva-alta, or Rialto. Here too was the Exchange where the merchants met. In process of time the bridge leading to this island was called the Rialto, and has at last become the sole proprietor of the name.

In the evening to the Opera. Venice is the land of late hours: the scene in St. Mark's Place at midnight is more gay and animated than at any hour of the day; and it is after the opera that evening parties and *conversazioni* commence. The Gondoliers no longer sing the verses of Tasso; but you are frequently regaled with beautiful music from parties of *dilettanti* musicians. I ought to record, as an instance of the obliging civility of the Italians, that I met a serenading party in a Gondola to-night, singing very beautifully to their guitars the songs of a favourite opera. Supposing they were professional people, and under the idea that I was to make them a recompense, I detained them half an hour; and it was not till they explained their refusal of any remuneration, that I found it was a nobleman's family returning from an excursion to Padua.

The cafés in the Place of St. Mark are brilliantly lighted, and you might fancy, when you see it for the first time, that it was a gala night of extraordinary occurrence. The shops under the arcades are very handsome, particularly those of jewellery. One of the principal manufactures is that of gold chain, which is brought to the greatest perfection. The price of the chain is in proportion to its diminutiveness. I gave twenty francs for a small specimen, not more than an inch and a half long, of the *ne plus ultra* of this manufacture: it is worked with the aid of microscopic glasses, and seems to be the absolute minimum of all that is little.

29th

I was awakened from my dreams of poetry this morning by a sharp east wind from the Adriatic; bringing with it, as usual to me, cough and fever, attended with most oppressive defluxion upon the lungs. What a miserable thing it is to depend upon the wind for the power to breathe!—especially at Venice, where you are not allowed to take what physic you please without the assistance of a physician. I sent a prescription to a druggist, and though the strongest ingredient in it was paregoric elixir, the answer he returned was, that he might not sell so potent a potion without medical sanction. I thought of Romeo's apothecary; but my friend was less compliant than his, for he persisted in his refusal; and as I was equally resolute not to comply with his condition, I must have gone without my draught—which perhaps would have been the best course of all—if my friend the Vice-Consul had not supplied me from the consular medicine chest.

Passed the morning at the Armenian convent;—a very interesting establishment, where, as long as the present librarian—Father Paschal Aucher—a man of great learning, very extensive knowledge of the world, and most amiable manners,—continues in office, a few hours may be passed most agreeably.

Went afterwards to the Campo di S. Maria Formosa to see the house of the "*proud Priuli*;" which still belongs to the family of that name. The east wind continues with such biting severity, that I feel I cannot stay here, and so, to-morrow—"I must away toward Padua."

30th

Left Venice in the courier's boat, and arrived at Padua in the evening. The voyage is dull and uninteresting. The banks of the Brenta are just high enough to prevent your view of the country, without possessing any beauty in themselves to render them interesting.

I found the apothecaries at Padua more accommodating than at Venice;—and if I had been inclined to swallow poison, I should have met with no obstruction.

31st

Engaged with a *vetturino* for a place in his carriage to Milan. I should have, as usual, engaged a small carriage to myself; but the pleasure of this mode of travelling depends much upon the state of the weather, and the character of the scenery through which you pass. In the present case, the rain is pouring down in torrents; and the plain of Lombardy offers no great promise of picturesque beauty; so that I prefer studying life and manners in the inside of a vetturino's coach. By the way, these vetturini are the greatest scoundrels upon earth excepting perhaps the jackals or *finders*,[2] who hunt down their prey for them. This is a regular profession in all the towns of Italy; and a tribe of these fellows is constantly on the look-out for travellers whom they cheat of course as much as they can;—for their own profit consists of so much per cent upon the bargain they make in behalf of their employers.

My companions are a ci-devant captain of infantry, in the army of the kingdom of Italy, who had served in Spain for many years, and who retired in disgust when his country was subjected to the government of Austria, and two Italian ladies of the *negoziante* class. We halted in the evening at Vicenza. The rain prevented my attempting to see any thing, but I console myself with hoping that there was nothing to see.

June 1st
Another day of rain. My military companion is a very intelligent man, and we have had much friendly discussion on all subjects, except politics—or, I should rather say except military topics. It is truly provoking, after the achievements of the English at Waterloo, that their countrymen should have to fight the battle over again, as one ever has to do, when the subject is canvassed out of England.

The truth in this as in most cases, will be found to lie in the middle; between the exaggerated pretensions of the English, who insist upon having gained a complete victory, and the ridiculous extravagancies of the French, who would wish to talk themselves and all the world into a belief that, *if* the Prussians had not robbed them of their prey, they should have annihilated the English. A calm retrospect of the objects that the two leaders proposed to themselves will, I think, show clearly how the question really stands between the English and the French, without embarrassing it with the Prussian co-operation.

Napoleon's object was to carry the English army by storm, and thus gain Brussels before the arrival of the Prussians;—he pointed out the road to his soldiers with exultation he triumphed by anticipation in the idea that, at last, he had got the English within his gripe;—"*Ah! pour le coup je les tiens donc, ces Anglais;*"—and so confident was he of success, that he had prepared printed proclamations, dated from the royal palace at Brussels. The Duke of Wellington's object seems to have been simply to prevent this, by standing his ground, and keeping the enemy at bay till he should be joined by his ally.

This is all that the Duke of Wellington proposed to himself to do, and this is what he did do most completely and triumphantly, *proprio marte*. It is to the having repulsed the enemy, and defeated his object, that the claims of the English should be limited;—and this is claim enough. Then come the Prussians, and convert this repulse into a rout; and now, those who ran away would fain hope, that between the English and the Prussians—as in the old fable of the stools—the glory of the day may rest upon neither.

The evening cleared up as we approached Verona, the environs of which are beautiful; and the town itself has a gay and pleasing appearance.

The amphitheatre has suffered little from the lapse of centuries, and it serves as an explanatory key to the great Coliseum at Rome. I have observed here again, that the mind is more impressed with the grandeur of what it has seen, by a subsequent comparison of its recollections with smaller objects of the same kind, than by the actual contemplation of the objects themselves. Thus the amphitheatre of Verona has made me more sensible of the prodigious scale of the Coliseum, than I was when within the walls of the Coliseum itself.

I went in the evening to the theatre; but the house was dull, dark, and dirty; and the audience seemed to come with any other object rather than to hear the play, for they talked amongst themselves as loud as the actors, on the stage.

When there is no sympathy between the actor and the audience, nothing can be more tiresome than a play. The re-action is wanting, to give it spirit; for when a play goes off well, it is, I believe, because the audience bring at least one-half the entertainment along with them.

2nd

Halted to breakfast at *Desenzano*, on the bank of the *Lago di Garda*. On the island in the lake are the remains of Catullus's villa. We were now passing over the scenes of Buonaparte's Italian campaigns, and my military companion was very eloquent in the praise of the ci-devant Emperor. It is truly surprising to witness the enthusiasm of feeling which this man has excited in his favour amongst those who have served under him. My companion spoke of the effect of his appearance on the field of battle, in its influence upon the spirits of his army, as something supernatural. No man could ever act the hero better, when it suited his purpose; and no man ever attained in greater perfection the art of gaining that ascendancy over his followers, which constitutes the spell that strong minds hold over weak ones.

He seems to have had a very happy knack in speaking as well as acting *the sublime*. The captain gave me two instances of this kind. At the battle of Lodi, there was a battery of the enemy which was making dreadful havoc amongst the French ranks, and repeated attempts had been made to storm it in vain. An officer came to Buonaparte to represent to him the importance of making another effort to silence it; when he put himself at the head of a party, exclaiming *Qu'elle se taise!* and carried it by storm. On another occasion, he was giving some impracticable orders, which were humbly represented to him to be *impossible*; when he burst out—*Comment? ce mot n'est pas Français.* The most remarkable feature in the character of this strange being is his inconsistency; displaying, as he does, at different times, the most opposite extremes of great and little—magnificence and meanness. This inconsistency, however, is sufficiently explained by his utter want of fixed principles of right and wrong. What can be expected from him who laughs at religion, and does not even possess a sense of honour to keep him steady in the path of greatness! Selfishness seems to have been the foundation of his system, the only principle which he acknowledged; and this will reconcile all the apparent inconsistencies of his conduct. Every thing was right to him that conduced to his own interest, by any means, however wrong; and as his mind seems to have had the power of expanding with his situation, so it had an equal power of contracting again; and he could at once descend from the elevation of his throne, to the pettiest considerations connected with his altered condition; accommodating himself in a moment to all the variations of fortune. In a word, he was the Garrick of the great stage of the world, who could play the leading part in imperial Tragedy—carrying terror and pity into all bosoms—and re-appearing in the part of Scrub in the after-piece, with equal truth and fidelity of representation. We might admire the equanimity of such a temperament, if we did not find it associated with such a selfish and exclusive attention to his own personal safety, as robs it of all claims to our applause. After all, he is a truly extraordinary being—a wonderful creature, furnishing the most curious subject for examination to those who, abstractedly from all the national and political feelings of the present time, can consider him merely as a singular phenomenon, an anomalous variety in the strange history of human nature.

Whatever *we* may think of him in England, he is the great idol of adoration in this country. The people carry a little bronze image of him—like a Roman household God—in their waistcoat pockets; which they kiss with every mark of affection; and yet this very people helped to pull down the statues of the Emperor at his abdication. How is this to be explained, and what could have been the charms of Napoleon's dominion? Is it the natural fickleness of mankind? Or is it that the people were taught to believe, when Napoleon should be put down, a better order of things would be established; but finding now, that though *he* has lost every thing, *they* have gained nothing, a re-action has taken place in public opinion, and the sentiment in his favour is increased, by mixing up their own disappointment along with it.

The Austrians rule Italy with a rod of iron; or, as the Italians say, they rule it as if they were to be turned out of possession to-morrow. The conscription, the taxes, the rigid exclusion of English manufactures are all continued; and the *manner* in which their oppressors exercise their rule is as offensive to the Italians as its spirit. They are utterly without the *suaviter in modo*, which made the French individually popular, in spite of their oppressions; and the Italians always speak of the *Tedeschi*, as *la brutta gente*.[3]

It is impossible not to sympathize with the Italians in their complaints; but the domestic jealousy of one another, that exists amongst the different States, will stand in the way of any general effort to throw off the foreign yoke, which galls them so severely; to say nothing of that softness of character, approaching to imbecility, which seems to incapacitate them from sustaining the perils of such a struggle. Though there is much more firmness of tone in the character of the northern than of the southern inhabitants of Italy, yet my companion inveighed with vehement bitterness against the apathy of his countrymen and his constant prayer was, that the Austrians might carry their tyranny so far, as to inflict daily a hundred blows of the bastinado upon every Italian, expressing his willingness to he the first to submit to this discipline. Upon my asking him what he meant, he explained, that he thought this, and nothing less than this, might rouse his countrymen to a general insurrection, to free Italy from the intolerable oppression of their German masters.

The spirit of the Austrian government was signally displayed, in conferring upon a *German* the Archbishopric of Milan, the highest ecclesiastical preferment in their Italian territory, and worth about 8000*l.* per annum.

We have had some taste of the rigour of their police, in the vexatious examination of our passports and baggage at every town through which we have passed.

The captain replies to all my sallies of impatience, by a significant shrug, adding, with a sort of sarcastic submission to his lot—*Væ victis!* and then exclaiming, with an indefinable expression,

Exoriare aliquis nostris ex ossibus ultor!

We arrived late in the evening at Brescia.

3rd

Off again at sun-rise. It perhaps may be reckoned among the advantages of travelling with a voiturier—with whom "*lucet, eamus!*" is a standing order of the day—that it soon accustoms you to rise at day-break without effort or fatigue. Nothing can be more uninteresting than the dull flat plain of Lombardy, where there is little to please any eye but the eye of the agriculturist. The land indeed is as rich and fat as land can be, yielding four hay-harvests in the year. Besides, the whole plain is almost one continued vineyard, and the vine is not here the little dwarfish plant that it is in other places, but is trained to hang from tree to tree in rich festoons, as it is described by Virgil.

The mulberry is the common tree of the soil, which is cultivated rather for the sake of the leaves than the fruit. These are stripped off, as soon as they arrive at maturity, to feed the silk-worms. This operation had just been performed, and the poor naked trees looked wofully out of fashion, at this season, when every scrub of a bramble is dressed out in a new suit of green livery; but nature soon provides another set of leaves, and the silk-worms get a second harvest.

Our vetturino crawled along more sluggishly than usual, and we had nothing to interest us in the way of novelty, but occasional fields of rice, which were a new sight to me.

Halted for the night at Caravaggio.

4th

Vive le Roi!—My female companions talked a great deal to-day of England, and of English manners. They made the same charge against us which is made by all the world, of pride and hauteur. In the course of our route to day, we saw a chariot at a distance advancing towards us. The ladies clapped their hands together and cried out *Eccolo! Eccolo! Inglesi! Inglesi!* I asked them how they knew at such a distance to what nation the carriage belonged, when they laughingly pointed to the female domestic on the box. They cannot see the propriety of the distance which is preserved between English masters and their domestics—especially female domestics. The sight of a *female* posted on the outside of the vehicle shocked their notions of the deference and courtesy due to the sex—all considerations of rank out of the question—and was considered by them as an unpardonable act of high-treason against the divine right of womanhood; nor could I make them understand that the Abigail was probably better pleased to accompany her fellow servant on the box, than to be admitted inside, subject to the constraint arising out of unequal association.

1. The *St. Peter and St. Paul,* which is at Milan, is another specimen of Guido's best manner.

2. The Italian designation of the *finder* is *Sensale.* He fleeces the Vetturino without mercy; and in some of the petty states the latter is *obliged* to have recourse to him, and not allowed to make his bargain for himself; the *Sensale* being the agent of the Police, who must also have their share of the plunder.

3. The popular sentiment was strongly manifested, during the late visit of the Emperor of Austria to his Lombardo-Venetian dominions. The Emperor was at the Opera at Venice, with Maria-Louisa, the wife of Napoleon. The audience were clamorous in their applause, and so particular in directing it to the Ex-Empress, that, as the best way of appeasing the tumult, Maria-Louisa quitted the theatre. The audience, however, rose with her, and accompanied her home, leaving the Emperor of Austria

With a beggarly account of empty boxes!

XI

MILAN TO LAUSANNE

The approach to Milan is very grand; as soon as you pass the gate, you enter a noble street, as broad as Piccadilly, with a wide trottoir on each side for foot-passengers. All this is the work of the French.

Established myself at the Albergo Imperiale; where I have engaged to give nine francs per day for my rooms, breakfast and dinner.

There is something disagreeable at first to English feelings, in making a previous bargain for your entertainment at an inn; but it is the only way of securing yourself from a greater evil—a final dispute. Those to whom economy is an object will find their advantage in this practice; for if the innkeeper is made to understand that you do not travel *en grand Seigneur*, as the great mass of English are supposed to do, he will moderate his demands to your own terms, rather than allow you to seek another inn. Amongst the minor mortifications of a limited purse, there are few more disagreeable than the necessity it imposes of attending to considerations from which the rich man is exempt. What's to pay? Is the only question he need ask upon his travels—and the answer to him is of small importance.

5th

The Cathedral;—a *new* cathedral, especially if it be built of white marble, as is the case at Milan, is an ugly staring thing. In the inside there is a curious subterranean chapel, in which the body of the Patron Saint, Charles of Borromeo, is deposited. He was one of the best and most amiable men of his time, and was committed quietly to the peace of the grave, amidst the respect and regret of his contemporaries. Some twenty years after his death, however, his canonization took place; upon which his body was removed from its former tenement, and deposited in state in this splendid tomb; where he is now exhibited as a spectacle to every curious stranger, at so much a head. This little chapel is all gold and silver, and the saint himself, arrayed in splendid robes, is laid in a case of transparent crystal. The face is visible—"grinning horribly a ghastly smile,"—as if he felt the bitter sarcasm conveyed by the contrast of his present situation with the motto of his life— *Humilitas*!

Went to the Mint; where you may see in a few minutes the whole process of coining, from the rough bar of silver to the finished piece of money.

The whole of the machinery is worked by water; that part of it which stamps the impression works 1500 pieces in an hour. The last act of the process is verifying the coin. The balance used for this purpose is so delicately constructed, that the eight-hundredth part of a grain is sufficient to turn the scale.

Napoleon certainly excelled all the world in money-making. His Italian coin is perfect—at once handsome, commodious, and intelligible—and this last article is of great use to a stranger. In our own imitation of this coinage, how is a stranger to know that a shilling is a shilling—except by inspiration? In the Italian Mint, the coin speaks for itself, and the value is inscribed on it in legible characters.

They still continue to stamp the gold pieces of forty and twenty francs, and the silver pieces of five francs, with the image of Napoleon.

The coinage of the smaller money is discontinued.

6th

Drove to the *Piazza Castello*, where there was a review of Austrian troops. The General rode on the ground, attended by his staff most sumptuously caparisoned. The infantry were all padded out about the chest, and screwed in about the waist; according to the fashion that has sprung up, of improving Nature's model.—"Heaven has given us one shape, and we make ourselves another."

From hence I went to the Amphitheatre of Napoleon, capable of containing 40,000 persons; the seats are cut out of the shelving bank, and are covered with living turf. Here were given, in imitation of the games of antiquity, splendid fêtes, with horse and chariot races, and naumachia. There are channels constructed for filling the area of the Amphitheatre with water.

A grand gala is now in preparation, to celebrate in the same place the birth-day of the present Vice-Roy, an Archduke of Austria. At the farther extremity of the town, at the commencement of the Simplon route, is the unfinished arch of Triumph which was designed to record the glory of Napoleon.

The *bas-relief* ornaments were all finished, representing his victories over the Austrians; the surrender of General Mack, and his own triumphal entry into Milan; and these things still remain, as if Austria thought the piece was not over, and that there might yet be

> A rare fifth set to crown this huffing play,

when these decorations would be called for.

Leonardo da Vinci's famous picture of the *Last Supper*, in the refectory of the convent of the *Madonna delle Grazie*, is almost gone. The magnificent copy of it in mosaic, which was undertaken under the auspices of Napoleon, is finished; but it has been sent off to Vienna! The excellencies of this great work, however, will still live in the admirable engraving of Morghen.

Lounged in the evening in the public gardens, which form an agreeable promenade. Here is a theatre without a roof, open to the heavens, where an Italian tragedy was performed.

One is so accustomed to *stage lights*, that a play by day strikes one as a monstrous performance. And indeed, all prejudice out of the question, day-light destroys entirely the illusion of the scene;—at least as long as the scenes are made of painted canvass, and the actor's dresses of tags and tinsel.

If the stage were indeed the marble palace that it is made to represent—as was probably the case in the ancient theatres, if we may judge from the marble of the proscenium that still remains—and if every other decoration "savoured equally of the reality"—the light of day and of truth might be safely admitted.

The play was dreadfully dull, and the actors "imitated nature most abominably."

In the evening I went to the theatre of Marionettes, a very clever exhibition, where puppets of four feet high moved about, and performed all the action of the scene with great spirit and propriety, while the voices were supplied by persons from behind the scene;—so that of the two entertainments it would be fair to say, that in the one the puppets acted like men, and in the other the men acted like puppets.

7th

Cold wet day. Italian gossips. Universal outcry against the "*paternal government*" of Austria. By the way, this cant phrase seems to be appropriated, as if in a spirit of mockery, to the very worst governments in Europe; unless, indeed, it be taken from the old adage of "he who spareth the rod spoileth the child," which seems to be the leading maxim of the paternal governments, in their conduct to their subject states.—Engaged a vetturino for twenty francs a day, to carry me to Lausanne, by any route I should choose, and to pay my board and lodging expenses on the road.

8th

Rose at day-break;—but my vetturino showed the caitiff so strongly at the very first step, by a breach of his agreement, that I was obliged to determine my contract with him at once.

Breakfasted at a café adjoining my hotel. Some hours afterwards, in an opposite quarter of the town, I missed my purse, containing about seventy Napoleons, which was all the money I had in the world. Remembering that I had taken it out at breakfast, I immediately set out on my return to the café, though with very little expectation of recovering it.—As I walked along, I bethought me of the physiognomy of the waiter, and drew the most unfavourable conclusions from the knavish expression which I began to recollect in it; and then I arranged the best mode of conducting my queries, with a view to arrive at the truth, in spite of the lies which I took it for granted I should have to encounter. Upon entering the café, however, before I had spoken a word, he advanced towards me, with my purse in his hand, saying,—*Ecco, Signore!*

I record this, as one of the many but perhaps the strongest instance that I have met with, of the honesty of the Italian people. This lad might have taken my purse without the possibility of detection, and almost without suspicion; for numbers of persons were then breakfasting in the room, and many others must have entered it during the time of my absence; and the confusion and crowd of an Italian café would have made it the easiest thing in the world for any one to take up the purse with the newspaper that I left with it on the table.

Went in the evening to the theatre; where Alfieri's tragedy of Mirra was performed. The subject is revolting; but Alfieri has managed it with great skill, and in the representation there is nothing to disgust. On the contrary, I have seldom seen a tragedy where the distress is more affecting. The actress who played Mirra did it to the life;—her first entrance told the whole story of the play; and the part is so managed, as to excite pity and sympathy for Mirra, in spite of the odious passion of which she is the victim. If terror and pity be the objects of tragedy, the part of Mirra is admirably contrived to excite both these feelings in the highest degree; for, while you shudder at the terrible workings and fearful energy of her passion, the struggles of her own native innocence of mind, and the horror with which she regards herself; make the strongest appeal to your compassion.

They manage their Theatres better, in one respect at least, than we do in England. The hour of commencement, instead of being the same all the year round, varies with the season,—and the curtain does not rise till the sun has set.

9th

Having accidentally encountered a voiturier, whose carriage and appointments are better than usual, I have engaged him to carry me, and me alone, whithersoever I will, for twenty francs a day; which is to include the common expenses on the road. My first stage has been to Como; and I have passed the day on the lake, enjoying all the pleasure that a fine landscape can give. What that pleasure is, would, perhaps, be more difficult to describe than the landscape itself, differing so much as it does in different people; for how much more will one person see in a landscape than another, and even the same person than himself, at different times He certainly made a notable discovery who first laid it down that beauty does not reside in things themselves, but in the eye that sees it; and every eye sees a different beauty. I have heard a man argue that there was nothing in nature equal to the *scenery* of Covent Garden; Dr. Johnson used to say there was nothing like Fleet street; and every man, I believe, thinks the finest prospect in the world is that which commands a view over his own land.

But he is little to be envied who is dead to the enthusiasm of nature, whose heart and feelings are out of the reach of her influence, and who is insensible to the tranquil enjoyment which is derived from the contemplation of such charming pictures as the Lake of Como will present to him.

The spot from which this noble lake is seen to most advantage, is from a point immediately opposite the *Fiume di Latte*, a romantic little waterfall, which forms a succession of miniature cascades, from a height of several hundred feet, amongst the vineyards with which the side of the mountain is planted. There is a spot, opposite to this waterfall; from which you command a prospect of the whole scene, without the disadvantage of a bird's-eye view. You have the three branches of the lake under your eye at once. The principal one extends northward, in the direction of Chiavenna; with the mountains of *Val Tellina*, and the Julian

Alps, for its more distant boundary. Full in front is the *Monte Legnone*; which, though not ranking, as Eustace ranks it, amongst the highest Alps, nor retaining its snow in summer, is yet, from its bold rugged form, and its insulated position, one of the grandest and most commanding of them. To the south you look upon the other two branches leading to Lecco, and to Como. This branch of the lake, from Menagio to Como, is of very different character from the northern branch; and though it is very beautiful, and at once wild and highly cultivated—with its banks studded with villas and villages—yet it wants the grander features of the northern prospect. At the villa Pliniana, the well, with its rustic masonry, is apparently in much the same state as in Pliny's time, whose descriptive epistle is engraven on a tablet in the wall. The lake abounds with fish. I came up with the boats of a party of fishermen as they were hauling in their nets, in which was a fine trout of fourteen pounds.

The inhabitants of the country about Como have a rage for seeing the world. They traverse all countries with pictures and barometers for sale; and when they have scraped together a little money, they return from their wanderings to pass the evenings of their days and lay their bones in their own country—a desire that seems to be natural to all mankind—"*dulces moriens reminiscitur Argos.*"

The itinerant Italians, who carry on this traffic in England, will nine times in ten be found to come from Como.

10th

Passed through Varese to Laveno, where I embarked my carriage to pass over the *Lago Maggiore* to Baveno, while I put myself into another boat to make a wider survey of the scenery of the lake.

There is nothing in this, nor perhaps in any other lake, that can be put in competition with the view from that point of the lake of Como which I have before alluded to; but the *Lago Maggiore* is, I think, more interesting than the southern branch of the Como lake; because, with the same soft features in the bosom scenery, there is, in the character of the hills immediately on its brink, a boldness and grandeur, which heighten the impression of the whole by the powerful aid of contrast.

Amongst this bosom scenery, if the expression may be allowed, are the Borromean Islands:—*Isola Bella* and *Isola Madre*;—the magic creation of labour and taste. Originally barren rocks, they have been furnished with soil, and planted with groves of cedar, cypress, citron, and orange trees, and decorated with gardens, grottoes, and terraces. In the midst of this fairy land, which might serve as a model for a description of the island of Calypso, is the Palace, as it is called; which is not the stately, comfortless pile usually designated by that name, but a delightful villa, combining elegance with comfort. I observed here, what I have not seen elsewhere; the statues have a drapery of real gauze thrown about them, which does not, in fact, conceal any thing, though it seems to do so. The effect is not unpleasing; and, if it be the result of prudery, it is a much better expedient than a fig-leaf.

I could have lingered at Baveno a month, during this delicious season; and I was on the point of dismissing my voiturier; but something is constantly whispering in my ear to hasten to Lausanne, where I expect letters from England. How are we to explain that presentiment of what is to come, or of what has already happened at a distance from us, whether of good or evil— though chiefly, I believe, of the latter—which every body has felt more or less? It may be doubted how much, or even whether any, deference should be paid to those secret intimations. For my own part, I am not prepared to disregard them altogether. If it be a delusion, it is as old as Socrates, and may rank him amongst its victims. There is something strange and inexplicable in it; but so there is in all the links of that mysterious chain of attraction and repulsion, affinity and hostility, sympathy and antipathy, by which all the parts of nature are united and separated. *Second-sight*, as it is called, by which, according to some, the fate of the absent has been often so unaccountably communicated, may be but one of the many phenomena of this mysterious system, of which we know so little. There may be nothing really more surprising in this—though we are less able to explain it—than in the common fact of striking upon the cord of a violin, which produces a corresponding vibration in another that is in unison with it; unless, indeed, we are prepared to decide that human heart-strings are made of less susceptible stuff than the strings of a fiddle.

11th
Baveno is on the grand Simplon road, which I now entered upon for the first time. It is lined on both sides with short granite pillars, about the size of a common English mile-stone, placed, in regular succession, at very short intervals—scarcely more than six feet apart—which, on the edge of a precipice, are also surmounted with a wooden rail. The scenery soon becomes interesting, but it is not till you pass Domo d'Ossola, and begin to wind up the Val Vedro, that you are introduced into the heart and core of the Alpine recesses.

Near *Crevola*, where you begin to ascend, there lies on one side of the road a vast column of granite, wrought from a neighbouring quarry; which was on its way to Milan, to form a part of Napoleon's triumphal arch, when the news of his reverses arrested its progress. It is, perhaps, in its present situation, a more striking monument of fallen greatness, than it would have been at Milan of prosperous ambition;

In passing through the sublime and stupendous scenery of this part of the Alps, Napoleon will have no inconsiderable share in exciting your wonder; especially if you are a disciple of that sect which sees nothing sublime or beautiful that is not founded on *utility*.

For while you gaze with astonishment at the monstrous masses which nature has here heaped one upon another, in every mode of shapeless desolation, and feel that sensation of awe which it is the effect of such scenery to produce, by impressing the mind with a vague but overwhelming idea of the power of the mighty Master of nature—it is impossible not to be filled with admiration of the man who had the boldness to undertake, and the genius to accomplish, a complete triumph over such fearful obstacles. In this, as in many other instances, he has far exceeded all former achievements. Hannibal, it is true, passed the Alps at the head of his army; but Napoleon not only did this, but, as a lasting record of his contempt of all impediments, physical as well as moral, that stood in the way of the execution of his purpose, he has left this "*royal road*," by which every puny whipster may do the same, without the precaution even of dragging the wheel of his carriage.

This great work does, I think, eclipse all the fabled exploits which *Græcia mendax*, or *Roma mendacior*, has handed down to us. Xerxes' adventure with Mount Athos was nothing to it. Napoleon has burst through solid rocks, that would have defied Hannibal with all his vinegar; he has *abridged rivers*—in a word— he has played the very devil. The rocks frown at you, and seem

> To wonder how the devil you got there;

while they hang over your head, as if preparing every moment to come thundering down with a tremendous "πεδονδε κυλινδετο" to punish you for daring to invade their secret and solemn solitudes, and make

> At once your murder and your monument.

In fact, Napoleon has so *catamaranned* the foundations, that more than one *écroulement* has already taken place. It is remarkable that he never traversed this road himself. It was begun and finished in five years; but it is to be feared, from the negligence evinced in repairing it, that the indolence or the policy of the present rulers may suffer it to fall into decay.

Austria, it is said, does not view with the same admiration that a traveller does the facility of ingress into Italy which is afforded by this and the Mont Cenis road—the sister work of Napoleon. She would much rather increase[1] than diminish the difficulty of access from that quarter of Europe, being quite content with her own approach through the Tyrol, by way of Trent and Verona.

This is very natural; and in this spirit, it is said, she has exercised her influence with Sardinia to prevent the further completion of the road from Genoa to Leghorn, which had been begun by Napoleon.

I lingered so long on the way, that darkness came upon us before I was aware, and I was obliged to halt at a wretched hovel at *Isella*.

12th

I was glad to rise as soon as it was light, and escape, from the filth and vermin of the cock-loft in which I had passed the night, to the fine fresh morning air of the mountains.

Soon after leaving Isella, we passed the Swiss frontier, and after a long ascent, reached the village of the Simplon. This part of the Valais was incorporated into the French empire, but has now returned to its ancient connexion with the Swiss confederacy. At the top of the hill is the unfinished *hôpital*, which was intended for the residence of the Capuchin monks, whose business and occupation it is to assist and provide entertainment for travellers, and who are now stationed in a less convenient situation. The new building is on a very large and handsome scale, but the progress of it has been arrested, like that of the granite column, by the downfall of Napoleon. There is now little hope of its ever being completed; at least the poverty of the state, to which it at present belongs—the Valais—is confessedly unequal to such works.

The zigzag ascent and descent are so skilfully managed, that you may trot up and down, without difficulty or danger. The character of the scenery, on the Swiss side, is much less bold and grand than on the Italian. The Val Vedro contains every ingredient of the sublime that can be found in natural scenery— Mountain—Rock—Precipice—Torrent—Water-fall—Forest— in all their wildest forms;—but when you arrive at the summit of the Simplon, you are presented with a softer scene, and look down upon the verdant valleys of Switzerland. The first impression of this land of liberty is very favourable. The little cottage inns, if I may judge from this of *Bryg* where I have concluded the journey of to-day, are neat even to elegance; and there is in every thing an attention to comfort and cleanliness, which will remind an Englishman of his own mother-country.

13th

Intensely hot. Pursued my course through the Valais;—but I must cease to "babble of green fields." As for natural scenery, even sketches convey but a faint idea;—and descriptive sketches are ten times worse. The poverty of language is never so apparent, as when you seek to represent by words the infinite varieties of nature.

Descriptions, to be of any value, should be peculiar and appropriate; but how general and indefinite are the terms which you must use, if you are obliged to *paint* in words; and how little is conveyed by the whole catalogue of phrases which the most fertile imagination can supply! If, indeed, by mixing up these phrases like colours on a pallet, you could produce the same variety of tints, it might be as easy to represent a landscape with the pen as the pencil. All however that the pen can do, I believe, is to give the poetical part of the picture; by which I mean that part of it which appeals to the eye of the imagination, in the associations which the mind connects with the contemplation of the scene described; and in this, the pen may perhaps have the advantage. But, as to presenting a clear and intelligible *picture* of a complicated landscape by verbal description, I believe it to be impossible. The best and most picturesque representations of this kind are perhaps to be found in the writings of the inimitable author of *Waverley*; but I doubt whether even his sketches ever present any distinct image to the mind of the reader. I do not deny that his charming descriptions of nature, in her loveliest and boldest aspects, afford the greatest pleasure in the perusal;—all I contend for is, that the pleasure is of a vague and general character, and not derived from a clear perception of the particular features of the scene described.— Slept at Sion.

14th

There is a great sameness in the views in the Vale of the Rhone. The road runs along the bank of the river the whole way; both pursuing their course in nearly a straight line.

The *Cretins* are sad disgusting objects. I was prepared to expect the *goitre*:—

> Quis tumidum *guttur* miratur in Alpibus?—Juv.

It would seem as if nature in these regions could not help breaking out into excrescence, as well in the animate as in the inanimate part of her creation.

This loathsome appendage has been attributed to many causes. It has been supposed, though without foundation, that it is peculiar to those valleys which run from east to west; and that it is not found in those that run from north to south. A more general notion has been, that it arises from the qualities of the water, which is here little more than melted snow. But the more probable supposition is, that it is the consequence of breathing the damp foggy air which is condensed in valleys situated between the ranges of high mountains;—for the same disease is found in mountainous regions where no snow exists.

This is the suggestion of Marsden, who, in his *History of Sumatra*, describes a similar disease in the hilly districts of that country; where the valleys are exposed to the *caboot*, or thick fog, to the influence of which cold vapour he very rationally at tributes the tumours in the throats of the inhabitants.

Cretinage seems also to be peculiar to mountainous regions, though the cause and connexion are, in this case, still more inexplicable. It is found in the Pyrenees; and also, according to Sir G. Staunton, in the mountainous parts of China; and, in these cases, there is no common similarity of situation or climate, to indicate a common cause—except the single circumstance of *hilliness*.

It is well for these poor helpless creatures, that the superstition of the country causes the to be regarded with more than common affection, as the peculiar favourites of Heaven; for, being incapable of criminal intention, they are considered as exempt from the obligations of moral responsibility, and as privileged exceptions from the common lot of man kind, who are doomed to be born in sin.

But Switzerland is not the only paradise of fools.[2] In Egypt an idiot is held in still higher estimation, and even worshipped as a saint:—

If ignorance is bliss, 'tis folly to be wise.

I have been much struck to-day with the neatness and personal beauty of the female peasantry, dressed in their Sunday costume. They still deserve the praises which St. Preux bestows upon them in his letter to Julie, describing the Haut-Valais, and they still retain "*leurs petites coiffures noires, et le reste de leur ajustement, qui ne manque ni de simplicité, ni d'élégance.*"

Dined at *Martigny*;—afterwards, in my way to *Bex*, stopped to examine the *pisse-vache*; a cascade, of which Coxe says, that "he had seen higher waterfalls, but none more beautiful." Since his time—forty years ago—its beauties have been diminished by the operations of a miller; who, having built a mill under the fall, found it convenient to break away much of the projecting rock, to prevent the dispersion of the stream. The mill exists no longer:—the mischief remains;—but it is still a beautiful waterfall. Situated as it is by the road-side, and therefore accessible without any trouble, it is perhaps for that very reason less valued and less visited. For there is a stimulant in difficulties to be overcome; and indeed it is certain, that retirement of situation would give an additional charm to the beauties of the *pisse-vache*. Arrived early in the evening at Bex, where there is one of the very best inns in the world, and truly characteristic of the neat and elegant simplicity of Switzerland.

In Italy all the domestics of an inn are men, who perform the offices of waiters and chambermaids: here it is directly the reverse; and while attended by the Swiss Hebes of Bex, you may feel the force of St. Preux's remark:—"*avec la figure des Valaisanes, des servantes mêmes rendroient leurs services embarrassants.*"

15th

At *Villeneuve* I came in full view of the lake of Geneva. From Villeneuve to Vevay the road is beautiful, and every step of it passes through the fairy land of poetry and romance. The "snow-white battlement" of Chillon—the "*séjour charmant*" of Clarens—and "Lake Leman with its crystal face," beautiful as they are in reality, speak to us with more than the dumb voice of nature, through the glowing periods of Rousseau, and the immortal verse of Byron.

At *Clarens*, the shrubberies, and walks, and the *bosquets*, so minutely described in Rousseau, exist no longer; they have long since given way to plantations of potatoes, corn, &c.; for, as my honest host at Vevay observed, in allusion to the Nouvelle Héloise—"Romances are good things, but bread is better."

From Vevay to Lausanne you pass through one continued vineyard all the way. The landscape is very pleasing, but it scarcely deserves the raptures of St. Preux, who, on his return from his tour round the world with Lord Anson to his native Pays de Vaud, describes it as "*ce paysage unique le plus beau dont l'œil humain fut jamais frappé, ce séjour charmant auquel je n'avais rien trouvé d'égal dans le tour du monde.*"

In arriving at Lausanne, I drove immediately to the house of M. de Seigneux, to whom I had been recommended, who receives strangers into his house *en pension.* My first inquiry was for my letters,—which quieted all my anxieties. Those only who have experienced them can form an idea of the feelings with which a traveller retires to his own room, to enjoy alone and at leisure the luxury of long-expected letters from home.

17th. Paid a visit to the house in which Gibbon resided, which is within a few doors of us. Paced his terrace, and explored the summer-house, of which he speaks in relating, with so much interesting detail, the conclusion of his historical labours:—"It was on the day, or rather night, of the 27th of June, 1787, between the hours of eleven and twelve, that I wrote the last lines of the last page, in a summer house in my garden. After laying down my pen, I took several turns in a *berceau*, or covered walk of acacias, which commands a prospect of the country, the lake, and the mountains. The air was temperate, the sky was serene, the silver orb of the moon was reflected from the waves, and all nature was silent." Gibbon's library still remains, but it is buried and lost to the world. It is the property of Mr. Beckford, and lies locked up in an uninhabited house at Lausanne.

18th

Excursion to *Martigny*—to witness the dreadful effects of the late inundation. The cause of this calamity was as follows. Some months ago a glacier had fallen down in the valley of *Bagne*, choking up the course of a small river, and forming the head of what in time became a very extensive lake. The inhabitants, fearing that as the warm weather advanced this dam might thaw and give way, had cut a gallery through the ice to let off the water; by which, if the dam had remained firm a few days longer, the whole lake would have been emptied without causing any damage. But on Tuesday the 16th the head of the lake gave way— and down came the waters with a prodigious rush, sweeping all before them.

> ——lapides adesos,
> Stirpesque raptas, et pecus, et domos
> Volventis unà.——

If it had happened in the night, all Martigny must have perished. Four hundred houses were washed away in a moment, as you knock down a building of cards. The poor host of the Swan inn, who presided at the table d'hôte where I dined on Sunday the 14th, was on Tuesday swallowed up in an instant, in his own garden;—and away went stables, carriages, and horses, in all directions. Perhaps it was my good genius that whispered me so constantly to hasten to Lausanne, and who prevented my halting at Martigny, as I had once thought of doing, in order to go from thence to Chamouny. If it were, I fear I am not so grateful to him as I ought to be; for I would willingly have been a spectator of this dreadful visitation, even at the risk of being its victim. A poor painter was in the valley of Bagne, sketching this lake, at the time the dam gave way, and his escape was little less than a miracle. He has made a drawing of the perils that surrounded him. If he were a man of talent, such a scene ought to furnish him with materials for a picture of the Deluge, which has probably never been painted from nature. The scene at Martigny beggars description;—ruin and havoc are every where. Water seems to be a more dreadful agent even than fire in the work of destruction. The operation of fire is at least gradual, and affords some chance of escape; but water is a *radical* destroyer, and jumps at once to the conclusion. A single fact will be sufficient to convey an idea of the rapidity with which the work of demolition was effected;—the water travelled at the rate of twenty miles an hour.

The loss of lives is great, and the loss of property still greater. Those who have escaped with life—and only life—are perhaps most to be pitied. They have not only lost their all; but the very ground, upon which their houses and crops stood, is a desert, covered with a coat of gravel and rubbish, and rendered utterly unfit for future cultivation. The despair of the poor creatures is very affecting; they rub their eyes—like the King in the Fairy Tale when he no longer saw Aladdin's Palace—as if they doubted the evidence of their senses.

What a passing world this is! and how foolish it is to fret and worry ourselves about the petty vexations of such a transient existence;—at least such is the lesson which the contemplation of a scene like that of Martigny preaches, with more than the eloquence of words.

20th

Excursion to *Mont St. Bernard*. The convent is situated about 8,000 feet above the level of the sea, and is the highest habitable spot in Europe. The approach to it, for the last hour of the ascent, is steep and difficult. The convent is not seen till you arrive within a few hundred yards of it. It breaks upon the view all at once, at a turn in the rock. Upon a projecting crag near it stood one of the celebrated dogs, baying at our advance, as if to give notice of strangers. These dogs are of large size, particularly high upon the legs, and generally of a milk-white, or of a tabby colour. They are most extraordinary creatures—if all the stories the monks tell you of them are true. They are used for the purpose of searching for travellers whom may be buried in the snow; and many persons are rescued annually from death by their means. During the last winter, a traveller arrived at the convent in the midst of a snow-storm, having been compelled to leave his wife, who was unable to proceed farther, at about a quarter of a mile's distance. A party of the Monks immediately set out to her assistance, and found her completely buried under the snow. The sagacity of the dogs alone was the cause of her deliverance, for there was no visible trace; and it is difficult to understand how the scent can be conveyed through a deep covering of snow.

It is stated that the Monks themselves, when out upon search for travellers, have frequently owed their preservation to their dogs, in a manner which would seem to show that the dogs are endued with a presentiment of danger.

Many stories of this kind have been told, and I was anxious to ascertain their truth. The Monks stated two or three cases where the dogs had actually prevented them from returning to the convent by their accustomed route; when it afterwards turned out, that, if they had not followed the guidance of their dog in his deviation, they would have been overwhelmed by an avalanche. Whether the dog may be endued with an intuitive foreboding of danger—or whether he may have the faculty of detecting symptoms not perceptible to our duller senses—must be determined by philosophers. Be this as it may—even the dogs are sometimes deceived, and, with their masters, are overwhelmed in the avalanches that are frequently falling in the spring of the year. About eighteen months ago, two of the domestics of the convent, with two or three dogs, and a party of travellers who had been waiting with the courier from Italy, were lost in an avalanche. The bodies of these unfortunate persons may now be seen in the Charnel-house of the Convent of St. Bernard, where they are preserved, in order that there may be chance of their being identified by their friends. The coldness of the climate tends to retard putrefaction; but, at this time, no feature is distinguishable.

Buonaparte crossed this mountain with 60,000 men, with whom he afterwards fought the battle of Marengo. He halted for two hours at the convent with a few of his staff, and took some refreshment, but forbad the soldiers to enter or disturb the retreat of the Monks. I saw the spot where his life was saved by his guide. Buonaparte passed on without noticing the obligation at the time; but, upon his return from the victory of Marengo, he sent for the man, and presented him a purse of sixty Napoleons. The guide still lives, and is called Buonaparte.

21st

We left the convent deeply impressed with the hospitable and kind manners of the superior and his brethren. The support of the establishment is greatly dependant on charitable contributions; but it has lately suffered considerable loss, by the swindling device of some impostors, who—assuming the garb of the missionaries which the convent is in the habit of sending annually round the country to solicit support—contrived to levy very extensive contributions.

In descending the hill, I looked into a sort of sheep-cot, about two miles below the convent. Here lay the skeleton of a man, in the garb in which he was originally deposited. The hat still remained on the skull, and his great coat lay spread beneath his bones.

24th

In my way back to Lausanne I halted at Vevay, took a boat with three watermen, and crossed the lake to *Meillerie*; but I sought in

vain for the secluded spot so romantically described by Rousseau,
where St. Preux is supposed to have led Madame de Wolmar, after
their escape from the storm.

Rousseau's description, however, of the view from the lake, is as
accurate as possible; and I was now in the track of St. Preux—

Nous avançames en pleine eau; je dirigeai tellement au milieu
du lac que nous nous trouvames bientôt à plus d'une lieue du
rivage. Là, j'expliquais a Julie toutes les parties du superbe horizon
qui nous entouroit. Je lui montrois de loin les embouchures du
Rhône, dont l'impétueux cours s'arrête tout-à-coup au bout
d'un quart de lieue, et semble craindre de souiller de ses eaux
bourbeuses le crystal azuré du lac. Je lui faisois observer les redans
des montagnes, dont les angles corréspondants et parrallèles
forment, dans l'espace qui les sépare, un lit digne du fleuve qui
le remplit. En l'écartant de nos côtes, j'aimois à lui faire admirer
les riches et charmantes rives du Pays de Vaud, où la quantité
des villes, l'innombrable foule de peuple, les côteaux verdoyants
et parés de toutes parts forment un tableau ravissant; où la
terre, partout cultivée et partout féconde offre au laboureur, au
pâtre, au vigneron, le fruit assure de leurs peines, que ne dévore
point l'avide publicain. Puis lui montrant le Chablais sur la côte
opposée, (pays non moins favorisé de la nature, et qui n'offre
pourtant qu'un spectacle de misère) je lui faisois sensiblement
distinguer les différents effets des deux gouvernements, pour la
richesse, le nombre, et le bonheur des hommes. C'est ainsi, lui
disoisje, que la terre ouvre son sein fertile, et prodigue ses trésors
aux heureux peuples qui la cultivent pour eux-mêmes.

The contrast between the coast of *Chablais*, and that of the *Pays
de Vaud*, still remains in full force, and, by way of commentary
upon the text of Rousseau, I might cite the decrees and regulations
stuck up in all the inns of Savoy, since the late changes; where,
amongst other arbitrary articles, there is one which strictly forbids
any person to be seen in the streets after ten at night; and the
other prohibits all assemblies from dancing in public. *Private*
balls in private families are graciously allowed, provided, however,
that it be done "*sans rumeur et avec décence.*" Conversing with an

inhabitant of the country, I asked him whether the people were contented and happy under the government of Sardinia: "Oh yes," said he, "we are as happy as fish in a frying-pan."

June 26th to August 15th
A life of idleness. M. de Seigneux's establishment combines every thing that can make a guest comfortable. Monsieur S. is a gentleman, in the whole extent of that term; and Madame has every quality that a guest would most desire in the mistress of such an establishment. Amongst all her attractions, there is perhaps none more remarkable, than that active, well-informed common-sense, which is awake at all times and on all subjects. This is the most companionable of all qualities; especially when, as in this case, it is joined with great good-nature, and unmixed with a single grain of affectation. The house opens into a garden, and on this side of it we are completely in the country; looking upon a fine expanse of water, backed by the hills of Savoy, with a rich fore-ground of meadows and vineyards descending to the lake, which is about a mile distant from us. By opening the street-door we are in the town, and in the best part of it. If a man wish to be alone, his own room is his castle; if he wish to mix with society, he will find the best company of Lausanne in M. de Seigneux's parlour. Perhaps society is never so free and unconstrained as in an establishment of this kind;—there can be no lurking mistrust in the mind of either host or guest, to poison the pleasure of their association. This assurance of welcome is well worth buying at any price; and, if either party be dissatisfied, the account is demanded or presented,—and there is an end of the matter.

Sterne says, if he were in a condition to stipulate with death, he should wish to encounter him at an inn;—but perhaps Sterne had never lived in such a pension as this; which is the very place for a man to live or die, in the most quiet and comfortable manner.

The Pays de Vaud, of which Lausanne is the capital, was for two centuries and a half under the dominion of Bern, if such a term can be applied to so mild a system of government. For, during the whole of this period, it would appear that no tax whatever was levied by the sovereign state upon the dependent province.

Bern, in possessing itself of the Pays de Vaud, took possession also of the estates, which the Dukes of Savoy and the Bishops of Lausanne held in this little territory; and the produce of these was sufficient to defray the expenses of the administration of the government.

Things were in this state when the French revolution broke out. Switzerland was too near not to catch the infection; and the contest between the have-somethings and the have-nothings— the two great parties into which Sancho divides mankind— ended, as usual in such contests, in a complete revolution of the government; which had hitherto been confined to the aristocracy, but which was now vested in a Landmann, and a representative council, chosen by the people at large.

But it perhaps may be doubted whether the Pays de Vaud have not lost more than she has gained by this revolution. She has, it is true, thrown off the yoke of Bern; she has gained the rank of an independent state; and she has obtained a free constitution; but the public property which used to defray the expenses of the state has been somehow or other lost in the scramble; and the acquirement of cantonal independence has been saddled with the imposition of taxes, which may lead the people to doubt whether their old robes did not sit easier than their new.

Much attention is paid in this, as in the other republics of Switzerland, to repress the growth of luxury; and to check by the interference of the police all fashionable innovations, which may seem to threaten the corruption of the simplicity of republican manners.

An English gentleman lately gave a private ball, at which the ladies of course continued dancing long after the hours prescribed by the plebeian laws of Lausanne. The police made some attempts to fine all the persons concerned; but finding it difficult to establish the proof, they contented themselves with imposing the usual fine upon the master of the house. He refused to pay it; and the issue of this question was expected with some interest, when it was set at rest by some friend of peace, who, as it would appear, secretly paid the penalty on behalf of the defendant. He was however so indignant, at having been supposed to comply with a demand which he considered unjust, that he offered a reward, by public advertisement in the Gazette of Lausanne, for the discovery of the person who had thus interfered.

The religion of Lausanne is Calvinistic;—but though we are so near the head-quarters of "Brother Jack"—there are no symptoms of that mortifying and ascetic spirit, which so often distinguishes the followers of Calvin.

To instance, for example, the observance of Sunday. Every body goes to church; and so sacred is the period considered which is consecrated to public worship, that it would be an offence of which the public would take cognizance, to disturb the streets, even by driving your carriage through the town, during the time of divine service.

But, the offices of worship at an end, the leisure hours of the day are devoted to rational recreations;—and if Sunday be distinguished at all, it is by a more than ordinary cheerfulness and gaiety. Music and the common domestic amusements proceed as usual, without any apprehensions that the recording angel is noting these things down as abominations. Sunday, in short, is kept without any of that gloomy formality, which seems to be thought by some essential to piety;—it is regarded rather as a feast than a fast,—being the day dedicated to the preaching of that gospel which brought "glad tidings of great joy to all people."

The difficulty in this, as in other cases, is to preserve a just medium; to remember the purpose for which the sabbath was instituted and "made holy," without falling into the sour seventies which were first introduced by the Puritans,—a sect that seems to have borne some affinity to the Pharisees of old, who reproached even the Saviour of the world with being "a Glutton and a Wine-bibber."

1. As an illustration of this, I might notice the vexatious requisition of an *Austrian signature* are to the passports of all strangers entering the Lombardo-Venetian territory, which has delayed or sent back so many travellers approaching from Switzerland; who, in ignorance of this regulation, often omit to get their passports countersigned by the Austrian Minister at Berne.

2. Sir Robert Wilson, in his *Expedition to Egypt*, says, "In Egypt a fool is worshipped as a saint, and at Cairo they have many particular privileges; but the most singular is the superstition which favours them so as to make their children considered the peculiar favourites of Heaven; therefore, in the public streets the most virtuous women have no scruples to them, and passengers, instead of disturbing, pray over their union. A woman so with child is highly esteemed amongst her own sex."

XII

TOUR OF SWITZERLAND

August 15th

The tour of Switzerland might well furnish occupation for a whole summer; but, if the object of the traveller be confined to the picturesque, a fortnight will perhaps suffice to survey the finest features of this interesting country, and skim the cream of the landscape. With this limited object in view, I left Lausanne, with my friend D. in a one-horse *Char*, which resembles an English gig, only that the body is placed, on account of the narrowness of the roads, sideways between the wheels. For this we agreed to pay 13½ francs per day; this was to include the keep of the driver and his horse on the road, and indeed all the current expenses of the equipage, except the *bonne-main* to the driver; which should always be contingent, and made to depend upon his good-conduct.

There is nothing between Lausanne and Payerne, our first day's journey, to excite observation.

16th

This day's drive brought us to Bern, the environs of which have an air of magnificence, that announces the approach to a capital. The situation of Bern is very striking. It is built upon a bold eminence, at the foot of which runs the Aar—clear and rapid— and in the distance is a bold range of the Alps, covered with eternal snows. The town is well-built, of handsome stone, but the arcades on each side of the street, with their projecting buttresses, give it a heavy and gloomy appearance. The leading feature of the place is cleanliness; nothing can be neater than the streets, which are freshened by streams of water, that flow down the middle of them, in channels prepared for their reception.

The Bear is the patron of Bern, and Bruin's portrait, as at the mansion of the worthy Laird of Bradwardine, meets you at every corner. A couple of these animals are entertained at the expense of the government in a court in the town-ditch, where a fir-tree has been planted, that they may exercise themselves in climbing; and perhaps there is not much in Bern that will amuse a stranger more than the gambols of this ponderous but active pair.

The costume of the women—for the men seem to be laying aside that distinctive dress which used to characterize the different cantons—is any thing but graceful. Nothing can be more absurd than the cap of a *Bernoise*, for it answers no purpose of utility, with a broad, starched, black lace frill standing up all round it, in which she flits about as with the wings of a dragon-fly; though this is a very bad comparison, for the rest of her dress gives her figure such a heavy Dutch look, that no wings could support it. The character of the Bernoise beauty might be given in the description which Henry the Eighth complainingly made of Anne of Cleves. With a delicacy of complexion that rivals the fair faces of England, there is a robustness almost amounting to clumsiness in their figures, which is irreconcileable with the graces. Madame Roland, in characterizing the beauty of the women of Bern, says wittily enough;—"C'est le *rosbif* des Anglais pour les estomacs à toute épreuve."

The ancient government of Bern was an absolute aristocracy;—but an aristocracy that furnished the singular example of exercising its power for the advantage of its subjects.

The French revolution, however, and its consequences, had deprived Bern of the rights of sovereignty, which it formerly exercised over its dependent states, and reduced it to the condition of a single canton in the new federal compact: in determining the principles of which, there was much opposition between the aristocratic and democratic parties, which might have led to serious consequences, if the Swiss had not received a pretty strong hint, that if they could not settle their constitution amongst themselves, quietly and peaceably, the Allied Powers would be obliged to step in and do it for them. Such an intimation from without had a wonderful effect in moderating the violence of party animosity within; and in 1814 the new constitution was concluded at Zurich.

The leading principle of this constitution was the equalization of rights, not only amongst the different states composing the confederation, but also amongst the citizens of each state. The first step towards this was the abolition of the name of subject in Switzerland; and accordingly, the same rights were given to the vassal districts, hitherto called subjects, as to the cantons to which they belonged. This principle was strongly opposed by the canton of Bern, which hoped to recover its ancient dominion over the Pays de Vaud and Argovie; but it was fully established by the eighth article of the constitution;—which also provides that the Diet, in whom the government of the confederacy is vested, shall consist of nineteen deputies, one from each canton, who shall vote according to their instructions, each canton having a voice by its deputy.

By the seventh article, the equalization of rights amongst individuals was established by the abolition of all exclusive privileges belonging to any particular class;—and thus the triumph of liberty and equality, in the only intelligible meaning of those words, was complete.

Since 1814, Geneva, Neufchatel, and the Valais, have been added to the confederacy; and liberty is thus again re-established in her stronghold; and here at least, amidst storms and whirlwinds, and poverty and precipices, she may hope to maintain her sanctuary.

17th

The road from Bern to Thun passes through a beautiful country which exhibits comfortable symptoms of the *general* distribution of property. There are no splendid chateaus; but the cottages are neat and elegant, and have all the appearance of plenty. Every village has its public walk; and wherever there is a fine view or a shady tree, you will find a *public* walk, and a *public* bench; where you may rest and enjoy yourself, without being afraid of an action of trespass. In short, you see every where a striking attention to the wants and comforts of the many. At Bern and Zurich, you may find equipages, and even liveries;—but these last are held in general abomination throughout this land of equality, as base badges of servitude. Bern and Zurich, however, are large and wealthy towns, and it seems to be the natural effect of wealth and luxury to destroy the true republican spirit.

At Thun we sent our carriage to the right-about to give us the meeting at Zug, while we made a boating and riding *detour* through the lakes and valleys that lie between Thun and that place; and hiring a boat for eleven francs, we embarked for Neuhaus.

The home scenery of the lake of Thun is picturesque and pleasing, and the range of the Oberland Alps, in the distance, furnishes a grander background to the picture than perhaps can be seen from any other lake in Switzerland. At Neuhaus you find people with the waggons of the country on the look-out for passengers to Interlaken. Interlaken is a charming village, situated in a retired and romantic spot, combining all that painters love to delineate, and poets to describe. The view from the hill behind the village, commanding the lakes of Thun and Brienz, is superb.

18th
Morning's drive to Lauterbrunn. Nothing can well be imagined more grand and sublime than the scenery of the valley of Lauterbrunn. Mountains rise on each side of you ten thousand feet high, and a torrent roars at the feet of them, tearing its course afterwards through the valley with a brawling noise, that alone disturbs the solemn silence of this profound retreat. Occasionally you encounter the summer cabin of a cow-herd, perched like an eagle's nest among the rocks;—which seem inaccessible to any animal without wings, except the chamois.

At last, the valley widens a little, and you arrive at the village of Lauterbrunn. Here you see the cascade of the Staubach, which comes down at one fall from a perpendicular rock 800 feet high,—nearly twice the height of St. Paul's. This cascade would be the grandest in the world, if the body of water were greater; but it is composed of so small a rivulet, that it is dispersed into thin spray before it reaches the ground. Instead, therefore, of the tremendous thunder of a raging cataract, the Staubach "droppeth like the gentle rain from heaven," and presents a picture of enchanting softness and beauty, which I should be loth to exchange for any more sublime and terrible display of the power of nature. Madame Roland, in comparing the fall of the Staubach with the fall of the Rhine, has expressed in a beautiful illustration the different impression which nature produces upon the imagination, as we contemplate her in her grand and fearful aspects, or in those soft and sunny spots, which, like an oasis in the desert, derive an additional beauty from the horrors that surround them, as in the sequestered seclusion of Lauterbrunn. "Il semble," says she, "qu'une divinité imposante et paisible, ouvre une cataracte du ciel, et en fasse couler le Staubach devant soi pour s'annoncer aux mortels:—on dirait, de la chûte du Rhin, que le maître des enfers, voulant effrayer la terre, la soulève avec le fleuve pour manifester son courroux."

While we sat at the foot of the rock within reach of this refreshing shower-bath, admiring the rainbows produced by the morning sun in the falling spray, we were surprised by the sound of music, which seemed to be a duet of two hautboys; and the echoes of the surrounding rocks produced the most pleasing effect. But here again the evil genius of reality appeared to dispel the illusion; for the enchantment was at once dissolved, on discovering the cause of this music in the persons of two dirty old women.

Their singing was from the throat, and the sounds resembled closely the tones of a flute. It is in the same manner that the famous *Kureiholen*, or *Ranz des Vaches*, the national air of the Swiss, is sung; which does not consist of articulated sounds, nor is it accompanied by words; but is a simple melody formed by the same kind of guttural intonations.

After lingering many hours in this romantic solitude, we retraced our steps for some way, and then turned to the right into the valley of Grindelwald. The wooden cabins of the peasantry are in appearance just what Goldsmith describes,

Dear is that *shed* to which his soul conforms.

In Grindelwald there is less of sublimity than in the valley of Lauterbrunn; though the absence of wood, of which there is abundance in Lauterbrunn, gives a more wild and savage character to the scenery.

19th.

We had arrived at Grindelwald in a *Char* with two horses, with an intention of pursuing our course with the horses alone—there being no road for a carriage any farther over the Scheidegg to Meyringen. But to avoid the unprofitable toil of climbing up one side of a hill merely to descend the other, we determined to return to Interlaken, and proceed by water to Brienz.

All that is worth seeing may thus be seen, almost without quitting your carriage, or the high road.

Grindelwald is surrounded by the mountains of Eiger, Mettenberg, and Wetterhorn; but neither of these will compare with the Jungfrau, and Picvierge, so called from its inaccessible height which are seen from Lauterbrunn. It is between the Mettenberg and Wetterhorn that the *glaciers* descend. These stupendous masses of ice, while they command our astonishment, afford additional proofs of the wisdom and goodness of the Author of Nature. They have been well described "as performing the most important offices of utility, and while they serve as magazines which nature keeps in reserve to replenish the rivers in Switzerland, the partial thaw which takes place in summer maintains the freshness and moisture necessary to promote the vegetation of those mountain-pastures, which in this country constitute the chief wealth of the inhabitants. As the snow disappears, the flocks ascend the mountains, following the productions of the spring, which rise to life under their feet from day to day, until the snows of autumn compel them to retire again into the valleys." The life of the *Senn*, or cow-keeper, is thus a life of constant migration. He suspends bells of different sizes to the necks of his cattle, in proportion to the merit of the cows; and it is said that these animals are so susceptible of feelings similar to our own, that if the leading cow fall into disgrace and be deprived of her honours, she exhibits all the mortification of wounded pride, and of angry jealousy at the promotion of a rival;—and the question of precedence excites as much bitterness in the pastures of the Alps, as it can do in the drawing-room of the Thuilleries or St. James's.

The greatest affection is described as subsisting between the *Senn* and his flock, which he is said to regard as a part of his family; and the bells of his cows are made to harmonize with the *Ranz des Vaches*, which is his constant strain. It is from the same icy mountains that Switzerland derives its mineral waters, its hot springs, its crystal mines, and its cold baths, which have been found so efficacious in the cure of various diseases.

On our return to Interlaken, we had a dispute with the voiturier of whom we hired our horses. We had bargained for a journey of three days, intending to go to Meyringen; but as we abandoned this plan, and brought him his horses back the second day, we thought ourselves entitled to some abatement. He argued that it was our own fault that we had not proceeded to the end of our journey—and stuck to his bond. As it was a rainy day, and we could not continue our route to Brienz immediately, we resolved to try the temper of Swiss law, and adjourned with the voiturier to the Bailli of the village. He ruled the case between us with ability and impartiality, and I was delighted at the quickness with which he seized the real *gist* of the question. The cause was soon over, and—what, seldom, I believe, happens—both parties retired perfectly satisfied with his arbitration. Having first brought us to an agreement as to the terms of our bargain, he decided that we were bound by our contract, and must pay the voiturier for three days; but he also kept the voiturier to his part of the contract, and ordered, that if we chose to stay at Interlaken, we might ride his horses as much as we pleased, till those three days were expired. This produced a compromise between the litigants; and we wished the honest Bailli good morning, and a long possession of the judgment-seat of Interlaken.

We paid six francs for a boat to carry us to Brienz. The upper part of the lake of Brienz is superior to any thing I have seen in Switzerland. It is a perfect picture, and completely satisfies the imagination;—approaching nearer to the gaiety which is the character of the Italian lakes, as opposed to those of Switzerland, which have for the most part a sombre and gloomy air. The Italian lakes are, as Eustace says, "on the right side of the Alps"—in a land of wine and oil, instead of milk and water—where you have vineyards instead of pine forests, and the villages, instead of being buried in holes, and thrust into corners, as in Switzerland, are hung out in the boldest and most prominent situations. Opposite to the village of Brienz is the fall of the Giesbach; which has been less celebrated, though it is, I think, beyond all comparison the most magnificent cascade in Switzerland, and second only to Terni. And even when compared with Terni, its inferiority is confined to the volume of water: for perhaps there is more variety in the falls of the Giesbach, which comes foaming down with furious impetuosity, through magnificent forest scenery; the effect of which is, to break the usual uniformity of a cascade view The view from the Alpine bridge, which has been constructed half way up the steep, commanding at once the look up and the look down, is perhaps unrivalled. It is in a spot like this that we feel the impossibility of conveying by words any idea of the sublime imagery of nature.

At Brienz, a party of female choristers offered their services to enliven our evening, by singing their national airs. Many of these were delightfully simple and plaintive, and they "warbled their wood-notes wild" so sweetly, that perhaps science and instruction could have added nothing to improve the harmony.

20th

We hired a couple of horses to cross the Brunig to Sarnen, the road being impassable for a carriage; and for this day's journey we paid thirty-six francs: for in Switzerland they always charge you for their horses' journey back, as well as for the journey you perform. Sarnen is the capital of the little canton of Unterwalden. If, as it has been objected, there is any natural connexion between the Roman Catholic religion and the doctrine of passive obedience, it would seem that the character of this religion is changed by the climate of Switzerland;—and here it loses even its intolerance. For the canton of Unterwalden was one of the first to assert and maintain the rights of liberty; yet it was, and is, firmly attached to the church of Rome: though this has not prevented it from extending the hand of good fellowship to the Protestant inhabitants of Upperwalden; and these two cantons have long been incorporated together. They sit in the same council, administer the same laws, and inter-marry with one another, without at all disturbing their political or domestic harmony.

It is pleasant, amidst the wild and savage recesses of the Alps, to find a moral scene of such a character;—where the bitterness of religious differences is softened by the kindly feelings of human brotherhood; and every sect enjoys a full and complete participation in all the privileges of society.

The costume of the peasantry in this canton is grotesque, but not unpleasing. The women walk about in flat straw hats, which bear the same proportion to their figure that the head of a large mushroom does to its stalk.

21st

The government of a pure democracy may still be contemplated amongst some of the little cantons of Switzerland; where the people meet *en masse*, in the plain, to legislate and choose their magistrates. Here too may be seen the singular spectacle of a government without taxes, the government lands paying all the expenses of the state; and this will not appear extraordinary, where we find that the salary of the Landmann, or chief officer of the state, is limited to eight pounds per annum. In this miniature shape, such a government may be conducted with moderation and justice; but the history of democracies has too fatally proved, that it is perhaps of all forms of government the worst, when tried upon a large scale. Cruelty and injustice may disgrace the best-formed constitutions; but it would seem that they must be the characteristics of democracies. The history of Athens, the seat of arts and sciences, the country of historians, poets, and philosophers, teaches us, in the banishment of Aristides, the condemnation of Socrates, and the death of Phocion, that the intellectual and moral character of a people affords no security against their abuse of power; while the annals of the French Revolution will record in its true colours the savage spirit of a democracy acting under the blind impulse of ignorance and vice. This detestable spirit is completely explained in the declaration of a favourite demagogue of that day—"that true republicans ought not to bear even the aristocracy of virtue"—a sentiment which seems to be lineally descended from the Athenian, who employed Aristides to inscribe his name on the shell that was to send him into exile.

It is plain that these observations are not meant to apply to such mixed governments as have been founded on the representative system—the effect of which is, to counteract the inherent vices of democracy; though it may well be doubted whether this beneficial effect would not be completely neutralized, if the right of suffrage were made universal, with a new election every year.

After a long conversation on Swiss politics with our worthy host at Sarnen—who held an important office in the magistracy of the canton, and who delighted us at once by his good-humour, and the strong resemblance he bore to the Welsh Captain Fluellen, of gallant memory—we proceeded in a char to Alpnach, where we hired a boat to take us to Lucerne, and afterwards to Gersau, for fifteen francs. There was a good deal of wind, and the boatman hoisted a sail; but this is a dangerous practice; for the boats are flat-bottomed, and the men very bad sailors, so that you run the risk of being upset by those puffs of wind to which you are constantly exposed on the lakes of Switzerland, from the nature of the surrounding mountains and valleys. There is little in Lucerne to detain you, except the model of the four cantons by General Pfiffer, which should not be omitted.

The scenery of the lake in the neighbourhood of Lucerne is rather tame, but as you advance towards Gersau it assumes a loftier character, and the view towards Altorf is full of rugged magnificence.

The little republic of Gersau, consisting of a territory of two leagues in length and one in breadth, was incorporated into the canton of Schwytz in 1798. There is an anecdote told by a French traveller to show how completely, in so small a community, the conduct of every individual is under the eye of the public;—upon entering the inn at this place, he found an advertisement posted up, prohibiting all persons from playing at any kind of game, or drinking, with two citizens of the republic specified by name; and the reason assigned for this prohibition was, that one of them was addicted to drunkenness, and the other to choler.

22nd

We proceeded up the lake, and disembarked at Brunen; from whence it is a short drive to Schwytz—the cradle of Switzerland. The inhabitants of this canton displayed the same enthusiastic courage at the battle of Montgarten, against the French, in 1799, which their ancestors had done on the same spot, against the Austrians, in 1315, in the memorable battle which established their liberty. The interval between these battles—nearly 500 years—was an interval of peace and prosperity; but the havoc and devastation committed by the contending armies of Russians, Austrians, and French, in 1799, reduced the poor Schwytzers to beggary and ruin. The town of Schwytz is situated in a charming green valley, backed by the sharp and rugged heights of the Mythen. The *Cerf* at Schwytz is a perfect inn so delightfully comfortable, that I should have been well contented to remain there for some time, if the time had permitted it. It is necessary to penetrate into the core of Switzerland to recognise the traces of that honest simplicity of character, which has been considered as peculiar to the Swiss people. In those places which are situated on the great high roads, the influx of travellers has produced the usual work of demoralization; and the only competition seems to be who shall cheat the traveller most. The female cap of this canton seems to be fashioned with still less attention to utility than that of Bern; and is, in fact, nothing but a stiff frill of muslin, disposed uprightly on the top of the head, like the comb of a cock.

In our route from Schwytz to Art, we passed over the valley of Goldau, the fatal scene of the terrible *écroulement* of the Rossberg; a mountain which in the year 1806 slipped from its foundations, literally fulfilling the emphatic description of the Psalmist—"The mountains skipped like rams."—This overwhelming catastrophe swallowed up in a moment five of the most industrious villages in Switzerland, with some hundreds of their inhabitants, and a party of unfortunate travellers. The moving masses which came thundering down are described as being a league in length, 1000 feet in breadth, and 200 feet high; which in a few minutes converted this once cheerful and populous valley into a shapeless chaos of rocks and desolation.

The weather was so bad when we arrived at Art, that we resolved to postpone our intended ascent of the Rigi till our return, and proceed at once to Schaffhausen, the ultimate object of our tour.

After a boisterous voyage along the lake from Art, we arrived at Zug, where we found our carriage; and as the rain prevented us from seeing any thing of that place, we pushed on to Thalwyl to sleep.

23rd

We proceeded as rapidly as possible, without making any halt at Zurich, in order to see the falls of the Rhine before sun-set. It had continued to rain during the whole day, but a short time before our *Char* stopped at the foot-path which leads to the falls, the weather suddenly cleared, and we were fortunate enough to contemplate this splendid prospect lighted up by the rays of the setting sun. As the morning is the most favourable season for seeing the Staubach, so, from the difference of the aspect, the evening is the best period for looking at the falls of the Rhine. The impression of the first *coup d'œil* perhaps disappoints expectation, and it seems to require a longer survey to take in the whole magnificence of the scene. The best point of view is, I think, from the room of an artist immediately opposite to it; in which he has constructed a *camera obscura* which transfers the whole scene with all its lights, and colours, and motion, upon the table of his apartment. One of the defects, which are incident to representations of cascades, is thus supplied, and the effect of this *moving* picture is very pleasing; the want of sound, however, is a defect which seems irremediable, for though in this in stance you have the roaring of the real water-fall in your ears, you cannot, by any cheating of the senses, connect it with the mimic imagery of the picture.

Twilight came upon us while we were yet gazing with undiminished admiration at the awful majesty of the scene before us. I find that we have delayed our tour too long. The beginning of July is perhaps the best period for an excursion in Switzerland; for it is very important to have the evening as long as possible. At present it is night at eight o'clock, and the thermometer, which was a fortnight ago at 55 in the shade, was this evening as low as 52.

We found shelter for the night at a wretched inn at Iestetten.

24th

There is nothing interesting in the country between Schaffhausen and Zurich, and it is upon a road like this, that one is tempted to complain of the want of post-horses in Switzerland. The Diet seem to consider that the establishment of posting would be too great an encouragement of luxury; and accordingly a traveller is doomed to the snail's pace of a voiturier's team whether he will or no.

It is impossible not to wish well to any regulations that have a tendency to promote and maintain uncorrupted the simple

manners of the peasantry; and it is, I fear, a serious deduction
from the advantages of good roads and mail coaches, that, while
they promote the diffusion of knowledge, they circulate the
poison of immorality, and contaminate the country with the
vices and licentiousness of the capital. Travellers have certainly
done no good to Switzerland; but perhaps she has more to fear
from the mistaken policy of the Diet in encouraging the growth
of manufactures.

To say nothing of the absurdity of manufacturing at home
cottons and muslins, which she might purchase cheaper and
better from England; the profits of these establishments will be a
poor compensation for the evil effects which they must produce
upon the morals of the people. The only hope of duration that
a democratical government can entertain must be founded upon
the moral qualities of the great body of its population.

It would surely be happier for Switzerland, that her population
was confined to the honest and hardy followers of pasturage
and agriculture, than that she should, by the establishment of
manufactures, breed up an excessive population in particular
places, depending for support and subsistence upon the fluctuating
prices of commerce, and infected with the vicious propensities
which seem to be the necessary consequence of any system, that
confines large numbers of human beings together in sedentary
employments.

The Swiss, and particularly the inhabitants of the neighbouring
canton of Appenzell, have always been celebrated for their skill in
mechanics. A remarkable instance of their mechanical genius was
furnished by Ulrich Grubenman. This man, who was a common
carpenter, was the inventor of that sort of wooden bridge, which
is in German called *hængwerk*.

In consequence of the repeated washing away of the bridges at
Schaffhausen, a committee was appointed to consider of a plan
for a new structure. Grubenman, in order to avoid the force of the
stream, proposed to erect a bridge which should consist of a single
arch. The idea of throwing an arch across a width of 300 feet, was
treated with ridicule; and the plan was about to be dismissed as

the project of a visionary; when Grubenthan, as the story runs, answered the objections by jumping with his whole weight upon the miniature model of his intended work, which bore him up triumphantly, and his plan was in the end adopted.

Zurich is celebrated for the literary characters it has produced, and has been called the Athens of Switzerland. Gessner and Lavater are amongst the names of which they are most proud.

The last fell by the bayonet of a French ruffian, when Zurich was taken by storm, during those terrible times which made the peaceful retirement of Switzerland the theatre of war and carnage; and presented the awful spectacle of contending armies of French and Russians fighting hand to hand upon the Devil's Bridge.

The public library is large and curious; but a traveller has seldom time to do more than look at the outsides of books. They show you an original manuscript of Quintilian, and a collection of original letters in Latin, from our Lady Jane Gray to Bullinguer. In the evening we proceeded to Zug, along the banks of the lake of Zurich, which are gay and cheerful, though entirely without any of the higher characteristics of the sublime and the beautiful.

25th

The little canton of Zug, like Schwytz and many others, proves, that there is no necessary hostility between the Catholic Religion, and liberal principles of government. We embarked for Art at day-break, in order to ascend the Rigi. The lake of Zug is famous for the variety and abundance of its fish. The season of carp fishing is drawing to a close. I am told they are sometimes caught of the prodigious weight of ninety pounds: and frequently of twenty pounds' weight. But the fish in greatest estimation is the *rætele* a sort of salmon-trout, which is found under different names in most of the lakes of Switzerland. The day had promised a fine sun-set, but, as is often the case, these expectations were disappointed. There are four different routes by which you may ascend the Rigi; but that from Art is perhaps, on the whole, the best; not only as regards the road itself, but because the views by the way are confined, and the grand panorama is reserved till you arrive at the summit.

It took four hours and a half good walking to reach the top. The evening was extremely cold, the wind at north-west, and Fahrenheit's thermometer stood at 40.

26th

We rose soon after four o'clock in order to see the sun rise, which he did in the fullest splendour; gilding the white summits of the Swiss Alps, of which you command a view from the Sentis in Appenzell, to the Gemmi in the canton of the Valais. Ebel says, that fourteen lakes are visible, but I could only make out eleven. It was a magnificent spectacle. A sun-rise upon the Rigi,—the *Regina Montium*,—forms an epoch in one's life, which can never he forgotten. No man can help feeling on such an occasion some of those sensations, which Rousseau so eloquently describes as the effect of the air of high mountains, though it perhaps may be doubted whether the cause be not altogether moral, rather than physical. "Ce fut là,—on the top of the Rigi for instance,—ce fut là, que je démelai sensiblement, dans la pureté de l'air où je me trouvais, la véritable cause du changement de mon humeur et du retour de cette paix intérieure, que j'avais perdue depuis si long tems. En effet, c'est une impression générale, qu'éprouvent tous les hommes,—quoiqu'ils ne l'observent pas tous,—que sur les hautes montagnes, où l'air est pur et subtil, on se sent plus de facilité dans la respiration, plus de légèreté dans le corps, plus de sérénité dans l'esprit; les plaisirs y sont moins ardens, les passions plus modérées. Les méditations y prennent—je ne sais quel caractère grand et sublime, proportionné aux objets qui nous frappent, je ne sais quelle volupté tranquille qui n'a rien d'âcre et de sensuel. Il semble qu'en s'élevant au-dessus du séjour des hommes, on y laisse tous les sentimens bas et terrestres, et qu'à mesure qu'on approche des régions éthérées, l'ame contracte quelque chose de leur inaltérable pureté. On y est grave sans mélancolie, paisible sans indolence, content d'être et de penser; tous les désirs trop vifs s'émoussent, ils perdent cette pointe aiguë qui les rend douloureux;. ils ne laissent au fond du cœur qu'une émotion légère et douce; et c'est ainsi qu'un heureux climat fait servir a la félicité de l'homme les passions qui font d'ailleurs son tourment."

Such is the description of Rousseau, of which every man has, more or less, felt the truth; and it is, no doubt, to enjoy in Platonic perfection such seraphic raptures, that a lady of Switzerland has fixed her residence on the summit of the Rigi during the summer; where she receives and entertains such pilgrim visitors as may be thought worthy to participate in them.

In descending, we took the road to Wegghis, which is the shortest and the steepest. Here we embarked to cross the lake of Lucerne, where we rejoined our carriage.

27th and 28th

The road from Lucerne to Bern, by way of Zofingen, passes through the most fertile and best cultivated part of Switzerland. The views are of a softer and richer character, and the landscape is constantly enlivened by herds of grazing cattle; a feature which is often wanting, especially in the Pays de Vaud; where the favourite system is to confine the cattle to the house. In the neighbourhood of Lausanne, there is a large grazing farm, where no less than a hundred cows are thus kept in the confinement of the stall during the whole year. The advantages of this mode, in a farming point of view, seem to be considerable. The grass which supplies them with food during the summer, instead of being wastefully trodden under foot, and daintily picked, is regularly and fairly cut,—fat and lean together,—and is thus made to go much further; while the vast quantity of manure which is accumulated from so large a stock, is sufficient to support the pastures under the constant exhaustion of the scythe.[1]

The animals on the other hand give more milk than if they were at liberty; and are in much better condition, in the grazier's sense of the word;—that is, they are always ready for the butcher. The only objections to this mode arise out of considerations for the happiness of the animals themselves, to whom we are disposed to attribute human feelings and sentiments, and to imagine that they derive the same pleasure from browsing freely in the sunshine of the meadow, or reposing in the protecting shade of the woodland surrounded by the beauties of nature, which we should ourselves feel if similarly situated.

But it may, I think, be fairly concluded that animals, though they may seem to participate with man to a certain extent in the faculty of reason, are utterly insensible to all the pleasures of taste and imagination. The *beautiful* has no charms for the brute creation; for even in the passion of sexual desire, where, if any where, it might be supposed to have some influence, we do not perceive that youth, beauty, and cleanliness, make a more forcible appeal to their feelings, than age, dirt, and deformity. And it may be doubted whether the tranquillity and protection from flies during the summer afforded by the stall, be not sources of greater gratification to these animals, with whom

> To live well means nothing but to eat,

than any which they could find in the enjoyment of liberty, or the contemplation of the landscape.

29th
After again exploring the beauties of Bern, and its promenades, we retraced our steps to Payerne.

30th
Returned to Lausanne;—the more one sees of Switzerland, the more one is pleased with the country, and the less one is pleased with the inhabitants.

Point d'argent point de Suisse is a maxim of which every day's experience demonstrates the truth. Our bill last night was just twice as much as it was a fortnight ago at the same place; and our host was somewhat confused, when we produced his former account, in opposition to his charge. Swiss honesty is a phrase that is much used, and it may have some application out of

Switzerland; but it is an article that seems to be cultivated solely for exportation, and none is retained for home consumption.

September *6th*. Packing up. Farewell visits. Last drive round the environs of Lausanne, which are studded with pretty villas; amongst which *La Chabliere* is conspicuously beautiful, the residence of Mr. Canning, the British minister, whose courteous and hospitable attentions will not be forgotten by any of his countrymen who have resided at Lausanne.

1. The Swiss are very attentive to the dressing of their pastures, and to the preservation of the means of doing so, particularly the urinary part of manure, by far the richest and most valuable, of which they collect and treasure up every drop with scrupulous care.

XIII

JOURNEY TO NISMES

September 8th.

Left Lausanne in a voiturier's carriage, consuming eight hours in the journey to Geneva. There is a metropolitan appearance about Geneva; and it would seem that the people had acquired a taste for military foppery during their long connexion with France.

The town is fortified;—and there is as much pomp and circumstance in the examination of your passport at the gate as if you were entering the capital of a military despot. In the lower and trading part of the town, the houses, which are very high, have arcades of wood supported by pillars carried up to the roofs, something after the manner of Chester. The upper part of the city, which is built on a gentle ascent, is clean and handsome; the houses are of fine stone; and the views from the public walks towards the lake and neighbouring mountains are magnificent. The Rhone issues out of the lake in two rapid streams of dark and transparent blue, which unite soon afterwards, before they join the muddy Arve. It is surprising how the notion could ever have prevailed, that the Rhone passed through the lake without mixing with its waters; but there is this very extraordinary fact,—at its going out, it resembles neither the muddy colour of its former stream, nor the crystal clearness of the lake through which it has passed, but is of as deep an indigo as the stream that runs from a dyer's furnace.

9th

Drove to *Les Délices*;—the residence of Voltaire before he fixed himself at Ferney; but there was nothing to be seen. Afterwards to Ferney. His bed-room and salon remain precisely in the state in which they were when he occupied them.

Under the canopy of his bed is a portrait of Le Kain; on one side of the hangings, a portrait of the King of Prussia—and on the other, one of Voltaire himself. On another side of the room is the Marquise de Chatelet, his mistress. On the third wall are the Empress of Russia; Clement XIV., better known by the name of Ganganelli; Voltaire's Sempstress; and his Little Savoyard Boy. On the remaining side are a collection of prints. The family of Calas—De Lille—Diderot—Sir Isaac Newton—Franklin—Racine—Milton—Corneille—Antoine Thomas—Leibnitz—De Mairan—Helvetius—Washington—D'Alembert—Marmontel. All these remain as he had placed them. Here, too, is a model of the monument which he prepared for the reception of his own heart, with this inscription:

> Mes manes sont consolés
> Puisque mon cœur
> Est au milieu de vous.

All the prints are very poor performances, of small size. The Sempstress and Savoyard Boy are beautiful subjects, and very prettily done in crayons. I could not hear that there was any tale of scandal relating to either. The portrait of Frederick is a vile daub in oil colours, which an ale-house in England would scarcely accept as a sign. That of the Marquise de Chatelet is not much better, though her countenance apparently deserved an abler artist. Catharine of Russia's portrait is executed in embroidery. Le Kain's is a wretched performance in crayons; and, if it was like him, there never was on actor who had to contend against greater disadvantages of person. Voltaire's portrait is by far the best of the collection; the face is full of vivacity and spirit. It must have been done when he was a very young man; and, placed here, it looks as if he had been the god of his own idolatry.

The portrait of Clement XIV. should have been inscribed with his memorable repartee to Voltaire, which has still higher merit than its wit to recommend it.

The Baron of *Gleichen*, in his way to Italy, stopped at Ferney, and inquired of Voltaire what he should say from him to the Pope?—"*His Holiness*," replied Voltaire, "favours me with presents of medals, and of indulgences, and even sends me his blessing: but I would rather that *Ganganelli* would send me the ears of the Grand Inquisitor."—The Baron delivered the message:—"Tell him," replied Clement, "that, as long as *Ganganelli* is Pope, the Grand Inquisitor shall have neither ears nor eyes."

The whole town of Ferney was of Voltaire's creation. His estate consisted of about 900 acres. I talked with an old pair who spoke of him with the greatest affection, and told me tales of his various charities;—of his portioning the poor, to enable them to marry—and of the kind interest which he took in all their concerns. He was very fond of rifle shooting, and encouraged popinjay contests amongst them, in which he himself took a part. An old domestic produced two relics of his master;—the cap which he used to wear in his study, made of white silk embroidered with tinsel—and a curious book, in which Voltaire had made a collection of the seals of all his correspondents. The seals were pasted in, and underneath each he had written the address of the writer. It seems that it was his practice, when be received a letter, to examine and verify the seal by referring to his book; and, if it came from a quarter he did not like, he refolded it in an *enveloppe*, and returned it unopened to the writer.

He built the church of Ferney close to his own gate, as if he had a mind to illustrate the old saying—the nearer the church, the further from G—.

So much for Voltaire, whose merits as an author seem to have been over-rated. Johnson's praise of Goldsmith might with some limitation be applied to him—*nullum fere scribendi genus non tetigit, nullum quod tetigit non ornavit*; but though he sparkled in almost every style of writing he did not perhaps shine pre-eminently in more than one. He had more wit than genius—and his forte rather lay in cooking up the thoughts of others with his own *sauce piquante*, than in producing new sources of knowledge. He is perhaps only *maximus in minimis*; an exquisite writer of a satiric tale; unrivalled in wit, raillery, and sarcasm:—and inimitable in "exposing knaves and painting fools." Beyond this, there is little to say. His epic poetry, his tragedies, and his histories are only extraordinary in their combination. Separately considered;—his epic poetry would be placed by all but Frenchmen in the very lowest class of epic poems, all that Lord Chesterfield says to the contrary notwithstanding;—his tragedies are inferior in force and grandeur to those of Corneille, and in sensibility and pathos to those of Racine. Of his history much is romance; and the Age of Louis XIV., upon which his claims as an historian are founded, is rather a collection of materials for a history than an historical work. On many subjects it is plain he had but a smattering. Perhaps a stronger instance could not be given of the difference between a mouthful and a belly-full of knowledge than would be afforded by a comparison of Voltaire's preface to Œdipe with Johnson's preface to Shakspeare.

His physiognomy, which is said to have been a combination of the eagle and the monkey, was illustrative of the character of his mind. If the soaring wing and piercing eye of the eagle opened to him all the regions of knowledge, it was only to collect materials for the gratification of that apish disposition, which seems to have delighted in grinning, with a malicious spirit of mockery, at the detected weaknesses and infirmities of human nature. Though a man may often rise the wiser, yet I believe none ever rose the *better*, from the perusal of Voltaire. The short but admirable epitaph on him may well conclude his character—

> Ci git l'enfant gâté du monde qu'il gâta.

On our return to Geneva we had as usual a battle to fight with the voiturier—a kind of animal, of all others the most nefarious—perhaps the Swiss species is the worst. The dispute ended, as most disputes do—by the fool submitting to the knave. I paid the rascal his demand, and proceeded to Bonneville to sleep;—and the next day brought us to St. Martin.

11th.

Rainy morning; nothing to be seen.—On entering the valley of Chamouni it cleared up. Stopped to examine the glacier of Bossons, which is perhaps the brightest glacier in Switzerland. But all glaciers look like frozen *snow*, rather than frozen water; and in fact they are all covered more or less with a thin coat of snow. Some of the pillars, or rather spires of ice in this glacier, are above a hundred feet high.

Arrived at Chamouni before dusk;—but Mont Blanc was invisible—enveloped in mist and clouds.

It is now nearly a century since Pococke explored this valley, which was till then as little known as the interior of Africa. There are now two well-appointed inns; and during the summer season it has become the fashionable resort of all the idle tourists of Europe.

12th

Beautiful day;—but before the sun appeared above the horizon, which it did not do till nine o'clock, it was bitterly cold. I had now, for the first time, a fine clear view of Mont Blanc

> ——soaring snow-clad through its native sky,
> In the wild pomp of mountain majesty—

with the whole range of *needles*; some of which appear higher to an unpractised eye than Mont Blanc itself. But the eye is of all witnesses the most inaccurate, and it is some time before it can be taught to distinguish which is really the summit of Mont Blanc.

Rode to the cross of the Flegere; a height on the opposite side of the valley to Mont Blanc. The best point of view to look at a mountain is from an opposite *elevation*, and not from the plain. From the height of the Flegere we enjoyed the prospect in full perfection;—Below, as Johnson would say, was "immeasurable profundity," and above, "inaccessible altitude." The needles now sunk to a level with ourselves, while the round head of Mont Blanc rose higher than ever.

After having inscribed our names on the cross of the Flegere, we prepared to descend, and in our way down stopped to refresh ourselves and our mules on the mossy bank of a clear spring, from whence the prospect on every side was superb;—"and all was rudeness, silence, and solitude." A tranquil and happy hour!—I was reminded of Johnson's hour of rest on a "bank such as a writer of romance would have delighted to feign" in his tour to the Hebrides.

A full view of Mont Blanc at midnight, by the light of a glorious moon.

13th

Ascended Montanvert, to go to the *Mer de Glace*. It is impossible to describe this scene better than in the words of Coxe, who compares it to "a raging sea suddenly frozen in the midst of a violent storm." The glaciers which terminate the *Mer de Glace* debouch fairly into the valley of Chamouni in enormous masses, overturning trees, protruding forward vast blocks of granite, and threatening to advance, notwithstanding the crosses which have been set up to check their progress; many of these the Glaciers have actually overturned; in spite of the religious processions, which the superstition of the people leads them to hope will interrupt the course of nature. Vast pyramids of ice of all forms and sizes are constantly giving way, as they are pushed forward by those behind, or rather by the insensible movement of the whole mass, and they fall down with the noise of a peal of thunder.

The *Mer de Glace*, or Valley of Ice, is one of those things which, like Vesuvius, does not disappoint expectation. As that represents "the fiery floods" of the place of punishment, so this is the other extreme—the "thrilling region of thick ribbed ice." Nothing can be more awfully sublime; and there is just enough of danger in the chasms that yawn under your feet, and the occasional cracking of the surface, to impress the mind in a manner that disposes it to feel in its full force all the grandeur of the scene. Amongst other effusions in the *Album* at Montinvert, the Empress Josephine had written a quatrain, with her own hand; but some unprincipled collector of autographs has torn out the leaf in which it had been inscribed. The registrar, however, retained the verses in his memory, and has re-written them in the book:

> Ah je sens qu'au milieu de ces grands phénomènes,
> De ces tableaux touchans, de ces terribles scènes,
> Tout élève l'esprit, tout occupe les yeux;
> Le cœur seul, un moment, se repose en ces lieux.
>
> 1810.

An imperial quatrain is too great a curiosity to be within the reach of criticism; but how shall we explain a sentence inscribed by Madame de Staël!

> Si les passions n'anéantissait—(probably anéantissaient)— la sensibilité du cœur, on verroit les hommes s'abstenir des choses impures, et que le sentiment reprouve, mais l'ame inclinée vers sa perfection ne sauroit composer avec ses principes, et jetter dans la vie une autre vie, qui conduiroit à un avenir sans avenir.
>
> DE STAEL HOLSTEIN, 17 Août 1815.

I own I am not Œdipus enough to understand what the Sphinx would be at here; though I have faithfully transcribed the sentence even to a fault. If the author of the Rejected Addresses had visited Chamouni, one might almost suspect it was a *quiz*. It is certainly very like the style of the lady in question, particularly when—as it often happens to her—she does not seem to understand her own meaning. This, I suspect, is frequently the case in the mystical and metaphysical parts of her writings; which continually remind us of our old friend the Vicar of Wakefield, with his "*anarchon ara kai ateleutaion to pan.*"

I record one more effusion, taken from the Album at Chamouni; which is more intelligible, and perhaps applies as strongly to the foregoing, as to any other piece of *galimatias* in such collections:

"J'ai pensé," says the writer, "que les grandes impressions que
l'on reçoit ici donneraient de grandes pensées; que la pureté,
la légèreté de l'air qu'on y respire les feroit rendre avec netteté;
par-suite j'ai donné en Juillet 1809 un registre au Montanvert,
pour que les Voyageurs y consignassent leurs reflexions:—Je m'en
repens. Ce que j'y ai lu,—ce que je lis ici, me désespère. On a du
bon sens quand on se détermine à voir la Vallée de Chamouni,
mais je vois qu'on le perd en y arrivant."

My guide was one of ten who a few weeks ago attended a
Polish count in an expedition to the summit of Mont Blanc. They
pitched their tent the first night in a sheltered spot about two
thirds of the way up; the second day they succeeded in reaching
the top, and rested again at night in the same spot; and the third
day they returned to Chamouni.

This was a mere excursion of pleasure and curiosity, unconnected
with scientific observation, which made great part of the object of
M. de Saussure's expedition in 1787. It was a short time before this,
that M. Paccard, the apothecary of Chamouni, and Jacques Balma
the Guide—ever afterwards called *Balma Montblanc*—went up
without any other companions, and had the glory of being the
first to explore the maiden snow of these uninhabited regions of
frost and silence, which had never been disturbed by the tread of
any living thing. M. de Saussure gives one caution to pedestrian
travellers, which may be found of use. He advises you, before you
enter upon a dangerous path, to familiarize your eye with the
precipice beneath; lest the sight of it should break upon the view
unexpectedly, and occasion a dizziness, that might be fatal. The
guides, on the contrary, always recommend you, when you are
passing the brink of a precipice, to turn your eyes away from it.
This may be the best rule, when it can be done; but sometimes the
precipice will obtrude itself upon you, whether you will or no, and
then it is certainly as well to be previously prepared for it.

14th
Returned to Geneva.—As the weather was fine, I had an
opportunity of seeing all that is to be seen between Chamouni

and St. Martin. Though the scenery is occasionally very grand, yet it cannot be compared with Lauterbrunn and Interlaken. Mont Blanc improves as one recedes from him. A mountain like a hero loses much from juxtaposition. I was disappointed in the impression he made upon me when I was face to face with him at Chamouni; but at the Torrentnoir, or on the bridge of St. Martin, he might—addressing me as the ghost of Banquo—say with Macbeth—"Why so—being gone I am myself again!"

15th

Arrived at Aix—a small town in Savoy. The hot springs are much celebrated for their effects in removing all chronic pains. The baths are well built, and the expense of bathing is very trifling. It is a sulphurated water so hot, that the thermometer stands at 110. The general mode of bathing is the douche, as it is called;—the water is made to fall from the height of some feet, and is conducted by a pipe, so as to play with considerable force upon the part affected. After being parboiled in this manner for twenty minutes, they wrap you up in a blanket, and carry you back to bed. The *douche* is very fatiguing. After a trial for ten days, the only effects it produced on me were nausea, headache, and general debility; so I resolved to change the scene.

26th

Drove to Chamberry;—passed the day in strolling with Rousseau's Confessions in my hand to *Les Charmettes*, the quiet retreat in which he lived with his *Maman*, Madame de Warens. His description of her person is one of the most animated pictures of grace and beauty that ever was penned; and her gentle and benevolent character is still more interesting than her beauty.

The house is situated in a valley surrounded by mountains; but scarcely a vestige remains of the garden, which he tells us he cultivated with his own hands.

27th.

I once more consigned myself to a voiturier to be conveyed to Lyons. The road across the mountains is romantic. This road is the work of Charles Emanuel, second Duke of Savoy, who has recorded his achievement in an inscription as—"*Romanis intentatum cæteris desperatum*"—but it has been thrown into the shade by the imperial road maker of the Simplon, who has here also cut his way in a straight line through the mountain by a subterraneous tunnel of many hundred yards long.

At *Pont-de-Beauvoisin* our baggage was strictly searched. The custom-house is in the habit of instituting a very rigorous examination on this frontier, for the ostensible purpose of preventing the introduction of Geneva goods, particularly watches and jewellery; but it is notorious that cases of watches are carried over the mountains by men on foot in large quantities; and the rate of insurance is so low, that it would lead one to suppose there must be a secret understanding between the custom-house and the smuggler.

The first impression of France is favourable, but as you approach Lyons, the country becomes more bleak and open.

28th

Arrived at Lyons before sun-set.—Lyons is the Manchester of France; filled with a manufacturing, money-getting tribe, who wear their hearts in their purses. The sight of an Englishman is wormwood to them; and well it may for we seem to be travelling fast towards surpassing them even in their own staple manufacture.

The first view of Lyons is grand; the Rhone and the Saone flow through it in parallel lines, and the broad-paved quays of the Rhone are magnificent.

First sight of French soldiery;—fine stout looking men; but their pale livery has a had effect.

29th

There are several interesting Roman antiquities in the neighbourhood of Lyons; and the aqueducts of Marc Anthony still remain on the mountain Fourvières.

At the Hotel de Ville are the celebrated bronze tablets which record a memorable speech of the Emperor Claudius.

Made a tour of the principal silk manufactories; and, without professing to be a very accurate judge, I thought not only their pocket-handerchiefs, but their silk stockings, very inferior to our own. The price of a handkerchief is five francs; a pair of silk stockings of the best quality costs twelve francs. In all their stuffs the inferiority of the French taste in the pattern is very conspicuous; at least it is generally what we should call staring, flaunting, and vulgar—but perhaps there is no disputing about taste in the patterns of silk.

Lyons seems to be full of Buonapartists. They received him with enthusiasm on his return from Elba; and yet one might have thought that the recollections of the reign of terror—of Collot d'Herbois, Fouché, and Châlier—would have given a bias to the Lyonese politics against this child and champion of the Revolution.

30th

Nothing can be more evident than the hostile feeling towards England and Englishmen, which manifests itself here on every occasion. Nor is it surprising, when we consider that the Lyonese regard us as the causes of the decline of their commerce; for the dulness of trade is as much the subject of complaint here as every where else, at the present moment; and the *odium mercatorium* is perhaps, next to the *odium theologicum*, one of the deadliest sources of enmity.

The Valets de Place pointed out with precision the spot where Hannibal crossed the Rhone; though Whittaker, who acts as moderator between Polybius and Livy, and occasionally sets them both right, would wish to make it quite clear that he crossed the river at Loriol in Dauphiny; and that he marched up the course of the Rhone, keeping the river on his left, all the way to Geneva.

The accounts I hear of the climate of this place dissuade me from thinking of passing the winter here. No place is more subject to sudden changes from heat to cold. There is also a great deal of rain, and the winter is cold and long. Besides, it is not pleasant to reside in a town where the public feeling is so hostile to you; and amongst a people who look daggers at you, though they may use none.

October 1st

The great hospital at Lyons is a noble establishment, and all the arrangements are calculated to promote the comfort of the patients. It is attended by the *Sœurs de la charité*, who officiate as nurses, with a kind spirit of benevolence that must be as beneficial to the minds as to the bodies of their patients.

One cannot look without respect and admiration at these devoted sisters of Christianity, whose profession of vows has been made with a view to enlarge rather than to contract the sphere of their utility.

None of the common objections to monastic institutions have any application to this order of nuns, which is founded on a practical imitation of the conduct of their Divine Master, who, according to the simple narrative of the Evangelist, "went about doing good."

2nd

While I was deliberating into what quarter of the world I should move, I stumbled on a voiturier, who was on the point of setting out for Montpellier. When you have no decided will of your own, the best way, I believe, is to commit yourself to the tide of events, and let them carry you *quocunque ferat tempestas.*—At least it was in this disposition of mind that I hurried back to my hotel to collect my packages,—and before I had time to consider whether I had done well or ill, I found myself at Vienne, where we slept. At this place, there are some relics of the Romans; and the people show you a house which they tell you belonged to Pontius Pilate, and in which they would have you believe that he died.

It was here that Pius VI. the late Pope, breathed his last, who confirmed by the misfortunes of his reign the presentiment to which his title had given rise; for the number six has always been considered at Rome as ominous.

Tarquinius *Sextus* was the very worst of the Tarquins, and his brutal conduct led to a revolution in the government; it was under Urban the sixth, that the great schism of the west broke out; and Alexander the *sixth* outdid in crime all that his predecessors amongst the Tarquins, or the Popes, had ventured to do before him. It was during his papacy, that the line was written, which in after times was applied to the election of his successor Pius VI.

Semper sub sextis perdita Roma fuit.

In Pius VI.'s life, "nothing became him like the leaving of it;" and he attracted more respect by the piety and resignation with which he bore the insults heaped upon him by the French during his captivity, than he could ever have commanded in the palace of the Vatican.

3rd

I should have embarked in the *Coche d'eau* at Lyons, and descended the Rhone to Avignon; but the pleasure of this scheme depends entirely upon the state of the wind. If this be adverse, as in the present case, you may be detained many days, and there is no certainty of arriving at any habitable inn to rest at night. The views of the river with the surrounding scenery have to-day been very pleasing; but it would be profanation to compare them with the lovely Wye, and "the dear blue hills of my own country."

The more I see of France, the less am I able to understand how it has gained the title of *La belle France*. The phrase cannot certainly refer to *picturesque* beauty, of which no country has less to boast. Perhaps this deficiency may in some measure account for the utter want of taste for the beauties of nature, in the English sense of that phrase, which is so remarkable a feature in the French character.

A Frenchman cannot understand the feeling that is delighted with the contemplation of picturesque beauty; it is as unintelligible to him, as the pleasure of music to a man who has no ear.

His *beau ideal* of landscape is that which produces the greatest quantity of corn, wine, and oil. He will indeed chatter about *les belles horreurs* of a Swiss scene; but the very terms he uses prove how incapable he is of communing with nature, and interpreting the language she speaks in the sublime scenes which she there addresses to the imagination.

4th

La belle France grows dirtier and dirtier. Sunday is no sabbath here. All the shops are open, and every thing goes on as usual. Even the butchers are at work, elbow-deep, in their horrid occupation. We halted in the middle of the day at the little town of Tain, near which are the vineyards so famous for their red and white Hermitage. This tract, however, cannot supply a tithe of the wine which is sold under that name. It is a small black grape, rough and unpleasant upon the palate. It would seem that all the good wine is exported, for the sample which was given me as the best was but ordinary stuff. The end of our day's journey brought us to Valence. It was at the military school of this place that Napoleon was educated, and he practised the first lessons of the art of war on the Champ de Mars of Valence.

There is a story current here, that, from want of means, he was reduced to the necessity of leaving his boarding-house without paying his *pension*.

5th.

As you advance towards the south, the country becomes richer, and begins to wear an Italian appearance.

Encountered a large troop of deserters. In England it requires three guards to prevent one deserter from running away. Here, fifty deserters are conducted by three *gens d'armes*, like so many beasts being driven to a fair. They were most of them mere boys, and apparently in great misery.

The military spirit seems to have evaporated; or the white flag has not the same fascination that the tri-coloured possessed. Under Napoleon, the military were every thing; and the only road to honour and power was through the profession of arms. The airs of consequence which the army assumed, and the tyranny which they exercised over all the rest of the world, to whom they applied the contemptuous appellation of pequins, were almost as intolerable as the old grievances of which the Roturiers complained against the Nobles.

This is no longer the case. The *prestige* of military glory received its death-blow at Waterloo; and the army feel now, that they no longer enjoy that paramount weight and consideration in public opinion, upon which their insolence was founded;

> Fortuna sævo læta negotio, et
> Ludum insolentem ludere pertinax,
>   Transmutat incertos honores—

Fame and honour are now to be gained by fighting the battles of the senate, towards which the public attention and public interest are almost exclusively directed.

I deviated from the road at Loriol, to examine the banks of the river at this point, where Whittaker would demonstrate that Hannibal passed with his army. He relies much upon a passage in Livy describing Hannibal's course after he had passed the river:

"*Postero die, profectus adversa ripa Rhodani, mediterranea Galliæ petit, non quia rectior ad Alpes via esset, sed, quantum a mari recessisset minus obvium fore Romanum credens, cum quo priusquam in Italiam ventum foret, non erat in animo manus conserere. Quartis castris, ad insulam pervenit; ibi Arar Rhodanusque amnes confluunt in unum.*"

So far so good.—Loriol would certainly be about four days' march from Lyons, where the Rhone and the Arar (now the Saone) unite, and where they once formed an island.

But, if the authourity of Livy is to be relied on, how shall we reconcile what he says afterwards, with the supposition of Hannibal's having marched up the Rhone to Lyons?—Livy says, that after leaving *this island*;—"*quum jam Alpes peteret, non recta regione iter instituit, sed ad lævam in Tricastinos flexit, unde per extremam oram Vocontiorum agri tetendit Tricorios, haud usquam impedita via priusquam ad Druentiam flumen pervenit.*" Now, the *Tricastini* were to the south of Loriol; and how he could have passed per extremam oram *Vocontiorum*, to arrive at the *Tricorii*, will puzzle any one who will examine the map. But the last is the greatest riddle of all; what could bring him to the *Druentia*, now *La Durance*? Again, if Livy be correct, Hannibal passed the river *in Volcarum agrum*, which can hardly be made to extend to Loriol. But I believe we must conclude, from reading Livy's account of this matter, which is throughout so inconsistent with itself, that he wrote it without his map of Gaul before him, or else, that our map of Gaul is very different from his.[1]

We halted at night at Montelimart.

6th

Near Montelimart was the *Chateau de Grignan*; where Madame de Sévigné fell a victim to maternal anxiety, and was buried in the family vault. The Chateau was destroyed during the fury of the Revolution, and the leaden coffins in the vaults presented too valuable a booty to be spared, by the brutal ruffians of those days. The body of Madame de Sévigné had been embalmed, and was found in a state of perfect preservation, richly dressed;—but no respect was paid to virtue even in the grave; every thing, even to the dress she wore, was pillaged and taken away; and the naked corpse left to mingle, as it might, with its native dust.

This unnatural war with the dead is one of the most revolting features of the French revolution. What must be the character of that people who could find gratification in rifling the sanctuary of the tomb; and who, carrying their enmity beyond the grave, could glut their brutal and cowardly revenge in offering insults to the defenceless remains of the most illustrious characters in the history of their country? No respect was paid to rank, or sex, or virtue; and this was not a solitary outrage, committed at a single place, but the general practice throughout France. A fellow passenger tells me that he saw the body of Laura, the mistress of

Petrarch, exposed to the most brutal indignities in the streets of Avignon. It had been embalmed, and was found in a mummy state, of a dark brown colour. It was the same every where; the best and the worst of the Bourbons—Henry IV.—and Louis XI. were exposed to equal indignities; nor could the deeds of Turenne himself protect his corpse from the profanation of these ferocious violators. All the cruelties committed upon the living, during the reign of blood and terror, will not stamp the French name with so indelible a stain, as these unmanly outrages upon the dead. The first may find some palliation, weak as it is, in the party rage, and political animosity, of an infuriated populace;—but what can be urged in extenuation of the last? It is worse than the fury of the beasts; for of the Lion at least we are told—that he "preys not upon carcasses." I blush, in venting my indignation against the French, at the recollection of the indignities that were offered in my own country, to the remains of Cromwell and of Blake, who were both taken from Westminster Abbey—the first, to be hanged at Tyburn and buried under the gallows—and the last, to be cast into a pit in St. Margaret's church; but I console myself with thinking, that this was done by the "express command" of the government of that day, in which the people had no share, and by which, I trust, our character as a nation cannot be affected.

We crossed the Rhone at the *Pont du St. Esprit*, which is 3000 feet long, being nearly three times the length of the bridge at Westminster. It is turned against the stream with a point like a bastion. From the road you command a view of the *Pont du Gard*, a splendid relic of Roman architecture, built to connect the ranges of an aqueduct which extends for seventeen miles;—fragments of which are still remaining in various parts of the hills.

The first entrance into Languedoc is not pre-possessing; as you travel to the south you find all the comforts of civilization decrease, and dirt and wretchedness flourish.—Slept at Bagnols.

7th

The kitchen of a village inn at Languedoc is enough to damp the strongest appetite. I wished for the pencil of Wilkie at

Remoulins, a little village where we breakfasted this morning. While the host, who played as many parts as Buskin in the farce, was killing the devoted fowl, his cat ran away with the sausages intended to garnish it. Poor Chanticleer was laid down to finish his death-song as he could, while the host pursued puss to her retreat, which was so well chosen, that a third of the sausages were gone before he discovered her. Puss however paid dearly for it in the end; for in endeavouring to make her escape under a door, the aperture was so small that her hinder legs and tail were left on the hither side of it, upon which mine host wreaked his vengeance, by stamping most unmercifully. At last we sat down to Grimalkin's leavings; and though the landlord had no "appliances and means" to help him, nor scarcely a stick of wood with which to make a fire, he did contrive, somehow or other, to furnish a very tolerable breakfast; and this seems to be the great merit of French cookery—that it can make something out of nothing. Molière observes that any body can dress a dinner with money and materials; and if a professed cook cannot do it without, his art is not worth a farthing.

This part of Languedoc may be very rich and productive, but nothing can be less pleasing to the eye, stone walls instead of hedges—no meadows—no cattle—and no trees, but the olive, which add little to the beauty of the landscape.

A poor Carmelite nun joined our party, who had been driven out of her convent in Spain by the French, and was now seeking an asylum.

The rigid austerities practised in her convent had not however extinguished entirely the vanity of her sex, some remains of which still lurked under her coarse black hood, breaking out in the delight with which she traced up the antiquity of her order, higher than all other monastic institutions, to Elijah, and mount Carmel.

Nismes, where we arrived in the evening, is full of Roman antiquities.[2] There is an amphitheatre in good preservation; and the *Maison Quarrée*, as it is called, is one of the most beautiful relics of ancient architecture that have come down to us. It has been supposed that this temple was built in the reign of Augustus; and Monsieur Seguier has contrived to decipher an inscription which contains the names of Marcus Agrippa, and his sons; but this inscription is not very satisfactorily made out; and those arguments seem to be the strongest, which, from a comparison of the minuteness and profusion of ornament of the *Maison Quarrée* with the more simple architecture of the Augustan age, would fix its date at a later period.

8th.

My first impression of the French character is, that it must be greatly changed from that gay and lively frivolity, of which we used to hear so much. My fellow-passengers are serious and reserved; each man seems to suspect his neighbour; and at the *Table d'Hôte*, where I have dined and supped during my route, the company could not have been more silent and sombre, if the scene had been laid in England during the month of November. There is a crest-fallen look about them, and they shake their heads and shrug their shoulders when they talk of the Congress, in gloomy apprehension of the future.

This seventh day's journey brought us to Montpellier; where, being heartily tired of the jumbling of the carriage, I was well disposed to make a halt.

1. Since writing the above, I have read an ingenious treatise, by M. de Luc of Geneva; who takes the text of Polybius for his guide, and gives very satisfactory reasons for setting Livy aside, wherever their authorities differ. M. de Luc makes Hannibal cross the Rhone lower down than Loriol, in the neighbourhood of Avignon. His four days' march then brings him to the *Isere*, at the point where it falls into the Rhone. This river, which in the different editions of Polybius is called *Iscar or Scoras*, by a corruption of the Latin text which puzzled the Commentators, has been converted by the editors of Livy, from *Bisarar*, into *Arar*. If, instead of three letters, they had been content with removing one, it would

leave left *Isarar*, which is very nearly its modern name. This then is the *Insula* at which Hannibal arrives; *viz.* that tract of country *insulated* on all sides but one, by the Rhone and the Isere. He then makes for the Alps, but not directly, on account of the mountains of *les Echelles* over which there was no road at that time. He turns therefore *ad lævam*; that is, instead of due east, he marches north-east round these mountains, until he comes to the *Druentia*, which is not the *Durance*, but the *Drance*. This river runs through Chamberry, and falls into the Rhone near Yenne—the ancient Ejanna. M. de Luc, whose reasoning is for the most part clear and convincing, conducts Hannibal from the Drance to the pass of the little St. Bernard, and so down the valley of Aoste to Ivrée. Here Hannibal is obliged to deviate from his direct road, in order to take Turin the capital of the ancient *Taurini*, whose alliance he had been unable to conciliate; after which he marches with all haste to encounter Scipio on the banks of the *Ticinus* now the Tesino; and there M. de Luc leaves him.

2. About twelve miles from Nismes is the Pont du Gard, one of the most perfect and magnificent Roman aqueducts remaining,—constructed to supply the city with pure water. (See Frontispiece.)

XIV

MONTPELLIER

October 9th

The situation of Montpellier is very fine; and the environs are pretty. The view from the *Place de Peyrou*, where from one spot you see the Mediterranean to the south, and on a fine day may command the Pyrenees to the west, and the Alps to the east, is superb. All the statues which once ornamented this place were destroyed during the iconoclastic fury of the revolution.

10th

Engaged a lodging in a clean protestant family on the *Boulevard de la Comedié*; and for two rooms am to pay sixty francs per month. I would rather have established myself in a *maison de pension*, but there is no such thing in Montpellier; so that one is forced to dine at a restaurateur's, which to an invalid in winter-time is a serious inconvenience.

There is a custom amongst the restaurateurs in this part of France, which to a resident is worth knowing. If you dine regularly at the same house, you may, by paying a certain sum in advance, have credit for one-fifth more than you have paid.

11th to 18th

A week of severe illness. It is difficult to conceive how Montpellier ever obtained a name for the salubrity of its climate. For pectoral complaints it is probably one of the worst in the world. It is true, there is almost always a clear blue sky; but the air is sharp and biting, and you are constantly assailed by the *bise*, or the *marin*—and it is difficult to say which of these two winds is the most annoying.

The one brings cold, and the other damp. The climates of Europe are but little understood in England, nor indeed is it an easy thing to ascertain the truth, with respect to climate. Travellers generally speak from the impression of a single season, and we all know how much seasons vary.

I believe that Pisa is the very best place on the continent during the winter for complaints of the chest; and Nice, of which I speak from good authority, is perhaps the very worst. The air of the first, which is situated in a low plain, is warm, mild, and muggy; that of the second is pure, keen, and piercing. The air of Montpellier is of this latter character;—it is as different from Pisa, as frisky cider from milk and water, and every mouthful of it irritates weak lungs, and sets them coughing. If there be any climate preferable to Pisa, it may perhaps be Rome; where the air is pure without being piercing; and, if one might illustrate it by a comparison with a liquor, I should compare it to cowslip wine.

19th

Nothing can be more dull than Montpellier is at present. There is nothing going on in the shape of amusement or instruction. It is vacation, and the lecture-rooms are shut. There is but little society; and the good people here, as if civil dudgeon were not enough to set folks together by the ears, have seasoned their dissensions with the *sauce piquante* of religious hatred—and are with difficulty restrained from cutting each other throats. While the present king lives, things may continue quiet; but the protestants seem to fear that, under his more orthodox brother, the tragedy of St. Bartholomew might be revived.

Nor do these fears seem to be wholly without foundation. The scenes that took place here and at Nismes, in 1815, after the second abdication of Napoleon, were dreadful. The triumph of a party in France is something more than a change of ministry; for the *re-action* that it produces amongst the inflammable inhabitants of the southern provinces is followed by proscriptions and massacres.

The party that is uppermost cannot be content without cutting the throats of their opponents. This they proceeded to do in 1815, but the king interposed to check the outrageous zeal of his ultra-adherents; and this is likely to happen again at any time, if, instead of endeavouring to be the common protector of all his people, the king, by the formation of an ultra-royalist ministry, were content to be the head of a faction.

The way in which the election of deputies for the department of Gard was conducted in the year 1815, shows the means by which the ruling party in this part of the world would wish to maintain its ascendency;—no less than thirteen protestant electors were assassinated in their way to the electoral college.

One is astonished by the amount of the population in the French towns; Nismes is said to contain forty thousand souls, and Montpellier five-and-thirty thousand; and you wonder where they can be stowed.

I am surprised to find at this place, which has been so long the resort of well-informed people, such a lamentable inattention to the most indispensable comforts and decencies of life. It would require the pen of Winifred Jenkins herself to describe some of the miserable expedients of *la belle France*!

Attended at the theatre, which was crowded to excess, to witness the drawing for the Conscription.

This law, which was held up as the great motive for resisting the tyranny of Napoleon, is nevertheless still continued by his successors.

The drawing was an amusing scene and truly French. The people assemble in a sort of amphitheatre. The *Préfet* presides. The names of all those of the prescribed age are called over; and every man of whatever rank, high or low, answers to his name, and draws his lot. If he is absent, the *Préfet* draws it for him. When any one drew a number above the complement required, thereby ensuring his own exemption, his antics of joy were in the highest degree comic; and when the number was within the complement, the exultation of the spectators, whose own prospects were thereby bettered, were expressed by the loudest applause, without any consideration for the feelings of the drawer. The present assessment is light enough, as may be collected from the price of a substitute, who may now be procured for 500 francs, whereas, in Napoleon's time, the price has been as high as 14,000 francs.

There needs but one law more—a property tax, which is a conscription of money, as the other is of men—the one operating on the purses, as the other does upon the persons of men—to complete a perfect system of despotism.

Wherever these two laws are thoroughly established, and the people trained to submit to them, the rights of personal security and private property are annihilated.

If governments would never raise more men or more money than the public interest required, both these laws are perhaps the best, because the simplest, the fairest, and the cheapest, in arriving at their object. But constituted as human nature is, none but an essentially popular government could be trusted with such a tremendous engine, which would place at its disposal every man, and every shilling that he has—in case of necessity;—a plea which was never yet wanting to justify any exercise of power.

Napoleon did in fact take away the whole population at one fell swoop, and there is no saying where a property tax might stop, on this side of ninety-nine per cent. For the principle of the tax once admitted, the *Sorites* argument would never be wanting, to furnish the minister of finance with a pretence for plucking out one more hair;

> Utor permisso, caudæque pilos ut equiæ
> Paullatim vello: et demo unum demo etiam unum;
> Dum cadat elusus retione ruentis acervi.

Still, however, there are so many arguments in favour of a property tax properly modified, that in a free government like England, where the people, through their representatives, exercise a control over the national expenditure, there seems but one condition wanting to make it the best, as it is unquestionably the fairest and cheapest mode of raising money, which is, that it should be the *only* tax. In this case, it might safely be trusted to the feelings of the representatives themselves, to take care that a tax, which came home so immediately to their own business and bosoms, was not unnecessarily increased

If this had been the system of raising the supplies in England during the last century, it may well be doubted whether such vast sums would have been expended;—sums which are easily voted, when it is proposed that they shall be raised by an increase of duty of a halfpenny upon this, and a penny on that article;—a proposal that is agreed to, as a matter of course, and nobody thinks it worth while to pause and consider from whose pocket the money is to come. If then all other taxes were abolished, the property tax might be hailed as a security for economy of expenditure, as it is in itself the least expensive of all taxes, in the collection. It has been calculated that a man already pays at least the half of his income, in some shape or other, to the support of government. If this be so, he would surely not fare the worse by paying the same sum openly as a 50 per cent duty upon property; which would then reach the exchequer without being subjected to the enormous deductions that are now made from it by all the various charges of collection.

This would then be the only shape in which the tax-gatherer would appear, and England might hope to become again, beyond all others, the land of cheapness and plenty.

But if the property tax be brought forward only when all other means fail; for there is a limit to indirect taxation—when two and two no longer make four—when increase of duty only produces decrease of consumption—if it be introduced as the *pincers*, to extract those sums which will not yield to the common *turn-screw* of taxation,—it must then be regarded as an additional weight to the already enormous burden, under the pressure of which the agriculture, the trade, and the prosperity of the country are now languishing.

It would not be one of the least advantages of such a system of taxation, that it would take away the arguments of those who, for their own purposes, seek to persuade the labouring classes that the principal part of the taxes, as at present imposed, is paid by them. These arguments, however, have manifestly no foundation; for no axiom of political economy seems more clear, than that the taxes upon the necessaries of life are not, in point of fact, paid by the labouring classes themselves; and that by increasing or diminishing the duty of any article of their necessary consumption, little more is done, as it regards them, than eventually to increase or diminish the rate of their wages. They do indeed feel all taxes, but it is remotely and in the same way that they would really feel the property tax;—namely, by the operation of that and every other tax upon capital, in abridging the means of employing them.

One of the conscripts behaved so riotously, that the gens d'armes took him into custody; but, as they were conducting him through the streets, his mother raised a mob in his favour, who, after a sharp struggle, succeeded in rescuing the prisoner from his keepers, and bore him off in triumph.

20th

While sitting at breakfast this morning, I saw my hero of yesterday with his mother, tied back to back in a cart, escorted by a large party of cavalry, who lodged them safely in the prison of the town.

Attended the drill of the recruits, which is constantly going on, as if France were preparing for an immediate campaign. The dishabille of the soldiers, especially of the cavalry, is very slovenly. The infantry march to the sound of the drum alone, for there are no fifers amongst them. The troops in this quarter are small, slight, and scraggy; and if I am not mistaken, there is more of muscle and sinew in one Englishman than in half a score of them. I speak only of the infantry for there is a great contrast between them and the cavalry, who seemed to be picked men. Went to the theatre for the first, and for the last time. The actors were worse than I ever saw in England.

21st to 28th

Confined to the house. Rambled through Buffon's *Discours sur la Nature des Animaux*—which is very ingenious and clever, excepting his blasphemy against love, of which he seems to have had a very low opinion. He seems to think that love and friendship cannot be identified, and felt for the same object. Did he judge from his experience of French women?

Buffon; with all his eloquence, is a remarkable instance of that national coarseness and grossness of feeling, which is so much the characteristic of the French. They are eminently deficient in sensibility, imagination, and enthusiasm; when they attempt to be sentimental, they do but talk it,—and cannot even *talk* it well. I doubt whether the *Pleasures of Imagination* could be made intelligible to them by any translation. Every man thinks he knows the meaning of sentiment;—and yet, it is a difficult word to define; without determining its application; but I believe it is commonly used in opposition to mere animal sense, which is all that the French word *sentiment* often signifies. For instance, the sentiment of love, in our use of the word, is something very different from the animal sense, which may be perhaps the foundation of the passion between the sexes. It is sense refined and exalted, through the influence of mind, by purer thoughts, and higher considerations; which, while they strip the passion of its grossness, increase its intensity and energy, and by expanding its views, convert the transitory enjoyment of animal desire into a feeling as durable and lasting as the mind itself.

But, let us hear Buffon on this subject. "Amour! Désir inné! Ame de la Nature!—Source féconde de tout plaisir, de toute volupté, pourquoi fais-tu l'état heureux de tous les êtres, et le malheur de l'homme?

"C'est qu'il n'y a que la physique de cette passion qui soit bon; c'est que, malgré ce que peuvent dire les gens épris, le moral n'en vaut rien.—Les animaux, guidés par le sentiment seul—leurs désirs sont toujours proportionnés à la puissance de jouir; ils sentent autant qu'ils jouissent, et ils ne jouissent qu'autant qu'ils sentent.

"L'homme, au contraire, en voulant inventer des plaisirs, n'a fait que gâter la Nature.——

"Tout ce qu'il y a de bon dans l'amour appartient donc aux animaux tout aussi bien qu'à nous."

Who but a *Frenchman* could have written thus? But a Frenchman cannot rise out of the mire of sensuality; and their literature is full of sneers and ridicule of that enthusiasm of heart, and elevation of soul, which seek to improve our nature,

And lift from earth our low desire.

29th

Inspection of soldiers, and grand field-day. Nothing can be less showy than the appearance of the infantry. They have no feathers or tufts in their caps, nor fifers in their band. In going through the manual exercise, the French seem to be much quicker than any soldiers I have seen. For instance—present arms—and—order arms—are performed at two motions; which in our own drill, I believe, employ three distinct acts.

The soldiers are as rapid in executing manœuvres, as in going through the exercise. But the word of command is much more noisy than with us; and it is repeated and vociferated by the officers, from the colonel downwards, so as to resemble the hallooing of cattle-drivers.

30th

Crawled round the botanical garden;—the pleasantest promenade in Montpellier. It was here that Young, the poet, buried his daughter. The longer I stay at Montpellier, the less I like it. The inhabitants are characterised in the proverbs of their own country. Pound seven Jews in a mortar, says one of these, and the juice will make one Montpelliard.—Proverbs must always be understood with some grains of allowance; though they have generally a foundation in truth. But, it would be unfair to judge of Montpellier during the vacation. It is a celebrated school of medicine; and the lectures, in that liberal spirit which distinguishes the public institutions of this country—and I am glad of an opportunity of speaking in favour of France—are open to all that choose to attend, without any expense.

31st

Stumbled, "in the course of my reading," upon an account of the taking of the Bastile, in which there is an attempt to clear up the mystery of the man in the iron mask. It is stated that a paper was found, recording the arrival of *Fouquet* in the Bastile from the island of St. Marguerite, in an iron mask.

This suggestion receives some corroboration from the history of Fouquet's disgrace and punishment; in which there are such remarkable coincidences with the history of the Iron Mask, that I am surprised Voltaire, who, in his Age of Louis XIV., relates Fouquet's fall immediately after his account of the mysterious prisoner, was not struck with them. For, he tells us that Fouquet was sent to the Isle of St. Marguerite, and that the Iron Mask was brought *from* the Isle of St. Marguerite; and, in concluding Fouquet's history, he adds this remarkable circumstance,—that while the smallest action of his life was celebrated with the most minute detail, nobody knew when or where he died.

Voltaire is unable to explain, and indeed there is something unaccountable, in the mystery and precaution which were thought necessary in the arrest and detention of Fouquet. The same reasons, what ever they were, might have suggested the continued concealment of his person in the iron mask, which has given rise to so much speculation.

Fouquet was arrested in 1661,—the precise date of the Iron Mask's arrival in the Island of St. Marguerite. We know that, after an imprisonment of twenty-nine years, the Iron Mask was remove from St. Marguerite, by the keeper of the prison in that island, to the Bastile, upon his appointment to the governorship of that fortress. Now, Voltaire tells us, that though nothing certain was known with respect to Fouquet's end, yet there was a notion amongst his friends, that he had quitted the Island of St. Marguerite before his death.

These are remarkable coincidences; nor is there any thing in Fouquet's age to make the identity of these two persons impossible. The removal of the Iron Mask to the Bastile took place in 1690, and he died in 1703, after a captivity of forty-two years. Fouquet was born in 1615, and was Intendant General of the Finances in 1643, at the age of twenty-eight. In 1661, the date of his arrest, he was forty-six, and forty-two years of captivity will make him eighty-eight at the time of his death;—that is, if he were indeed the Iron Mask who died in 1703.

November 1st to 8th
A week of confinement. Rambled through Voltaire, Bayle, and Rousseau. Rousseau's "Confession of a Savoyard Curate," though written, as it would seem, to invalidate the authority of Christianity, leaves behind an impression in its favour, stronger perhaps than is produced by most works written purposely to defend it.

And indeed, Bishop Porteus has not disdained to quote it from the pulpit, to advocate the cause of religion. It is one of the most splendid specimens of eloquence extant in any language, and the whole tone of the sentiments illustrates a passage in one of Voltaire's letters to Hume. "You are mistaken," says he, "in Rousseau; he has a hankering after the Bible,—and is little better than a Christian after a fashion of his own."

After all, what is there that can be urged against Christianity, which may not be directed with equal force against Deism? The doubts of the Atheist, considered as a question of abstract reasoning, can only perhaps be answered,—as Berkeley's reasoning against the existence of the material world was answered—by boldly begging the question at issue, and resolving the cause of our belief into an original principle of our constitution. For the existence of an infinite First Cause can never be made a matter of demonstration. The *physical* proof, derived from the order and arrangement of the universe, is manifestly inconclusive. The intelligence of the work may prove an intelligent contriver:— but it cannot *therefore* follow, that the contriver is Eternal—

Almighty—Infinite—all, in a word, that we include under the sacred name. Again, the *metaphysical* proof, as it is called, which, from the consciousness of our own existence, would trace it up to some necessarily existing first cause, is not a jot more satisfactory. The sum and substance of the whole argument amounts to this. I exist—therefore something exists. If something exists—something must have existed from all eternity; for "*Nothing can come of nothing*;"—and this something is the first cause, of which we are in search. But the axiom on which this argument is founded, *ex nihilo nihil fit*, will cut both ways; and it is perhaps more incomprehensible to human faculties to conceive an uncaused first cause, than to meet the difficulty in the first stage;—and consider the world itself as uncaused and eternal. The Atheist indeed neither affirms nor denies; but suggests that the existence of a Deity is an arbitrary hypothesis, to account for the phenomena of the universe. Can the Deist confute him by argument? Must he not at last be brought to acknowledge that his own belief is founded upon *faith*?—and the speculative Atheist will probably not deny that it is a faith, which we all feel impelled, by the very constitution of our nature, to admit intuitively, as soon as we can comprehend the terms of the proposition;—for Atheism is a doctrine which, however the head may be amused with its subtleties, the heart rejects. But does the faith of the Deist go far enough? Will Deism satisfy the head, or administer consolation to the heart? Is it not a cold and comfortless creed, alike unsatisfactory to both?—unless indeed we could return again to Paradise. Adam might have been a Deist, and contentedly a deist; but fallen man has need of something more. The world is no longer a happy garden. Evil assaults us on every side; and we need not look farther than our own hearts, for evidence of the continued existence of that rebellious opposition to sense of duty, which we are taught was the cause of its introduction into the world. But be the cause what it might—the existence of evil, in every appalling form, cannot be denied; here it is; and how will the Deist reconcile these phenomena with his abstract ideas of a Deity, without having recourse to the Revelation that he denies?—which not only explains the fearful mystery of our present situation, but at the same time points out the remedy; and furnishes us with assurances, which unassisted reason could never have suggested, by which we are enabled to look forward with faith and hope to a better state of existence hereafter.

9th
Left Montpellier in the diligence at night; and arrived at Beziers to breakfast next morning.

The French diligences have been very much improved of late years, but there is still room for further progress. The carrying six inside, which is the usual complement, is detestable. The conducteur, answering to our *guard*, rides in the cabriolet; while the vehicle is driven by a postillion, who manœuvres his five horses, which are marshalled two at wheel and three leaders abreast, with admirable dexterity, riding on the near side wheel-horse. The horses seem to be trained with great care, and obey the word of command like a troop of soldiers.

In Italy and France, the voice is much more used than the whip, in the government of horses; indeed it is, I believe, with beasts as with men,—mild treatment will often reclaim tempers that kicks and blows would only tend to make more brutal and vicious.

My companions in the diligence were all on the *qui vive*, for the carriage had been stopped and robbed two evenings before, by a single footpad. This fellow had practised a most ingenious stratagem to effect his purpose. He manufactured ten men of straw, and drew them up in the road in battle array;—then, having taken his post a little in advance, he ordered the diligence to stop; threatening, if the least resistance was offered, to call up his companions, and put all the passengers to death. In this manner he laid the whole party under contribution, amongst whom were two Spanish merchants, whose purses were heavily laden.

10th

Beziers is situated on a commanding eminence, from whence there is a beautiful view of the river Orbe, and a rich and cultivated valley, for many miles. Its situation would have tempted me to make some stay, but the streets were so dirty, and the appearance of the people so miserable, that I despaired of finding a decent residence.

There is a *coche d'eau*, which goes every day from Beziers at twelve o'clock, by the famous canal of Languedoc, to Toulouse. Finding that this passage-boat would be four days in making the voyage, as the weather was very bad, I decided to continue in the diligence. In fine weather the boat offers a pleasant and most economical mode of traversing this country. The fare of each day's passage is 30 sous, and the universal price throughout France, regulated by law, for supper at the table d'hôte and lodging, is three francs and a half; though an Englishman is generally charged as much again; but if he travels by a public conveyance, he *need* never pay more than the above named sum.

This canal was the work of Paul Riquet under the auspices of Louis XIV., and has been of more use to France than all his victories, and a more splendid monument of his glory than all his plaything waterworks at Versailles. It connects the Atlantic and the Mediterranean; near this town it is carried through a mountain by means of a tunnel, which, however common now, was an extraordinary enterprise then. In some places it is conveyed by aqueducts over bridges, under which other rivers pursue their course.

In order to secure a supply of water in dry seasons a basin has been constructed at Ferreol, which is perhaps the most extraordinary part of the whole undertaking. This immense reservoir, built of granite, is an English mile in length, and about half that distance in breadth, and contains an area of 595 acres—collecting the waters of the various springs that rise in the Black Mountain.

The road from Beziers offers little worthy of observation. Languedoc is very different in reality from the charming pictures which Mrs. Radcliffe has drawn of it in her "Mysteries of Udolpho."

The people have a miserable look, denoting poverty and wretchedness. Shoes and stockings are very generally dispensed with; or if shoes are worn, it is the wooden *sabot*, which is a sad clumsy contrivance.

Manure seems an article in great request in this province. Boys run after the diligence for a mile after changing horses, to catch the first fruits of exercise upon a full stomach; and I observed that a handful of this precious commodity was a common stake set between two lads in playing at quoits.

The country improves as you approach Toulouse; a neatly painted cottage occasionally meets the eye, and something like an attention to comfort is observable. After two nights and two days in the diligence, we arrived at Toulouse. I remember the time when the very idea of two days and two nights in a stage-coach, carrying six inside and full all the way, would have made me ill. But, travelling "brings us acquainted with strange bedfellows," and is the best receipt I know for curing a fine gentleman.

XV

TOULOUSE

The first impression of Toulouse is favourable, though it has a deserted appearance. It has lost much of its consequence by the Revolution, which has swept away its Parliament; grass now grows in some of the streets; and the population, which was formerly as high as 80,000, is now not computed at more than 55,000. It is built of brick, and this gives it a warmer look than the cold white stone of Montpellier. The bold line of the Pyrenees forms a noble background to the view from the bridge, which is one of the chief ornaments of the town; the Garonne being here above 800 feet wide

Established myself in a pleasant lodging in the *Rue des Cordeliers*, looking due south into a large garden. Two rooms—30 francs per month.

13th

Explored the town. In the great square is the capitol, containing the apartments in which the estates-general of Languedoc used to hold their sessions. There are two public libraries, one or other of which is open to the public every day, containing large and valuable collections of ancient and modern books in all languages, with every accommodation for reading. At Toulouse there is an University containing at least 1500 students, and there are daily lectures in chemistry, botany, and all branches of natural philosophy; and these, like the libraries, are thrown open to all who have an inclination to benefit by them *gratis*.

These are resources which make Toulouse a more agreeable residence than most provincial towns; but, a provincial town is bad at best. If one must live in a town, it should be in a capital;—provincial politics and parish scandal are intolerably tiresome.

The promenades here are extensive and pretty; though the beauty of these is sadly defiled by the abominably filthy habits of the people. But this is the case throughout France; the streets and the public walks are scarcely passable, owing to the disgraceful and disgusting practices of a people, who set themselves up as models of politeness and *bienséance*.

14th to 18th

Rain. My neighbour in my lodging-house is a fine old veteran of seventy-two, whose history would furnish the materials for a novel. He tells me he was present at the execution of poor Calas, in the square of St. George in this town.

The successful efforts of Voltaire to establish his innocence, and to save his family from sharing his fate, have given notoriety to the tragic history of this venerable victim of bigotry and injustice, who, at the age of 65, was condemned to be broken alive on the wheel, for the supposed murder of his son, without a shadow of proof. It was urged against him, that he had conspired with the rest of his family to put his son to death, to prevent him from becoming a convert from the protestant to the catholic religion, as one of his brothers had become before him. The, truth seems to have been, that the son, who was of a melancholy temperament, had hanged himself.

Poor Calas supported the agonies of his punishment, which lasted two hours, with the most patient resignation; and while he calmly protested his own innocence, spoke with charity and forgiveness of his judges.

Nor were the blows of the executioner all that he had to endure during these two dreadful hours; for he was also subjected to the mental racking of a catholic priest, who was torturing him with exhortations to confess his guilt.

At last the signal was given to the executioner to inflict the *coup de grace*; when the priest himself, convinced by the calm and steady denial of the dying father, addressed the surrounding populace in the following words, which seem to have been riveted in the memory of my old friend—"*Voilà l'ame du juste qui s'envole.*"

19th

Went over the scene of the battle of Toulouse. Soult's position seems to have been admirably chosen, and as strong as nature and art could make it. The difficulty of ascertaining the truth upon any one point makes one doubt of all the details of history. The French, with their usual hardihood of assertion, would fain persuade you that the Duke of Wellington was informed of the events that had happened at Paris when he attacked Soult's position, and fought the battle of Toulouse; but that he was anxious to gather one more wreath of laurel. Napoleon abdicated on the 4th of April, and the battle of Toulouse was fought on the 10th. It has however been clearly proved in this case, that the officers despatched from Paris to inform the Duke of Wellington of the revolution in the government were arrested and detained at Montauban by Bouvier Dumoulart, Prefect of the district; and they did not reach the Duke till the evening of the 12th;—and hence this fruitless effusion of blood six days after the abdication of Napoleon, which in fact put an end to the war.

20th

I find I have committed a great mistake in coming to Toulouse. I ought to have returned to Italy from Chamberry; for I see that a winter in France will be intolerable, after dear delightful Italy; but it is now too late to correct this error—and so I must e'en make the best of it. The English are regarded here with an evil eye, and it is not surprising that there should exist a soreness of spirit in this quarter, where the national vanity received so bitter an humiliation. I have heard my old neighbour describe the horror, indignation, astonishment, and shame, that he felt, on seeing an army of Englishmen profaning *"the sacred territory,"* and marching into Toulouse *en maîtres*; though history might have furnished him with sufficient examples of similar invasions to diminish his surprise;—and even here, our Wellington was pursuing the very track which our Black Prince had traversed as a conqueror before him. But a Frenchman reads no history that does not furnish gratification to his national vanity; and to talk to him of any thing anterior to the reign of Louis XIV. is to talk of what he knows as little, as of what happened before the Deluge.

Though the French cannot forget or forgive the battle of Toulouse, yet they speak in terms of the highest of the good conduct of individuals, and with admiration of the discipline of the army. It seems, that they had been so accustomed to associate war with plunder and contribution, that the good old-fashioned mode which the English have never forsaken, of softening as much as possible the evils of war by paying for the supplies they demanded, struck them as something new and unheard of;—though I doubt whether this admiration be not generally accompanied with a suspicion of the motive, or a sneer at the folly of such conduct. "Few people," says Fielding, "think better of others than of themselves, nor do they really allow the existence of any virtue of which they perceive, no traces in their own minds; for which reason, it is next to impossible to persuade a rogue that you are an honest man; nor would you ever succeed by the strongest evidence, was it not for the comfortable conclusion which the rogue draws, that he who proves himself honest proves himself a fool at the same time." And yet the French ought to have learned, if nations could learn any thing from experience—that honesty, in the end, is the best policy; and that the policy of wisdom is, after all, the policy of virtue.

21st

Napoleon is not in the south of France the idol of that blind adoration which the Italians still pay him. His character seems here to be very correctly appreciated, and every body is fully aware of the enormous evils which he inflicted upon France by his return from Elba. The king is denounced by the ultra-royalists as a Jacobin; but the Jacobins do not recognise him as a true brother; still, I believe, he has the great mass of the people on his side. United with the *Charte*, he will always have the majority with him; but then he must not use the *Charte* like an umbrella, which is only brought out in foul weather, to ward off the pelting storm; for the people consider it equally necessary as a parasol, to shelter them in fair weather from the scorching rays of royalty. If the king have not a greater majority now, it is because there are some who see, or fancy they see, in the first acts of his reign, a disposition to establish principles, tending to invalidate the very existence of the compact between king and people which they were certainly justified in believing had been solemnly accepted as the terms of his restoration. Thus, his dating his reign from the death of Louis XVII., his abandonment of the national colour which he had himself worn as Monsieur in 1789, and his second restoration at the point of foreign bayonets, have raised a spirit against him which nothing but time, and the most prudent conduct on his part, can soften.

Mr. Fox has pronounced, that of all revolutions a restoration is the worst. Generally speaking it must be so; for the restored family, bred up in ancient prejudices, can seldom forget the power which they once enjoyed; and the people will be for ever suspecting them of forming designs to recover it, whether they have such intentions or not. This want of good understanding between king and people must be greatly increased, when, as in France, the restoration has taken place by foreign interference; and when the people must feel that they have sinned beyond the bounds of forgiveness. It is indeed impossible, that there should be a cordial union between *revolutionized* France, and the *legitimate* claims of the Bourbons. Who can expect that the King, or the Comte d'Artois, should divest themselves of all fraternal feelings; or who can be surprised that the Duchess d'Angoulême should shudder with horror at the sight of the murderers of her father, and at the recollection of the sufferings of her brother and herself? On the other side, it is equally natural that the French people, according to the maxim which lays it down that we never forgive those whom we have injured, should entertain a strong prejudice against the Bourbon family. The leading feature in the national character is vanity;—now their national vanity has been humbled in the dust, and this humiliation is, unfortunately for the Bourbons, inseparably connected with their restoration. The feeling against them was so strong on their second restoration, that proposals, it is said, were made to the Allies, offering rather to receive the King of Saxony, or the Prince of Orange, or any other King that the Allies would have vouchsafed to give them.

The throne of the Bourbons seems then to be placed upon a barrel of gunpowder; nothing but consummate prudence can reconcile the people to their sway, and prevent a fatal explosion.

It is a common notion, and the enemies of the Bourbons are at the greatest pains to strengthen it, that the Comte d'Artois disapproves entirely of the system of the King; and that he is determined to restore the ancient regime in church and state, and to be *aut Cæsar aut nullus*. It matters little whether this be true, or not; the effect is the same if the people can be persuaded to believe it. Accordingly, you hear a revolution talked of as a thing of course at the death of the King; and there is no saying what might happen if he were to die immediately. But if he should continue to live a few years, the system which he has commenced will so have established itself; and the people will be so sensible of the advantages which they have obtained from the Charte that the future king, be he who or what he may, will be compelled to pursue the same course, and will be without the power, whatever his inclination may be, to disturb the order of the machine of government, or endanger the tranquillity of the nation.

22nd

Attended the church of the French Protestants. Heard a most excellent sermon, on the text "*Je laverai mes mains dans l'innocence, et je m'approcherai à ton autel, o Eternel.*" The service consisted of a lesson from the Old Testament, a few prayers, a good deal of psalmody, and a sermon which was preached *memoriter*. But in the prayers, and the sermon, there was a little too much onction for my taste. The priest pitched his voice in a recitative key, which must become tiresome in a long service.

The congregation was numerous; each person had a chair; and there was no kneeling down. The church was cold, and the men wore their hats without ceremony.

23d

I am pleased to hear, in attending the lectures in chemistry and experimental philosophy, the constant mention of English names, and English improvements, and discoveries, with the highest eulogiums upon those of our countrymen, from Newton downwards, who have advanced the progress of knowledge. In the library to-day I discovered an Æschylus and Euripides, which had belonged to Racine, with marginal notes in his own handwriting; but the notes were rather curious than valuable.

In the evening to the theatre; which is newly built and very handsome. *Le parti de Chasse de Henri IV.* was well acted. The air of Vive Henri Quatre, which was introduced in the supper scene, was very feebly applauded.

24th to 30th

Confined at home by severe indisposition.—Amused myself with La Fontaine. Charming style;—"He seems to produce without labour, what no labour could improve." This facility of production is essential to poetry, and perhaps gave rise to the maxim *Poeta nascilur*; for if there be any appearance of effort or labour—if the numbers come from the brains like bird-lime from frieze—the whole charm is destroyed. Poetry has been well defined to be

> Thoughts that *voluntary* move
> Harmonious numbers.

This definition is well enough as far as it goes; but to thoughts should also perhaps he added feelings, for brains alone *without heart* will never make a poet. For example, Pope, with all the requisite qualities of mind, wanted the deep and fervid feelings which are necessary to the perfection of the poetical character; without which, the poet can never ascend the brightest heaven of invention. The character of his poetry may be well illustrated by one of his own lines. It

> Plays round the head but comes not near the heart.

He delights us by the fertility of his fancy, the elegance of his imagination, the point and playfulness of his wit, the keen discrimination of his satire, and the moral good sense of his reasoning; but he is seldom pathetic, and never sublime. If Eloisa to Abelard be an exception to this observation, it is a solitary one—and *exceptio probat regulam*; and even in that poem the sentiment seems rather to be adopted, than to be the genuine offspring of the poet's heart.

What that soul of feeling is, that poetical verve, by which alone the poet can rise to sublimity, and which Pope wanted, will be understood at once, by comparing his ode on music with Dryden's divine effusion on the same subject.

His merit even in versification seems to have been over-rated. Pope may perhaps be said to have done for verses, what Arkwright did for stockings, by the invention of a sort of mechanical process in their composition. His couplets are as regular, as if they had been made with the unerring precision of a spinning jenny;— and, indeed, in speaking of his own talent, he himself makes use of a similar illustration;

> If every wheel of that unwearied mill
> That turn'd ten thousand verses now stand still!

The effect of this has been to supersede the necessity of much skill in the individual workman; and accordingly, we see every day how easy it is to imitate the versification of Pope—for the mechanism was too simple to elude discovery; but where shall we look for the freedom and variety of Dryden?

But to return to La Fontaine;—what can be more affecting than his tale of the "*Two Pigeons*"? It breathes the very soul of tenderness; and there are throughout his writings touches of pathos and sensibility that will rarely be found in French poetry. What *heart* there is in the lines beginning with

> Qu'un ami véritable est me douce chose!

And his love of rural retreat is expressed with almost the force and feeling of Cowper:—

> Solitude où je trouve une douceur secrète
> Lieux que j'aimai toujours, ne pourrai-je jamais
> Loin du monde et du bruit, gouter l'ombre et le frais?
> Oh! qui m'arrêtera dans vos sombres asiles? &c. &c.

December 1st

Now that the Congress has broken up, and the Allied troops are withdrawn, the attention of all parties is directed to the meeting of the Chambers. The Upper Chamber consists of 150 Peers; the Chamber of Deputies of 250 Representatives, one-fifth of which is dissolved every year. The qualification for a deputy is the payment of direct taxes to the amount of 1,000 francs per annum; and it is also required that he should be 40 years of age. The qualification of an elector is the annual payment of taxes to the amount of 300 francs, and the full age of 30 years. And yet this is the new law of elections which the *ultra* royalists have denounced as being too democratical!

The chamber, which was dissolved by the king in 1815 for its ultra royalism, had been elected under the imperial system of electoral colleges;—the people electing in the first instance the electors, and the electors then nominating the representatives. The abuses which had crept into this system so utterly unfitted for its purpose—for it seems absolutely essential to a popular assembly that it should emanate immediately from the people—threw the whole power of election into the hands of the government; but it is to this system that the *Ultras* wish to return, for the result of the late elections has been very much in favour of the liberal party. That this should have been the case is sufficiently extraordinary, if we consider the very limited number of the whole body of electors in France, which is said not to exceed 100,000;—a number so small, that it might be supposed—from the experience of what happens in England where the right of suffrage extends so much more widely—the influence of power and patronage would have been brought to bear against it with overpowering success. Though the popular spirit of the electors may be partly explained from the infancy of their institutions, which corruption has scarcely yet had time to contaminate; yet perhaps the real secret of their conduct may be found in their mode of voting by *ballot.* It is true that where the voting is secret, bribery may continue to be carried on, to a certain extent, by the reliance which will always be placed in the performance of promises; but the more pernicious influence of *intimidation* is effectually annihilated. It is this voting by ballot, indeed, which is the only saving virtue in the French law of elections, and to which they ought to cling as the sheet anchor of their liberties; for, without this, a system which vests the right of electing deputies for a nation of thirty millions in so small a body as 100,000 electors, can afford no security for a real representation of the people.

The other objects of contention between the *Ultras* and the *Libbéraux* are the laws of recruiting, public instruction, and the appointment of mayors.

The law of recruiting has been passed to continue the conscription; but it must be confessed that it is no longer the same terrible warrant of death and destruction which formerly bore that name. On the restoration of the king an attempt was made, but made in vain, to fill up the ranks of the army by voluntary enlistment. It was decided that France must have an army, and the present law was passed. This law subjects all the male population, who shall have attained their twentieth year, to the operation of the conscription. But it limits the period of their service to five years, when they have a right to their discharge;

and it throws open to the lowest ranks the hope of advancement. The *equality* of this law, in the obligation to serve and the right to promotion, is very distasteful to the Ultras, who can think only of the glorious privileges which the Nobles enjoyed in the army of the ancient regime.

With respect to public instruction, the Ultras wish to return to the old system of *Frères Chrètiens*; while the *Libéraux* patronise the *Enseignement mutuel*, or system of Bell and Lancaster.

The crown at present appoints the Mayors. The Libéraux would wish to introduce the *système municipal*, by which the people would elect their own Mayors.

There is a very general cry also against the extravagant emoluments of the *Préfets*, who are the creation of the Consular government. This officer is the head of his department, and is in himself what the Lord Lieutenant and the Sheriff are in our counties. The *Préfets* were of great use to Buonaparte in oiling the wheels of despotism, and their salaries were in proportion to their utility. The Prefecture of Toulouse is said to be worth 40,000 francs per annum.

Went in the evening to the theatre. The play was *Turcaret*, an admired comedy of Le Sage;—but it is a comedy of the old school, and the bags and swords of the ancient *bon-ton* will not make the modern *canaille* of the theatre look like gentlemen. I am surprised to see the waiting-maids in the French comedy as well or perhaps better dressed than their mistresses. "This is o'erdoing termagant."

2nd

Went over *L'école royale de Toulouse*. The establishment consists of the *Proviseur*, who is the *Chef de la Maison*; the *Censeur*, who is second in authority; eleven professors of Latin; three of mathematics; one of Latin and French literature; one of natural history; one of natural and experimental philosophy; one of history; and seven *Maîtres d'étude* or assistant masters. *L'Aumonier*, with a long train of assistants, tradesmen, and servants, from the surgeon to the shoeblack—complete the establishment.

The whole number of *élèves* is 400. Those within the walls amount to 160. The terms of the school are 650 francs per annum—about 27*l*. For this the boy is lodged and fed in sickness and in health, clothed, and instructed in all that the above-named professors can teach him. The dress is a uniform of dark blue. Each boy has a small bed-cell to himself by night; and a desk in the school-room by day Their breakfast is bread and water; dinner—bread, soup, meat, and wine—supper—bread, cold meat, and wine—bread always *à discretion*.

Nine hours per day are devoted to application. There are two months of vacation—September and October. With the exception of this vacation, the boys are kept under lock and key during the whole year within the walls of the college, beyond which they cannot stir without express permission. Their play-ground is within the walls, and to break these bounds without leave would be punished by expulsion. The internal discipline is conducted without having recourse to that brutal and degrading punishment, which, to the common disgrace of those that inflict and those who receive it, is still practised upon lads of all ages in the public schools of England There is a sense of self-respect in every rational being, that revolts at the insult of being subjected to blows; and this sense is recognised and encouraged in the French schools, where no sort of corporal punishment is allowed; nor do I believe it is ever necessary—except perhaps in early childhood, before the rational faculty has began to develop itself. But blows present so easy a mode of carrying on the business of school-government, that it is not wonderful schoolmasters should be desirous to retain their birchen sceptre, in defiance of decency and common sense. But it is surprising, when the systems of Pestalozzi and others have been explained to all Europe, that the public opinion of England should not have operated some change in this, as well as in some other particulars of school government.

The common means in the hands of the Professors of Toulouse for maintaining order are impositions of tasks; *pain-sec*, i.e. bread and water; and *pénitence*, which is confinement to the school-room under the *surveillance* of a *Maître d'Etude*. Solitary imprisonment, the heaviest of their punishments, cannot he inflicted without the sanction of the *Proviseur*, or the *Censeur*. Some disorders have lately broken out in many of the French schools, but these seem to have arisen from temporary causes. Party-spirit, which has so convulsed the political world, has not been entirely shut out of schools; where Bourbon and Buonaparte have been words of discord, and the question *Qui vive?* has given rise to many a juvenile battle. Dame Religion too, who is seldom idle when discord is abroad, has not been without her share in these disturbances, some of which have originated in the jealousies between Catholic and Protestant.

3rd.

Toulouse is the land of cheap living, and all sorts of provisions are excellent of their kind. Bread is at two-pence a pound;—wine, that is, the *vin du pays*, of very good quality, four-pence a bottle; —meat from two-pence to three-pence. The poultry is very fine; you may buy a good turkey for 3s. 6d;—a capon for 1s. 9d;—a fowl for a shilling;—and a goose for 2s. 6d. Servants' wages are also very low;—I hire the attendance of a female servant to officiate as bed-maker, at half-a-crown per month. They have a custom here of fostering a liver complaint in their geese, which encourages its growth to the enormous weight of some pounds; and this diseased viscus is considered a great delicacy. You get an excellent dinner at the table d'hôte of either of the hotels, of two courses, dessert and wine, *à discretion*, for 2s. 6d. I have established myself *en pension* with a family next door; where I have my breakfast, dinner, wine, café, and *liqueur*, for 80 francs a month.

In comparing French and English cookery, I think the balance is greatly in favour of the former. We may beat them in a few dishes, but they excel us in fifty. We have the advantage in soup—though they are fond of saying that our soups are nothing but hot water and pepper; and we beat them in fish, because most fish cannot be dressed too simply. But they have an infinity of good things; and if happiness consisted in good-eating, I should recommend a man to live in France. It is quite a mistake to suppose that roast beef is confined to Old England, though the French do not present it in such enormous masses as we do. Nor indeed is there any great treat in sitting down to a huge limb hacked off its parent carcass, with an intimation, that "You see your dinner;"—always excepting however a haunch of venison, or a round of corned beef, which are two of those precious *morceaux* peculiar to England that constitute a dinner in themselves.

When you laugh at a Frenchman for eating frogs, he retaliates upon you for breakfasting upon warm water and sugar. Nothing can be more incorrect than to suppose that the French live upon *soup maigre*;—the lower orders indeed, I believe, are very temperate, and seldom taste meat; but, amongst the higher classes, one might almost parody one of our national maxims, and say—that one Frenchman would out-eat three Englishmen.

Their déjeuner *à la fourchette*, when well served up, is, as they term it, *superbe*, *magnifique*; and wants only the addition of tea to rival the excellence of a Scotch breakfast.

In comparing the cookery of the two nations, it is the *general* excellence of the French that is so much beyond our own. The *best* cooks in the various countries in Europe are nearly the same, for they are formed more or less after the French model; but in France *all* are good.

Man has been defined to be a cooking, superstitious, self-killing animal. I know not whether the outward signs of these inward propensities have yet been discovered, in cranial protuberances peculiar to the human head; but when they are, the organ of superstition will probably be found to predominate in the Spanish, as that of suicide may perhaps prevail in the English, whilst, if there be any truth in craniology, the organ of cookery must be the leading feature of the French skull.

So much for cookery. With respect to cleanliness,—the balance here will incline very much in favour of England; though in many particulars the observances of the French evince a greater niceness of feeling than our own. A napkin is as indispensable to a Frenchman at dinner, as a knife or fork. In the lowest inn you will always find this luxury, and, though it may be coarse, it is always clean; nor is it confined to the parlour—all ranks must have their napkin, and all classes are equally nice in the use of a separate drinking glass. The silver fork too is almost universal, but their knives are villanous; and the use which even the ladies make of their sharp points, in performing the office of a toothpick, is worse.

The ablutions of the bath are perhaps more generally practised in France than in England; though you seldom see a Frenchman with his face cleanly shaved, or his hands well washed. With regard to the ladies of the two nations their pretensions to superiority in this respect were submitted to an emigré bishop, as an experienced judge of both countries, who answered—"*Les Anglaises sont plus propres aux yeux des hommes et les Françaises aux yeux de Dieu!*"

But though in some few instances the French seem to show a more delicate sense of *personal* comfort than ourselves, yet in the general estimate they will be found far behind us. Their houses would shock our neat and tidy house-wives; and their attached and detached offices are too filthy for description. In their persons too—though the bath may be used, the tooth and nail brush seem to be forgotten; and they are always either smart or slovenly, as you see them in their evening dress, or in their morning dishabille.

Lastly; some of their habits must be condemned as shockingly offensive,—what shall we say of the spitting about the floor, which is the common practice of women as well as men, at all times and seasons, not only in domestic life, but also upon the stage, in the characters of heroes and heroines even in high imperial tragedy?—to say nothing of the manœuvres of a French pocket-handkerchief—called expressively by Young "a flag of abomination"—which would disgust the feelings of any Englishman, without supposing him a fastidious *élève* of Lord Chesterfield.

In conversation too, though there is much of what may be called *moral* delicacy, which is shown in little attentions to oblige, and a nice tact in avoiding whatever can give offence, yet there seems a total want of *physical* delicacy on the part of the French.

This will perhaps explain what has been much remarked upon by travellers;—that the French rarely smile at the blunders of foreigners. An Englishman feels his muscles irresistibly moved when a foreigner unwittingly touches in conversation upon *forbidden* ground;—but here, where there is scarcely any forbidden ground, similar mistakes cannot of course have the same effect.

Feast of Sainte Barbe;—military fête. The regiments of artillery had a feast, and the soldiers in the evening cried *Vive l'Empereur*, in the great square. They were drunk, to be sure; but *in vino veritas*. The name of Napoleon is made to stand for any thing. In the mouths of the army it is only another word for military government and a military chief, without much individual attachment to him; and in politics, if the cry of *Vive Buonaparte* have any influence, it can only be because it is considered as the badge of the Revolution, and the changes which the Revolution has effected; in opposition to the powers and privileges of the *ancien régime*.

5th

The more I see of France and Frenchmen, the more I am struck with the serious and sombre complexion of their manners, so different from the pictures of other times. Nothing can be more dull than their theatre; that is, than the theatre of Toulouse. There seems to be no sympathy of feeling, no connecting link, between the audience and the actors. The laughter of the scene produces no correspondent emotion in the house. There is no applause, and scarcely any attention;—the spectators sit by in sullen silence. But it must be owned that the actors are not the best in the world.

The young students of the University, with little respect to the well-behaved part of the audience, throw *bouquets* of flowers on the stage to their favourite actresses.

6th

The dullness of the theatre has been explained to me. The audience is constantly made up of the same persons, and they are of course too familiar with the pieces and the actors to take much interest either in the one or the other.

In the provincial towns of France every body subscribes to the theatre. The *spectacle* is absolutely necessary to fill up the evening of a Frenchman; for neither conviviality nor social domestic parties are the fashion of the country. The theatre therefore is open every night, without excepting Sunday; on which day, indeed, it is most crowded. Economy is the object of many of those who attend; for it is cheaper to subscribe, and pass the evening from dinner till bed-time at the play, than to burn fire and candle at home.

The subscription, to the military who are quartered here, is one day's pay per month;—this was a regulation introduced by Napoleon. The students are admitted for eleven francs, and all other persons for fifteen francs per month. For this you have a free admission to all parts of the house.

The actors seem to be tolerably well paid, for a provincial theatre. There are none who have less than 1,200 francs per annum, and the leading actors have as much as 8,000 francs. But then the *premiers roles* in France are saddled with the expense of finding their own dresses.

23rd

Attended the assizes. A prisoner was brought up for horse-stealing. The president of the court and three other judges were present, dressed in robes of scarlet; but without any flowing horse-hair on their heads. The *Procureur Général*, or public accuser on the part of the crown, in the same costume, sat at the same table with the judges, so close to the jury, that he was continually communicating with them in an under tone, and even during the defence he from time to time suggested something aside to them, as it seemed, to do away the impression of what was urged in the prisoner's favour. The jury consisted of the principal inhabitants of Toulouse, and of the professors of the university. The whole court seemed to consider themselves as *pitted* against the poor devil at the bar. The president acted throughout as counsel against him; and even his manner, in the frequent cross-examination to which he made the prisoner submit, was what in England would be called unfeeling and indecent. Though the charge involved so serious a punishment, the judges and Monsieur le Procureur seemed to think it a very facetious circumstance, and laughed heartily—when the culprit aided his own conviction by some ill-considered answer.

Even the jury and the spectators seemed to be without any feelings of sympathy for the accused, and the address of his counsel was not listened to with a decent attention by any body;—though it ought to be added in their excuse, that the address was a villanously stupid one. Still it was impossible not to be shocked at the apparent want of fair play in the whole procedure.

The spirit of *equality*, which pervades every thing in France since the revolution, seems to have found its way into the courts of Justice in some of their observances; and in these instances, at least, we cannot condemn its influence. The prisoner and the witnesses are accommodated with seats, not as matter of favour, but as matter of right; and the witnesses give their evidence sitting. This is surely nothing more than just; it is a sufficient evil that a man, without any fault of his own, should be liable to the inconvenience of attending as a witness, without being subjected to the additional punishment of standing up in a witness-box, during an examination of as many hours as it may please the counsel to inflict upon him.

The witness is not sworn upon the Bible; but he holds up his hand, and to the charge of the president—Vous jurez, sans haine, et sans crainte, de dire la vérité, toute la vérité, et rien que la vérité —he answers—Je le jure.

No evidence was taken down; and the summing up of the judge was only a recapitulation of the proofs *against* the prisoner.

The jury retire to deliberate, and bring in their verdict in writing.

The prisoner was found guilty, and sentenced to five years' imprisonment.

29th

Assizes again.—A very interesting trial of a man for shooting at another, with an intent to kill him. Before the commencement of a trial the names of the witnesses are called over; and they are then sent out of court, that one may not hear the evidence of the other. The *President* opened the case to the jury. The proof was defective; at least, it was a very nice case as to the identity of the man; and yet one of the questions of the *Procureur Général* to the prisoner, in a cross-examination in aid of the proof against him, was – Are you possessed of a gun?!!! No evidence was taken down. When the evidence closed, the Procureur Général spoke in support of the prosecution; the prisoner's counsel then spoke in his defence, and lastly the President summed up, remarking, in this instance, upon what had been advanced on both sides; but still it was the speech of an advocate against the prisoner, in which character the French judge seems to consider himself. In the course of this trial, the President examined the witnesses *for the prosecution*, as to the character of the prisoner, in this sort of way:—

"Do you know any thing of the prisoner's character?"

"Have you ever heard any thing against him?"

"Do you think it likely from what you know of him, that he would commit the crime with which he is charged?"

In another trial, the judge, in his opening of the case, in order to influence the jury against the prisoner, commenced his speech by telling them—that the same culprit had, very lately appeared at the bar, and had been acquitted by the jury on the score of his youth, as he was only one day beyond the age which made him liable to legal penalty; and that, in addition to this lenity, the jury had made a subscription for him, in order that he might have something with which to begin the world again. This was the opening statement of the judge, unsupported by a tittle of evidence.

So much for the criminal jurisprudence of the French; of the very first principles of which they seem to be utterly ignorant.

The golden maxim of the English law, which presumes that every man is innocent till it has been proved that he is guilty, and which shields the accused from the obligation of replying to any question lest he should criminate himself, has no influence in their criminal procedure. The prisoner, though not absolutely stretched upon the rack, is subjected to the terrible *screw* of cross-examination; and a most powerful engine it is for extracting the truth. But it may sometimes confound the innocent, as well as convict the guilty. If indeed a prisoner be really innocent, and if he have coolness and good sense enough to adhere strictly to the truth, he may have nothing to fear from the legal inquisition of the French—which is certainly well adapted for unravelling the intricacies of a complicated case. But as it is surely better that many guilty should escape rather than one innocent man should suffer, the spirit of the English system is infinitely preferable, in spite of the facilities it affords to the clever rascal of escaping from justice.

XVI.

CHURCH AND STATE

January 1st, 1819

The weather for the last ten days has been bitterly cold; the thermometer has been below the freezing point, with snow, and sleet, and fog. This is a day of great bustle in France. All the equipages in Toulouse are rattling about, leaving cards of congratulation; for it would be a breach of politeness amongst acquaintance not to exchange visits on this day.—New year's gifts seem more in vogue in France than in England.

16th

The agitation of the public mind, produced by the late reports of changes in the ministry, seems at last to be tranquillized by the appointment of M. de Cazes and his friends. The heat and irritation produced here by the rumour of the appointment of an ultra-royalist ministry, which was believed for four-and-twenty hours, was excessive. The ultra-royalist party awaited the arrival of the next courier with the most intense anxiety; and if it had brought a confirmation of their hopes, there is no saying what outrages and excesses might not have been committed. The ultra-royalist party in the south of France is characterized by the spirit which massacred the protestants at Nismes; the green cockade is its ensign, and this party is more royalist than the king himself, who is regarded by them as an apostate from the old principles of the ancient régime. These then say, as the friends of our second Charles said, that Louis has interpreted the *oubli* and *pardon* of his brother's dying injunctions, into an act of amnesty to his enemies, and an act of oblivion of his friends. On the other hand, the anxiety of those who have benefited by the Revolution—that is, the great mass of the people—was equally evident; for they are taught to regard the appointment of an ultra-royalist ministry as synonymous with a re-establishment of the tithes of the clergy, and the feudal rights of the seigneur, and a resumption of all the property which has been purchased under edicts of confiscation.

This last is the tenderest point of all; and it is certainly a hard case, that a man who was obliged either to fly his country or lose his head, should upon his return find his estate in the possession of one of his own servants, who perhaps purchased it for almost nothing during the troubles of the Revolution. But this, it is to be feared, is one of those instances of injustice, which, by being committed and defended by numbers, is placed beyond the reach of punishment; for it is impossible to "indict a whole nation." The sentence of *Fiat justitia* would be accompanied with a popular convulsion, equivalent to the *ruat cœlum* of the original maxim; which however true in morals, will not always hold good in politics, of which expediency is the basis: and in which, I believe, we must be contented with what is practicable when we cannot attain what is desirable.

18th

Le Préfet's ball. The Prefect, who is considered, like our Lord Lieutenant, as the representative of the sovereign in the department over which he presides, keeps up a certain state, and amongst other entertainments gives a ball every Monday. The ball was but a shabby business;—three fiddlers, and no supper. Cotillions and quadrilles are so soon over, and the ladies are pledged so many deep, that every French beau is armed with his pencil and tablets to record his engagements, which he claims by presenting his partner with a bouquet of flowers. There is a very striking contrast between the fashion of the English and French ladies' dress, in disposing the drapery of the neck; and the advantage is for once so much on the side of the latter, in decorum and propriety, that I am surprised our countrywomen are not shamed into an imitation of it.

21st

Solemn service at the cathedral for the repose of the soul of Louis XVI.—The Prefect and the municipality, and the whole body of the professors of the university, attended this mourning ceremonial in grand costume. The church was hung with black, and the funeral anthem was beautiful.

The king's will was read from the pulpit; but, as far as it is possible to judge of the tone and sentiment of a public assembly, it did not appear to me that the impression produced upon the multitude was such as the authors of the ceremony must have contemplated. It might have been different at the *first* celebration of the anniversary of his murder; and perhaps it would have been better to have limited the mourning to one single occasion; for such feelings must in their nature be transient, and in time pass away altogether. What, for instance, can be more ridiculous than the pretended mournful observance of the 30th of January in England? By the way, it is rather a singular coincidence that January was the month fatal alike to Louis and Charles, as May was the common month of the restoration of their successors;—it will be for the Comte d'Artois to take care that the parallel between the families does not continue farther.

22nd

In the evening to the theatre. The play was *Edouard en Ecosse*; founded on the adventures of the Pretender in England, the work of M. Duval, who is fond of dramatising English story. The part of Charles Edward was admirably played by Beauchamp. His face and appearance, when he first comes in, pale and worn out with fatigue, presented a striking resemblance of Napoleon. The political allusions, with which the play abounds, were eagerly seized throughout, and applied to the Ex-Emperor.—"*Je n'ai fait que des ingrats*" was long and loudly applauded. In the last act of the play the air of "God save the King" was incidentally introduced; which afforded the audience an opportunity of manifesting their feeling towards England, which they did not neglect—and an universal hiss broke out. A pantomime followed, but a very faint imitation of the inimitable entertainment which is called by that name in England. The first dancer is called Harlequin, without his wand or his tricks; the first female dancer is Columbine; and the unfortunate Pantaloon, in addition to his own part, is Clown also; so that besides the kicks on the breeches which he receives in quality of the first character, he has also to endure the slaps of the face which fall to the lot of the second. His mock dance was excellent; and his animated sack, for he jumps into a sack and displays wonderful locomotive powers therein, was worthy of Grimaldi himself.

February 1st

It is a subject of great complaint that the time of the carnival should have been selected by the missionaries, who have lately made their appearance at Toulouse, for the period of their visit; as their arrival and preaching have cast a gloom over the usual festivities of this season of the year. There is a sort of mystery in the institution and appointment of these peripatetic preachers, who traverse France from one end to the other, as if there were no local clergy to provide for the religious instruction of their flocks. They preach twice a day, at the principal churches in the town; and in order that this may not interfere with the labouring pursuits of the lower classes, the morning hour is as early as five, and the evening as late as six o'clock. There seems to be a great craving after religion at present, as if there were a re-action after the long reign of infidelity during the Revolution. The churches are filled long before the service begins, and the receipts at the rate of three sous a chair will amount to a considerable sum, if the zeal of the congregations should continue.

The missionaries are represented in the most opposite colours, by the two parties of the state; if you listen to the royalists, they work nothing but good, and only excite the jealousy of the opposite party, because it is feared that they will restore the tone of the public mind, and bring back the people to "fear God and honour the king;" While the liberal party represents them as the preachers of fanaticism, and the promoters of domestic dissension. For myself I must say, that I have attended the missionary who preaches at the cathedral, and have heard the best and purest precepts of Christianity enforced by very extraordinary eloquence; but a friend has told me that he heard, at one of the minor churches, a sermon on the doctrine of tran-substantiation, in which the missionary preacher related the following story in confirmation of his doctrine. "There was a woman," said he, "who being in want of a decent attire to go to communion, went to a Jew to hire a dress; and the Jew would only consent to let it, upon condition that she would bring him back a piece of the consecrated wafer. After much difficulty, his terms were granted. The Jew, as soon as he had got possession of the wafer, trampled it under his feet; when, to his great surprise, he perceived drops of blood to issue from it. Astonished at this, he put it into a saucepan and boiled it upon the fire;—when the surface of the water became covered with fat. This second miracle so wrought upon him, that he was convinced and converted, and forthwith became a Christian." If such is the mode of expounding the mysteries of Christianity, in the nineteenth century, it is no wonder that the enlightened part of the nation condemn missions, and refuse to listen to missionaries.

5th

In the evening to the theatre. M. Huet from the Opera Comique of Paris drew a full house. He played *Adolphe*, and *Jean de Paris*, in the originals, from which Matrimony and John of Paris have been translated; but I thought him very tame and insipid after the delightfully spirited performance of Elliston in the same parts;—who is so happy in the combination of heart and feeling with vivacity and whim; and inimitable in the management of dry humour and playful raillery.

10th

The French seem to carry politics farther even than ourselves. Who ever heard in England of inquiring the politics of an actor? Yet here, the arrival of M. Huet, who it seems is recognized as a staunch royalist, has been sufficient to throw the town of Nismes into a state of agitation. The royalist party made a point of attending the theatre to support their champion; in the same party spirit which had been shown by the opposite faction upon a late visit of Talma, whose intimate friendship with the ex-Emperor is well known. A spark is sufficient to kindle the flame of civil war between parties composed of such inflammable materials, and nothing but the prudence of the police prevented an explosion.

March 16th

The *coup d'état* of creating fifty new peers has at last quieted the apprehension and anxiety which had been occasioned by the success of the Marquis Barthelemy's motion in the Chamber of Peers. The object of the motion was to consider the propriety of altering the law of elections; and it was carried by a majority of thirty-four voices against the ministry. This new creation of peers, which amounts almost to a revolution in the government, ought to convince all parties of the king's sincerity and good faith, and of his determination to oppose by any means the overheated zeal of his own adherents. The friends of M. Barthelemy affect to consider the public alarm as unfounded and unreasonable, since his motion was confined to a mere consideration of the propriety of making an alteration in the law. But it is surely not surprising that a people just entering upon the enjoyment of political privileges should be tremblingly alive to any attempt to tamper with a law which they are taught to consider as the great security of their rights. How for example would the king feel, if a member of the Chamber of Deputies were to succeed in a motion for considering the propriety of making some alteration in the settlement of the crown? There are certain fundamental points in all constitutions, which ought not, and cannot be made the subjects of debate, without disturbing the stability of the whole edifice.

It is only necessary to consider what the French have gained by the Revolution, to sympathize with the alarm excited by any measure that seems to indicate a disposition to return to the principles of the ancient government.

Liberty and equality was a cry peculiarly calculated to produce an effect in France; and however it might have been afterwards abused, its original import meant a liberation from the intolerable grievances of feudal oppression, and an abolition of the injurious privileges of the nobles;—who not only possessed an exclusive claim to all the honours and emoluments of the army and the church, but were also exempt from taxation; and, even in the article justice, were placed above the level of their inferiors—for there was one tribunal and one measure of justice for the high, and another for the low.

The direct power of the monarch was the least evil of which the French had to complain, and the rule of a single despot, in the person of Napoleon, must have seemed light to those, who remembered all the grievances of the *ancien régime*;—namely, the partial and oppressive imposts of the *taille* and the *corvée*; and the *capitaineries*, by which a sort of *free-warren* was conferred over the lands of others, taking away the rights of the proprietors themselves, and vesting the game of a whole district—with the power of *preserving* deer and wild boars—in any single Nimrod whom the king might appoint.

Last, and worst of all, were the feudal claims, and oppressive expedients—for an account of which see Arthur Young—by which the Seigneur might extort money from his vassals. But these and all the other sufferings of the people seem to be forgotten by all but themselves; and nothing is now remembered of the French Revolution, but the crimes and excesses by which the cause of liberty was disgraced.

This Revolution teaches indeed an awful lesson. But while we learn from it the dangers of popular excess, and the impossibility of effecting a beneficial reform by the agency of the mob, we shall derive but little profit from it if it do not also teach us the necessity of accommodating the institutions of government to the progress of information, so that they may be always kept in unison with public opinion.

If such had been the conduct of the French government, we should never have heard of the French Revolution. The rulers who refuse to make those alterations which the progress of the age demands, seem to act as imprudently as the debtor who neglects to pay interest of his debt. It is true he may delay paying any thing for a certain time, but in the mean time the arrears go on accumulating at compound interest, and when the day of reckoning does come, as come it must sooner or later, it comes with a vengeance, and brings ruin along with it. Those who have the direction of the machine of government would do well to watch the signs of the times, and by a regular payment of the claims of society maintain a constant good understanding between debtor and creditor;—for this is the sort of relation in which the government and the people seem to stand towards each other.

25th

The Annunciation. Attended the ceremony of professing a novice, in the chapel of the Benedictine Convent. The victim was a young and pretty girl, who had been on the point of marriage, for which the preparations had been made, and the day fixed. The destined bride however suddenly changed her mind, without any assignable reason; and, in spite of the entreaties of her friends, resolved to renounce the world; and, according to the French phrase, *épouser le bon Dieu*. She was arrayed in a superb dress of satin, with a profusion of lace, and wore a wreath of flowers upon her head.

The service was long and tedious. After receiving the communion, and hearing a sermon particularly addressed to her, which was dull and unfeeling beyond belief, the ceremony began. She was asked in the face of the congregation, whether it was from her own sincere and unbiased inclination that she sought the seclusion of a convent; and having answered in the affirmative, the *cierge* and *crucifix* were delivered to her. She was then led out of the chapel by her two bridemaids, and re-appeared within the grate of the convent. Here her hair was cut off; and quitting her worldly dress and worldly ornaments, she was invested with the coarse uniform of the order to which she was to belong. The novice then gave the kiss of peace all round to the sisters of the convent, and the ceremony concluded. At the expiration of a year, she repeats her vows, and takes the black veil: it is then that the convent becomes her tomb; and being considered as dead to the world, she is wrapped in a black shroud, and the funeral service is performed over her. The father of the novice attended the ceremony, and seemed to be overwhelmed with affliction. It was a melancholy scene; but less affecting than it would have been, if the profession of vows were now, as in former times, an irrevocable sentence of perpetual seclusion. This is no longer the case; for as the law at present stands, no vows are binding for more than a year; so that if a nun, availing herself of the privilege of her sex, should think fit to change her mind, she may have her cage-door opened, and return to the world.

27th

There was an intention of concluding the mission to Toulouse by a grand ceremony and procession, in which the missionaries were to walk barefoot, and plant a cross in one of the squares of the town; but it has been prevented by the interference of the police, and postponed *sine die*. It is difficult to form a judgment of the general effects of these missions from the opposite representations of their friends and enemies. The only *fact* that has come under my own knowledge speaks in their favour. As we were sitting at dinner one day, the host of my *pension* was called out to speak to a young woman, who desired particularly to see him alone. Upon his return, he recounted his interview to us. It seems that the woman had formerly lived in his service, and the object of her visit was to confess to him sundry petty acts of theft, and to make him restitution of their amount. This, she said, she was led to do from the representations of one of the missionaries, to whom she had confessed, and who had convinced her that repentance and absolution were of no avail, unless founded upon sincere resolutions of amendment; and that the best pledge of future good conduct would be the atonement and reparation of past sins, as far as it could be done. My kind-hearted host forgave his contrite domestic, and she had all the merit of good intention, without making any pecuniary sacrifice.

30th

Finished a course of Racine. The delineation of female characters seems to be his forte. Phèdre, Hermione, Agrippine, and Clytemnestre, are, I think, master-pieces in their way. All the faults of Racine must be attributed to the taste of his age and nation; and, considering the tight stays in which the tragic muse is confined upon the French stage, Racine has done wonders. His heroes, to be sure, whether taken from Greek or Roman story, are all Frenchmen. This is the common fault of all the French tragic writers; and it is exquisitely ridiculed by Grimm. "Le célèbre Hogarth, connu par le génie et l'esprit de ses compositions, a écrit un ouvrage sur le beau, rempli d'idées extraordinaires. On y voit entre autres une estampe où un maître de danse Français est vis-à-vis la belle statue d'Antinoüs; il s'occupe à lui relever la tête, a lui effacer les épaules, à lui placer les bras et les jambes, à la transformer, en un mot, en petit maître élégant et agréable: cette satire est aussi fine qu'originale. Je doute ce-pendant que notre célèbre Marcel eût touché a la contenance d'Antinoüs; mais mettez à la place d'Antinoüs la statue de Melpomène l'Athenienne, et nommez les maîtres de danse Corneille et Racine, et le symbole ne s'écartera pas trop de la vérité!"

His heroines are less national, the reason of which perhaps may be, that there is less *national* distinction amongst women, who have, as Pope has said, "no characters at all;" a remark, which, though Pope meant it as a satire, needs not I think offend the sex; on the contrary, it is perhaps the highest merit in a woman, that she is without those strongly-marked peculiarities which constitute what is called character in man;—for in her, to be prominent is to be offensive; and her most engaging qualities are of that unobtrusive kind, which belong rather to the sex than to the individual.

Racine's women are the women of high life. We must not look for the charming effusions of natural feeling which Shakspeare has given, in Juliet, Imogen, Cordelia, and the divine Desdemona. Such characters as these the French poet had not the head to conceive; nor, if he had, would a French audience have the heart to feel their beauty; but Racine has given most powerful and affecting delineations of the frailties and passions of the factitious beings amongst whom his scene is laid. It is to the distresses of such beings that the sympathy of a French audience seems confined. It would appear as if there were only a *royal road* to their hearts, for the idea of a *tragédie bourgeoise* is to them ridiculous; and not satisfied with confining tragedy to the great, they have also prescribed such rigorous rules of *bienséance*, that all the mighty play of the passions, which form the elements of tragedy, is limited in their expression by the arbitrary laws of poetic diction, and the strict modes of politeness, as they happened to exist in the time of Louis XIV.

Grimm in his Correspondence has pointed out with great discrimination the defects of French tragedy; but a few sentences of Rousseau comprehend the substance of all that can be said on the subject.

"Communément tout se passe en beaux dialogues, bien agencés, bien ronflans, où l'on voit d'abord que le premier soin de chaque interlocuteur, est toujours celui de briller. Presque tout s'énonce en maximes générales Quelque agités qu'ils puissent être, ils songent toujours plus au public qu'à eux mêmes.

"Il y a encore une certaine dignité maniérée dans le geste et dans le propos, qui ne permet jamais à la passion de parler exactement son langage, ni a l'auteur de revêtir son personnage, et de se transporter au lieu de la scène."

We English contend that Shakspeare is the reverse of all this; that his plays, instead of being poetical *descriptions*, are genuine *expressions* of the passions; that his characters do not talk like poets, but like men; that he has the faculty which Rousseau says the French poets want; and that he does, to use Schlegel's illustration, after the manner of a ventriloquist, transport his imagination out of himself, and successively animate every personage of his scene; that his characters speak in the very language in which their living prototypes might be supposed to have spoken; so that in fact it appears as if he had stood by an eye-witness of the scenes he describes, and had taken down in writing what actually passed between the parties; that instead of the cold generalities which are bandied about by the "intellectual gladiators" of the French stage, there is an individuality in Shakspeare's characters which gives to his scenes almost the effect of reality, and makes us regard the actors in them rather as real personages than as mere fictions of his imagination.

It is thus that we praise Shakspeare,—and for the most part justly; though perhaps we may overdo it a little. If the French have too much bienseance, Shakspeare had too little; and it may be doubted whether Johnson was not right when he boldly said, that no one of his plays, if now produced as the work of a living author, would be heard to a conclusion; but his faults are as "dew drops on the lion's mane," and may be easily shaken off.

Again,—when we challenge for him so peremptorily and exclusively the claim of the poet of nature,—is he always natural? Does he never make his characters speak rather like poets, than like men?

The language of highly-excited passion will often rise into poetry; and I will not question the propriety of the figurative imagery in which he delights to clothe the effusions of grief and despair. But, to give one instance out of many, let us turn to the dagger scene of Macbeth. The air-drawn dagger is a grand conception, and the execution is a mighty proof of the genius of Shakspeare. The scene is awfully sublime,—yet, verging as it does on the border of extravagance, in any other hands it would probably have been ridiculous; but, what shall we say to the description of night, which follows? As a Poet's description of night, admirably adapted to the circumstances of the scene, it is excellent, and in a descriptive poem it would be strictly in place; but what is the condition of Macbeth's mind?

Is it *natural* that his imagination should be at leisure to furnish the terrible accompaniments of a murderer's night, which are there enumerated with a somewhat laboured detail? To show how a Frenchman's mind is impressed by Shakspeare, let me record the sentiments of my friend Mons. B. C., to whom I gave this scene to read aloud, as a sample of Shakspeare's best manner. He read the dagger speech with great admiration, and though a little shocked at the coarseness of Lady Macbeth's language while she is waiting for the reappearance of her husband, he went on very well till he came to

> I heard the Owl scream and the Cricket cry.—

The cricket was too much for his risible nerves;—here he threw down the book, and fairly laughed out. He considered the introduction of so ignoble an image, as a high misdemeanor against the gorgeous dignity of tragedy, to say nothing of the absurdity of allowing Lady Macbeth to have leisure to listen to it. What would he have said to "*not a mouse stirring?*" The whole scene that follows, which I have always thought at once so natural and so terrible, he considered as utterly out of nature, and childishly ridiculous.

Figurez-vous, said he, an ambitious chieftain, who has, under the impulse of that passion, conceived and perpetrated the murder of his sovereign; yet,—in the very moment of its accomplishment, instead of being engrossed with those aspiring thoughts and anticipations natural to his situation, he has no better employment than to entertain his wife with the conversation and cries of the drunken domestics, who had been disturbed from their sleep by his proceedings.

> One cried God bless us! and Amen! the other,

was to his ears the very acmé of the ridiculous.

Such was the impression made upon an intelligent Frenchman, who understood English very well, by one of the finest scenes in Shakspeare. Racine would certainly have managed the whole business very differently. It would have been much less terrible, but much more polite and well-bred; and Monsieur and Madame Macbeth would have rhymed it away through some scores of fine verses. Racine however is full of beauties, and, though he sinks into insignificance when compared with Shakspeare, may perhaps challenge a comparison with any other English tragic writer, excepting Otway.

His knowledge of human nature too is considerable; though it is not the knowledge of Shakspeare, who was profoundly intimate with the heart of man in all its passions and affections, as it exists in all times and all countries, and who painted with the nicest discrimination all tempers and dispositions,—the gay and the joyous—the generous and the gallant—the serious and the sorrowful—the moody and the mad—the drunken and the desperate. The knowledge of Racine is more like that which has been displayed by Pope, and seems to be confined to factitious nature; but this is beautifully and faithfully delineated. His distress is often very affecting; and when the heart is not affected, the mind may generally find amusement and instruction, in the beauty of his verses and the force of his reasoning.

Though we generally begin by preferring Voltaire's tragedies, the beauties of which are more showy, Racine will in the end establish his superiority. Racine seems to have been fitted for the strict rules of the French drama, and he writes *con amore*. Voltaire, who understood English, had a taste for something better. Though he abuses Shakspeare, he was not above stealing from him very copiously; and then, as Steevens wittily remarked, like a midnight thief, he sets fire to the house he has robbed, in the hope of preventing the detection of his guilt.

There is something in Voltaire's tragedies which seems to show that his genius was embarrassed by the cramp and confinement of the French literary laws; of which indeed he himself complains:—

"Je regrettais cette heureuse liberté que vous avez d'écrire vos tragédies en vers non rimés;" though he maintains elsewhere that rhyme is absolutely necessary to the French verse, and gives, by way of example and proof, a very fine passage, which, by being stripped of these appendages, loses all its pretensions to poetry. If this be so, what more severe could be urged in the way of sarcasm against French poetry? For in fact it amounts to this,—that there is so little of the soul and spirit of poetry in their writers, that poetry would be converted into prose by Porson's receipt of removing the final syllable of each line.

Voltaire is the last man who ought to have depredated Shakspeare; for if his *Zaire* be superior in animation and energy to his other tragedies, the superiority will be due to Shakspeare, from whose fire he has caught a few sparks. But his thefts are not always turned to so good account. He sometimes meddles with materials beyond his strength. The bow of Ulysses would have been of no use to a vulgar thief. The Ghost of Hamlet's Father, under Shakspeare's management, is awful and sublime; but his counterpart in Semiramis is almost ridiculous.

The question of the unities—so differently treated in the theatres of the two nations—has been nearly set at rest by Johnson in his admirable preface to Shakspeare. None will deny the necessity of unity of action; and the unity of time cannot obviously admit of much latitude of interpretation, without violating probability, and destroying the closeness of, imitation, upon which much of the merit of a dramatic piece depends. The French contend, that their rigid adherence to the unity of place rests upon the same ground of closeness of imitation;—but it is evident that this is founded upon a mistaken idea of illusion.

For the fact is, that the imitation is not at all closer by the preservation of this unity,—but the contrary. For instance, would not the imagination of the spectator be more easily reconciled to occasional shifting of the scene, in the tragedy of Cato, than to the monstrous absurdity of bringing all sorts of people, on all sorts of errands, to talk of love, and treason, in the same public hall? The only effect of practice has been to change the drama—from the representation of an action—into a series of conversations. The difference, says Grimm, between the English and the French stage is, that, in England, "*On fait courir le spectateur après les évènemens;* in France, *ce sont les évènemens qui courent après les spectateurs.*" In this, as in most other instances, the truth will lie somewhere between the two extremes. Change of scene may surely take place without any violation of the illusion, if there be no objection on the score of time;—and, with all due deference to Dr. Johnson, it is rather *the intervention of time,* than *the change of place*, that ought to separate one act from another; and this, however small, should always make a pause in the drama.

If there could exist any real doubt of the *dramatic* superiority of the English muse, what strong proof might be adduced from the practice of the French actors themselves! Why is it that Talma prefers Hamlet and Manlius, to Orestes and Ninias, and other characters of the same kind, which are confessedly the *chefs-d' œuvre* of the French theatre; while Hamlet and Manlius are poor imitations of our own Hamlet and Pierre? Is it not that Talma has studied these characters in their native language, and contrived to impart to the cold copy some portion of the life and spirit of the divine originals? But more of French acting hereafter.

31st
Bancal, the woman concerned in the murder of Fualdes, was brought before the court of assize, to hear her pardon read. When this was over, she was exhibited as a spectacle to the gentle-folks of the town, French and English.

She conversed on the subject of the murder, and persisted in maintaining the guilt of Yence, and Bessière Veysac, who were lately rescued from the hands of justice by a host of perjuries.

Packing up;—this is a melancholy part of a traveller's life;—to arrive and hear no welcome—to depart and hear no farewell—or, if he remain stationary for a time, to be called away just as he is beginning to form new connexions.

Farewell visits;—to Dr. Thomas, from whose medical skill, and friendly attentions, my health has derived the greatest benefit;

and to Mr. Kemble, to, whom I have been indebted for many pleasant evenings of social intercourse. It is delightful to see the father of the English stage enjoying the evening of life in the tranquillity of literary leisure; a man to whose public exertions we have all been indebted for the highest intellectual gratification; who, by the charm of his art, has become so identified in our imaginations with the ideal characters of Shakspeare, that those who have seen him can scarcely think of Macbeth—King John—Wolsey—Hotspur—Brutus—or Coriolanus, without embodying them in the form and features of—John Philip Kemble.

XVII

BOURDEAUX
TO VERSAILLES

April 1st
Voyage down the Garonne to Bordeaux.—The duration of this voyage depends entirely upon the state of the river. In flood time it may be done in two days; but the ordinary time required is four. There is little in the scenery of the banks to demand notice. In so long a course, it is impossible that there should not be a few picturesque spots, but there are very few. It is but a comfortless voyage; there is no regular passage-boat, and the only vessels are small flat-bottomed barges, without any deck, or other protection from the weather, than such a tent as you may be able to construct. Again—if the water be low, you are constantly liable to get a-ground; and it can never be a matter of certainty where you may halt for the night. Still, if the weather is fine, it is well enough. There is a sort of mill for grinding corn in use on the Garonne, which might perhaps be introduced with advantage on our own rivers. It is a simple wooden structure, containing also the miller's house, built upon a solid flat-bottomed boat, which is moored on the stream by means of strong iron chains. The *streams* are very rapid, and the Garonne is subject to sudden and violent floods nevertheless, these mills stand their ground; and there is scarcely a stream in the river without one between Toulouse and Bourdeaux.

There are some fine points of view; particularly at the embouchure of the Lot, where you command a prospect of the town and château of Aiguillon; and again at La Réole where there

is an ancient Benedictine convent, of late turned into the residence
of the Prefect, which, with the surrounding scenery, forms a
beautiful picture. But these points are of rare occurrence. It was
not till the evening of the fifth day that we arrived within sight of
Bourdeaux. The character of the scenery improves as you descend
the river, and the approach to Bourdeaux is magnificent. I doubt
whether it be not equal to Lisbon: the river, which is rather an
arm of the sea, is nearly as broad again as the Thames at London.
It takes a bend at this point, and the town and the quays form a
splendid crescent on the left bank, the whole circuit of which is
taken in at one *coup d'œil*, while the opposite bank is rich with
woods, and vineyards, and villas. The piers of a stone bridge are
finished; and the superstructure will soon be completed, which
will form a magnificent feature in the prospect. The execution
of this project, the possibility of which was long contested, is a
splendid proof of the genius and ability of the architect.

Such is the approach to Bourdeaux. The town itself will be by
far the handsomest town in France, if the new buildings in the
faubourg of Chartron are carried on upon the scale which is at
present designed. The Chapeau-Rouge is already, as far as it goes,
one of the finest streets in Europe. Here is the theatre, the façade
of which is a model of architectural beauty; and the bottom of
the street terminates in the exchange, the quay, the river, and the
shipping. Vessels of any size can come up to Bourdeaux; a frigate
and two brigs have been lately built for Ferdinand of Spain, and
are now fitting out for the grand expedition to South America.

10th
Every thing at Bourdeaux is on a grand scale; the promenades are
beautiful, and the public buildings are numerous and splendid.
The cathedral, as is the case with many of the handsomest Gothic
buildings in France, was the work of the English, during the
time they occupied this country as masters. The price of lodging
and provisions is somewhat dearer here than at Toulouse. The
ordinary price of a *pension* at Bourdeaux, including board and
lodging, is eight francs per day.

17th

Attended the theatre—which is splendid. The boxes project like
hanging balconies, in a manner that I have seen no where else,
which brings out the company as it were in *alto relievo*, and gives
a very pleasing effect. Talma played *Nero*, in the *Britannicus* of
Racine. The part is not a very prominent one, but he made the
most of it.

His style of acting is more like Kean's than any other of our
actors; that is, he deals in electric shocks, which come flashing
through the sublimity of the storm. His concluding words
"*Narcisse!—suivez-moi!*" were given with tremendous effect. His
voice is magnificent, though perhaps none of his cadences are
superior to the quiet low tones of Kean, when he is in his saddest
mood, as in parts of Othello and Hamlet. Upon the whole, I
was much delighted. He is a great actor—in spite of the French
tragedy. He does all he can to bring it down to nature, and it
is a proof of the charm of nature, to witness the effect which
his delivery of the text produces, relieved as it is by occasional
touches of nature and feeling, when compared with the tedious
and tiresome uniformity of that declamatory recitative, which
is the general practice of the French stage. But great taste and
discretion are necessary in the introduction and management
of this familiar tone, which certainly may be carried too far for
nothing is worse than the affectation of being natural. Hear
Voltaire on this subject:—"On s'est piqué de réciter des vers
comme de la prose; on n'a pas considéré qu'un langage au-dessus
du langage ordinaire, doit être débité d'un ton au-dessus du ton
familier."

18th

Saw Talma again, in *Oreste*, in the *Andromaque* of Racine. He has
in an extraordinary manner the faculty of altering his appearance,
and one could scarcely recognise him as the same person who had
played Nero, till he spoke; but his voice is not to be mistaken—it
is divine, and possesses every variety of expression;—his whisper
is wonderfully impressive. There is something unhappy in the

contour of his countenance. A thick double chin encumbers his physiognomy and injures its expression, when the features are at rest; but when his face is agitated by the tempest and whirlwind of the passions, or when all expression is as it were annihilated, by the wild vacancy of despair, the effect is overwhelming. His action is overdone to an English taste; the constant shaking of the arms, and then slapping them violently against the thighs, has something ridiculously vehement in it to us; but those modes of expression are different in different countries, and it would be prejudice to assume our own as the standard of propriety. Still ,till you are habituated to this gesticulation, it looks like tearing a passion to tatters, and has something of the effect of burlesque. His management of soliloquy is admirable. It is just what it ought to be—thinking aloud.

It is impossible to conceive any thing more awfully terrible than his scene in the fifth act. Raving madness is generally disgusting on the stage; shocking the feelings by an exhibition of frightful bodily writhings, and nothing more,—"the contortions of the Sibyl without her inspiration." But there is a dreadful reality in Talma's fury; and the ghastly changes which affect his features seem to arise from the internal agonies of his soul. He made the blood run cold, and one might have fancied it was indeed Orestes *furiis agitatus*, the victim of divine vengeance, that was on the scene.

Though Talma is very fond of contrast, and puts forth his whole strength in particular passages, which resemble Kean's bursts of passion, yet he is also more attentive to the general effect of the character than our own actors are. From the moment of his entrance he seems to forget that he is Talma. No look or motion ever escapes him that betrays a consciousness that he is *acting* to an audience. This complete identification with his part is the great charm of his style. Nothing destroys this identity more, than the appearance of any consciousness of the presence of an audience, on the part of an actor. Yet on our own stage the illusion is dispelled at his very first entrance, by the acknowledgments which custom compels him to make to the plaudits of the spectators;—a frightful solecism in our theatrical practice, which we should do well to reform, from the example of our neighbours.

24th

Voyage in the steam-boat to *Pavillac*, ten leagues down the river. The banks are tame and uninteresting. At the junction of the Dordogne and the Garonne, the confluence takes place in such a manner, that it is difficult to say which river it is that runs into the other; and their magnitude is nearly the same. Hence, it is said, arose a great controversy between the partisans of the Garonne and the Dordogne, which of the two should give its name to the united stream. This was at last decided by the adoption of *La Gironde*—the name of the territory common to both rivers.

House rent in the neighbourhood of Bourdeaux is low enough; a ready-furnished house, containing every suitable accommodation for a small family, with five acres of vineyard yielding fruit enough to make a considerable quantity of wine, was offered me to-day for 500 francs per annum; and there was a peasant residing on the estate, who for half the produce would have undertaken the care and management of the whole.

It is more difficult to *buy* claret of the best quality at Bourdeaux than in London. The fact is, that all the produce of the vineyards is in the hands of a few merchants; and it would scarcely answer their purpose to sell the very best quality, unadulterated, at any price—necessary as it is to them to leaven their whole stock. For the increasing demand for the wines of Bourdeaux, occasioned by the growing consumption of Russia and the East Indies, augments the proportion of inferior wine which is mixed up in the general mass. The common wine of the *Pays de Medoc*—whence by the way comes our cherry whose name we have corrupted into *May Duke*—is light and pleasant, and may be bought for about tenpence a bottle; but it has little resemblance to our English claret, which derives its peculiar flavour from being seasoned with a mixture of a strong wine of Burgundy.

One of the best wines of the south of France is the wine of Cahors, which is rich and strong, and well calculated to please the English taste; but unfortunately the system of commerce which we have so long acted upon has transferred the wine trade to Portugal, where we buy worse liquor at a higher price. "There are few Englishmen," said Hume eighty years ago, "who would not think their country absolutely ruined, were French wines sold in England so cheap and in such abundance, as to supplant in some measure all ale and home-brewed liquors. But, would we lay aside prejudice, it would not be difficult to prove that nothing could be more innocent, perhaps advantageous." The misfortune is that now, when the true principles of commerce are generally understood and acknowledged, it is difficult to introduce them into practice, on account of the long establishment of the old system of restraints and prohibitions; the effect of which has been well described by Hume—as serving no purpose but to check industry, and to rob ourselves and our neighbours of the common benefits of art and nature.

May 1st

Talma's Hamlet is a *chef d'œuvre*; in his hands it is the most affecting picture of filial piety that can be imagined. His power of expressing grief is beyond every thing I ever witnessed on the stage, or in real life. As Hamlet, there is an appearance of concentrated sorrow impressed upon his features and figure, which never leaves him from beginning to end. He is—like the Niobe of whom his prototype speaks—"all tears"—to the utter exclusion of that "antic disposition" which the English Hamlet assumes, to the prejudice perhaps of our sympathy with his sorrows. The other alterations are chiefly these: Ducis makes Ophelie the daughter of Claudius, who is not brother to the murdered king, but only *premier prince du sang*; and this certainly heightens the *embarras* of the French Hamlet, who is as much in love with Ophelie as the English;—

Immoler Claudius,—punir cet inhumain,
C'est plonger à sa fille un poignard dan le sein;
C'est la tuer moi-même!

The madness and death of Ophelie are also avoided. The lovers however quarrel violently; the lady being determined to save her father, and Hamlet equally bent upon his destruction. Then for Gertrude—she does not marry Claudius;—the infidelity has preceded the murder of the king, and she is thenceforward all penitence and horror. The Hamlet of Ducis too is fonder of his mother than the Hamlet of Shakspeare; and the French hobgoblin is a much bloodier fellow than the English ghost: he insists upon it that Hamlet shall not only speak daggers, but use them also; and his bloody commission extends to the punishment of both the guilty parties. It is in vain however that Hamlet attempts the assassination of his mother—his hand and heart fail him;—ultimately however she saves him the trouble, and the Spirit is appeased and satisfied. The stage effect of the invisible speechless spectre of Ducis—which is seen only in the expressive eye of Talma—is certainly superior to the "too solid flesh" of the "honest ghost" of Shakspeare. The moment the English ghost enters with his "martial stalk"—the illusion is over. But perhaps the finest part of the French play is the scene where Hamlet relates to his friend Norceste his interview with his father's spirit;—this is the *ne plus ultra* of acting. Instead of Shakspeare's expedient of the play "to catch the conscience" or the guilty parties, Hamlet causes Norceste to announce to them, as news from England, a similar story of treason and murder, perpetrated there.

Ducis makes the conscience of Claudius immoveable; "*il n'est point troublé*," exclaims Norceste in doubt; "*Non!*" replies Hamlet, "*Non!—mais regarde ma mere!*" the effect of these words as delivered by Talma was truly astonishing. At the end of the play, the hostile approach of Claudius is announced to Hamlet, while he is engaged in a most affecting *éclaircissement* with his mother: he starts up, exclaiming—*Lui! ce monstre!—qu'il vienne!*

and then, after a pause, and a long start, à la Kean;—*Qu'il vienne! je l'attends! ma vengeance est certaine!*

This burst—*qu'il vienne! je l'attends!* is perhaps the most electrifying thing on any stage;—and then the *voice* of Talma!—*non hominem sonat!* There is a supernatural impressiveness about it, that affects the soul in the most awful manner, while it can melt in a moment into tones of the truest and most touching pathos. Talma stands alone upon the French stage, with no rival near the throne, at an immeasurable elevation above all competitors. It is a common, and I believe in general a just notion, that actors are stimulated by mutual excellence, and play better for being "acted up to"—as the phrase is. But though this may be true of the superior actor in relation to the inferior, I doubt whether it be ever true *vice versâ*; and it is easy to perceive that the powers of the inferior actors are paralyzed as they approach the "intolerable day" which Talma sheds around him, and "'gin to pale their ineffectual fire."

In a word, Talma's Hamlet is "the thing itself;" and may be classed with the Coriolanus of Kemble—the Queen Catherine of Siddons—the Othello of Kean; and though last not least—the Sir Pertinax Macsycophant of Cooke.

5th

Left Bourdeaux in a voiturier's carriage, in which we had not proceeded far before we discovered that one of the mules had almost the agility of Tickle-Toby's mare in curvetting with her heels, and that our driver was a Provençal brute, of the true Marseillois breed,—much more vicious and headstrong than the beast he drove.

There is little in the route from Bourdeaux to Tours, to make one wish to linger on the way; and I had often occasion to wish that I had adopted a more rapid conveyance. The public walk at Angoulême commands a fine prospect; and the view from Poitiers is superb, independently of the historical recollections which make it interesting to an Englishman. Every town of France seems to have its promenade. The public walk at Poitiers is delightful;

and its situation on a lofty height affords facilities, which have not been neglected, in laying it out to the best advantage.

On the sixth day of our journey we made a halt at Ormes, in order to see the château of M. d'Argenson. This is the only château I have seen in France that can bear any comparison with the country residence of an English nobleman. It is situated on the bank of the Vienne; and the disposition and laying out of the ground, from the back of the house to the river, which is within 200 yards, is in the true style of English gardening;—and I could have almost fancied myself on the banks of my own native Wye.

12th

We this morning reached Tours, chiefly remarkable for a very handsome well-built street, which is a rarity in France. The view from the hill before you arrive at Tours commands the greater part of the Touraine. The character of the scenery is made up of that calm kind of beauty consistent with fertility, without any pretensions to the grand or the romantic.

Soon after leaving Tours, our kicking mule had nearly played us a jade's trick. The road lies on the bank of the Loire, under a range of rocks on one side, and with a shelving steep descending to the river on the other, from which the road is protected by a low wall. Our mule, being on the side farthest from the river, seemed to think this a favourable opportunity for venting its malice; and after a desperate effort, succeeded in forcing its companion over the wall. Our situation was one of great danger; for the struggles of the poor animal, who remained suspended in the air by the harness, nearly dragged carriage and all over together. We succeeded however in cutting the traces, and the beast, thus set free, rolled down the steep without suffering any material injury;—and here we left our voiturier and his mule to settle their affairs as they pleased. We might have had some difficulty in arranging our own affairs with him, but for that ready assistance which the law affords to every one who wants its aid in France. The mayors are invested with powers which have a much wider range than those of our own magistrates; and in all petty disagreements, you may at once summon your adversary, and have an immediate and summary decision of the matter in dispute. This, to travellers at least, is a very great comfort, for to them a *delay* of justice would amount to a *refusal*.

13th

At Amboise there is a castle, the principal curiosity of which is a tower, by which they say the king used to ascend into the castle in his carriage. Here are the horns of a stag, eight feet long; and there is a joint of the same animal's neck, as large round as a man's body. This stag, whose horns are, if I remember rightly, still larger than those in Warwick Castle, is said to have been killed in the time of Charles VIII. The château of Chanteloup ought to be seen, as affording a superb specimen of the wretchedness of French taste. There is however an artificial rock there, which, if it were not crowned with a Chinese temple, would be worthy of an English garden.

It is impossible not to be disappointed with the boasted scenery of the Loire. The road and the river as far as Blois are well enough, and the views are occasionally very striking; but after you leave Blois, nothing can well be more uninteresting.

The peasantry, too, do not realize the pictures which the imagination would draw of the "festive choir," whom Goldsmith describes as having led

> With tuneless pipe beside the murm'ring Loire.

I have in vain looked for any specimens of female beauty amongst the lower classes; and, indeed, the hard labour and exposure to the sun, to which they are subject, will sufficiently account for the want of symmetry of form, and beauty of complexion, so observable in the female peasantry of France.

Blois is well calculated for an English residence. The people are said to be better disposed towards us than in most other parts of France; and it is particularly rich in all the productions of the soil.

The price of a pension, including all the comforts of board and lodging, does not exceed 90 francs per month.

This too is a part of France which seems to have suffered less than most other places from the fury of the Revolution. And this is a great consideration; for, whatever political advantages France may have derived from the Revolution, it will require a long time to repair the havoc and confusion which that tremendous explosion has made in the strata of society—elevating the lower, depressing the higher, and disturbing all. The axe of equality has levelled every thing in France, and to look for a gentleman is to lose your labour. All the distinctions of rank have been cut down, like the old trees of the forest, and the new generation that have sprung up, like the coppice, are all on a level; by which the social scene is as much disfigured, as the landscape would be by a similar process. You will seek in vain for that high-bred polish of manners which has been so much the boast, as peculiar to the *haut-ton* of France. The young men have, generally speaking, a *roué*, rake-helly demeanour;—the officers in the army are only to be distinguished by their epaulets; and there is throughout society a coarseness of manners, which savours strongly of *sans-culotism*. In losing the external *simagrées* of the old school, the French have lost the greater part of their politeness; for if politeness consist, as Fielding has beautifully defined it, in an extension of the great rule of Christian conduct to behaviour—so as to behave to all as you would they should behave to you—the French had never at any time more of this true benevolence in trifles than their neighbours.

True politeness indeed can only be associated with principle and honour; for it must be founded as well on self-respect, as on a sense of respect for others; and this can scarcely be expected in a country where it has been long a favourite maxim that every man has his price, and that every woman is no better than she should be. The decline of morals has indeed been greater than the decline of manners; and the whole history of France, since the Revolution, exhibits a lamentable picture of the most degrading want of principle. The French were formerly distinguished, if by no very strict principles of religion, at least, by a high sense of honour. But the age of chivalry is gone; France is no longer the country of "high thoughts seated in a heart of courtesy;"—and we shall in vain seek in the campaigns of the soldiers of Napoleon for any portion of that generosity of sentiment which animated the knight "*sans peur et sans reproche.*" It is common to hear the conduct of French officers in breaking their parole not only mentioned without censure, but praised and applauded—like a successful theft might have been in Sparta—as a justifiable and meritorious act of dexterity. It is to be hoped that the continuance of tranquillity, the progress of education, and the revival of religious principles, may restore to the moral sense of the French people that sensibility which has been almost destroyed by the long reign of license during the Revolution. There are, however, many obstacles that will prevent the reorganization of the "Corinthian capital" of society in France; which it is desirable should exist in all countries—if it consist, as it ought, of a class elevated above the vulgar herd, not only by the amount of their possessions, but by their intellectual and moral superiority.

One obstacle may be found in the spirit of equality, which it would be difficult to eradicate; and which in France is associated with that individual vanity which has no respect for high rank, or high station.

Again, there is the law of inheritance; the effect of which is to prevent the establishment of a permanent aristocracy of families, whose hereditary weight and influence serve as *ballast* in keeping the vessel of society steady.

Though a man may do what he pleases with his property during his life, this law limits his power of disposing of it after his death. If he have only one child, he is allowed the absolute disposal of a moiety—the child inheriting the other as matter of right; if he have two children, he can only dispose of a third; and if he have more than two, three-fourths of his property must be equally divided amongst the children, and one-fourth only is left to his own disposal; either to leave to a stranger, or to increase the portion of the child of his preference. If the father die intestate, the whole property is divided equally amongst the children.

The law of general division, if confined to cases of *intestacy*, might, perhaps, be rational enough, as far as it is founded in the interests of the many, in opposition to the exclusive right of primogeniture. But any interference with the right of a man to dispose of his property at his death—excepting so far as the general good of society may make it necessary to guard against perpetual entails—is manifestly impolitic, as removing one of the greatest stimulants of human industry. The relations of private life, indeed, can never be the proper objects of legislative interference. The interests of children may safely be left to the natural operation of parental affection; and the evil tendency of a law which makes children to a great degree independent of their parents, has already been very extensively felt in France.

While such has been the effect of this law upon domestic life, its consequences, in a national point of view, will probably be still more pernicious. The poor-laws of England have been well characterized by a French writer, as "*la vérole politique de l'Angleterre*;" but by what single term shall we designate the complicated evils which may be expected to flow from the French law of inheritance? For while, on the one hand, its natural operation will be to produce an excess of population, by the equal facilities for marrying which it affords to all the members of a family, it must, at the same time, be diminishing the means of support, by its constant attacks upon capital, in the continual division and sub-division of property. Such a system, if permitted to continue, must, in the end, produce universal beggary; for, if we follow it to its natural conclusion, every acre in France will finally be divided, to the utter extinction of all capital, and every Frenchman eventually reduced to the condition of a pauper.

Though the morals and manners of the highest class of society have suffered much from the Revolution,—though you will occasionally meet in the parlour with something that savours of the servants' hall,—you will perhaps meet with more of High Life below Stairs in France, than in any other country in the world. There is in France an universal quickness of intellect and apprehension, and a perfect freedom from that awkward embarrassment of manner, which is in England, I believe, denominated clownishness. As far therefore as the mere outward air of good breeding goes, almost every Frenchman is well-bred; and you may enter into conversation with a French servant or a French cobbler, upon any of the topics that are common to the mixed company of rational and intelligent people all over the world, without any fear of being disgusted by coarseness or vulgarity.

14th

Orleans;—the cathedral is a beautiful structure, and the view from the tower will well repay the trouble of ascending it, which cannot be said of all such expeditions. A walk of three miles will carry you to the source of the *Loiret*, which is considered an object of curiosity. This river rises in a plain; it is said to be navigable to its source, though no boats are to be seen; and they tell you its source is unfathomable.

15th

We diverged from the road this morning to the left; and, passing through a very interesting country, arrived to breakfast at Versailles. On the highest ground in the town stands the palace. The old front next the town, built by Louis XIII., is heavy and ugly. In the courts on this side were performed the tragic scenes that disgraced the 5th and 6th of October, 1789. The façade of the palace on the garden side is very fine; but the waste of expense in formal alleys, a mob of statues, and unmeaning buildings, hurts an English eye. We walked to *Le petit Trianon*, the favourite retreat of Marie Antoinette. The gardens are a tolerable imitation of the English taste, but still too artificial. The *Tour de Malbrook* is a foolish thing enough;—but the cottages are very pretty, and one might admire the taste which designed them, if they had been intended for the real habitations of clean and decent peasantry;— instead of retreats in which the queen and her favourites might play at shepherdesses.

The approach to Paris from Versailles is extremely grand. You come at once upon the *Place Louis Quinze*, which is the finest spot in Paris, or perhaps in any other town.

Drove immediately to the *Hotel de Boston* in the Rue Vivienne; an excellent house in every respect.

XVIII.

PARIS AND HOME

May 19th

In comparing Paris with London, the latter has, I think, decidedly the advantage in general magnificence, and all the attributes of a metropolis; though perhaps the former may have the greater number of *beau morceaux* in proportion to its size. But then, it must be remembered, that Paris is not much more than half the size of London.

Paris has certainly nothing that can be put in competition with our squares; nor are there such places for riding and walking as the Park and Kensington Gardens. The Thames would be degraded by a comparison with the Seine; and Waterloo Bridge is worth all the bridges in Paris put together. The Pantheon,—fine building as it is,—would not even by a Frenchman be placed upon a level with St. Paul's; nor can any Englishman allow Notre Dame to be mentioned in the same sentence with Westminster Abbey. Still, however, I think we must own that a walk from the Boulevards, down the Rue de la Paix, through the Place Vendôme, to the Place Louis Quinze, and so on to the river, proceeding thence along the Quai to the Thuileries and the Louvre, would present an assemblage of magnificent objects, which exceed any thing that London has to show within the same compass.

In making a survey of both capitals, one cannot help being struck with the distinctive differences of national character, which are so strongly marked in the leading features of the one and the other. *Comfort* seems to have presided at the building of London, and *show* at that of Paris. A drive through the streets of Paris will explain to you at once, that it is the capital of a people who have no taste for the privacy of home; but who prefer to live in the glare and glitter of public amusements. The houses are of an immense height, but then no man's "house is his castle;" each story has its tenants, and if the effect of such wholesale buildings be magnificent, it is obtained at a prodigious sacrifice of domestic comfort. But, to make comfortable homes is not the object in Paris; on the contrary, it is upon public places that attention and expense are almost exclusively employed;—and these are made as luxurious as possible The *cafés*, the *restaurateurs*, and the thousand establishments for the entertainment and recreation of the public, will be found in the highest state of perfection; and it is to enjoy themselves in such places, that the French escape from the comfortless retreat of their own dwellings. In London we find the reverse of all this. For, though our public buildings are in the grandest style of magnificence; yet, perhaps, the most striking feature in London is the evident and paramount object of all the vast sums expended in its improvement;—namely, the individual comfort of the inhabitants. Witness the paving and lighting the streets; the admirable though invisible works, by means of which water is circulated through all the veins of the metropolis;—works of which Paris is wholly destitute—and the spacious laying out of the squares which, splendid as they are, seem less intended for show, than for the health and enjoyment of those that *live* in them.

If the houses in London are not uniformly so high as those in Paris, it is because they are adapted for the use of different classes of people; and they rise, according to the rank of their possessors, from the humble scale of the Suburbs, to the magnificent proportions of Grosvenor-square. I can easily believe that a traveller may be more struck with the *coup d'œil* of Paris, than of London. But he has seen the least striking part of London, who has only seen the outside of the streets;—"there is that within which passeth show;"—for London must be seen in the luxury and comfort of its private society, which will furnish scenes of enjoyment, such as cannot be found, I believe, in any other metropolis in the world.

If the two towns however be merely considered as scenes of gaiety, as places of holiday recreation, it is not surprising that Paris should be almost universally preferred by strangers. One may certainly say of it, as I believe, was said of Seneca's style—*abundat dulcibus vitiis*—in other words, it is a charming place to play the fool in. But, whatever superiority it may have over London is derived chiefly from its very inferiority of scale and grandeur; for this gives it an advantage of the same kind with that which a small theatre has over a large one; in as much as the spectacle with all its details is compressed within a smaller compass, and brought nearer to the spectator. Thus the gardens of the Thuileries are very inferior in extent and beauty to those of Kensington; but the former are in the very heart of Paris; while the latter, for any useful purpose to the majority of the inhabitants of London, might as well be at York.

Again—Tivoli is certainly not equal to Vauxhall; but then you may walk to Tivoli in ten minutes from the Palais Royal, see all that is to be seen, walk back again, and be in bed before midnight, without any of the fuss and trouble attendant upon an expedition to Vauxhall. Every thing, in a word, that Paris contains is *come-atable* at pleasure; and if you add, that there is no smoke, that a dollar will go as far as a guinea does in London, and that it has not, as far as I could see, the horrid nests of human vermin which are to be found in Wapping and St. Giles's, you will have said nearly all that can be said in its favour. In the essential points of eating and drinking, indeed, the Parisians may claim the most unquestionable superiority over us. It is impossible not to admit, that cider cannot vie with champagne, and that burgundy is better than beer. *Vive Paris pour qui a de l'argent!* says somebody; but one might almost cry, *Vive Paris pour qui n'en a pas!*

Witness the culinary *affiches* with which the walls are placarded.

"Tabar, Restaurateur: Diner à 30 sols (15d. English)—On a Potage, 3 Plats très forts, une demi-bouteille de bon vin, Pain à discrétion, un beau dessert,—ou un petit verre de vieille eau-de-vie de Cognac. Le tout au choix. Le service se fait en beau linge; argenterie; et porcelaine, &c."

If this should he too dear, you are tempted by another affiche close by.

Unique dans son genre! Diner copieux à 22 sols (11d. English) par tête, servi en couvert et bols d'argent, en beau linge blanc. On a potage, 3 plats au choix, dessert, ua carafon d'excellent vin. Pain à discretion. On remplace le dessert par un petit verre d'eau-de-vie.

Le public est prévenu qu'afin de mériter sa confiance et flatter son gout, il trouvera la carte bien détaillée et variée tous les jours, tant en volaille, gibier, poisson, que patisserie et dessert."

This will suffice to show, that the Parisians understand the art of puffing and placarding, at least as well as the Londoners. It may be possible, in London, to get the *substance* of a dinner at a chop-house for as small a sum as two shillings; but in a wretched *form*, and without any of the accessories of luxury, or even comfort. In Paris, however, you may dine at the Salon Français in the Palais Royal, in a superb *salon*, as well fitted up, and better lighted, than the Piazza coffee-house in Covent- garden, and be served with soup, three dishes *au choix*, bread *à discrétion*, a pint of Burgundy, and dessert, all for the sum of eighteen pence;—and the waiter makes you a low bow for the gratuity of three-halfpence!

20th

There is another advantage in Paris, which is derived from its inferiority of size;—a walk of half an hour will take you from the centre of the town into the country. In London this is the work of half-a-day. And when you are once clear of the *barrières*, you are as much in the country, and breathe as pure an air, as if you were a hundred miles off. This facility of uniting the pleasures of town and country makes Paris very agreeable. St. Cloud, for instance, is a mere walk, and a more romantic scene can scarcely be conceived.

The park at St. Cloud during a fête might be compared with a scene in FairyLand. To compare it with something nearer home; —imagine several thousand people in Windsor Forest—though perhaps the wood at St. Cloud may be flattered by the comparison —temporary shops erected without number on each side of a fine alley of trees—and the whole forest animated by people amusing themselves in all sorts of ways;—here dancing in troops under the shade—there riding in *round-about* machines, with ships attached to the extremity of their poles, which sail round and round with an undulating motion, like that of a vessel under a steady breeze; —here enjoying the jokes of Punch and Merry Andrew—and there climbing paths that would not ill become the pleasure-ground of an Esquimaux. The whole combination is enchantingly picturesque, and realizes the descriptions that I have read in some foreign novels, in which I always thought there was something too poetical to be fact; but the fact is not less poetical, if one may so say, than the description.

The French, though without any taste for the *romantic* in nature, have a happy knack in the *imitation* of it. The gardens of Tivoli, for instance, though so inferior to Vauxhall in capabilities, are rendered much more rural and romantic; and this is extraordinary enough, considering the different tastes of the two nations. Instead of taking your refreshment in boxes, as at Vauxhall, you here take it under the trees, or in arbours; the walks too are delightfully solitary, and the whole scheme of the entertainments is got up in a better taste, than the *fêtes champêtres* on our side of the water.

21st
Visit to the Catacombs. Our descent into these mansions of the dead was less impressive than it might have been, owing to the association of numbers.

The effect which such a scene is calculated to produce upon the imagination is almost entirely destroyed, by the din and distraction of a large party. As, however, it requires some time to explore these Cimmerian regions, the Custos limits his labours to a single exhibition per day;—so that all those who wish to accompany him assemble at the hour appointed for opening the door, and proceed together.

Armed with tapers, we descended a flight of steps to the depth of about a hundred feet below the surface, and entered one of the low passages leading to the catacombs: These vaults are the work of ages, having been formed by excavating for the stone with which Paris was built. They are of prodigious extent, and there are melancholy instances to prove how fatally a stranger may lose himself in the labyrinth of passages into which they are divided.

To prevent a recurrence of such accidents, the proper route is indicated by a black line, marked upon the roof, which would furnish a straggler with a clue to retrace his steps, if he should happen to lose his way.

After some time we arrived at a small black door, over which was the following inscription:—

> Has ultra metas requiescant
> Beatam spem expectantes.

This is the entrance into the Cavern of Death, where the contents of the various cemeteries of Paris have been deposited; and, as the door is locked behind you, it is difficult to prevent an involuntary shudder from creeping over you, at the thought of being shut up with—two millions of skulls!

Here they are—grinning all around you; piled up in every form of fanciful arrangement; though the common mode of stowing them is in bins—like bottles in a cellar; in which the thigh bones answer the purposes of laths. Upon the whole, it is a painful sight. You feel as if you were guilty of profanation, by intruding upon that privacy which ought to be sacred—for the dead should not be made a spectacle to the living. We do not meet on even terms. They had tongues, and could sing—once! but their gibes and their flashes of merriment are gone; "not one left to mock their own grinning!—Quite chap-fallen."

Wherever you turn, you encounter something to excite disagreeable sensations. In one chamber is a disgusting assortment of the osteological remains of disease and deformity; in another, the surgeon may study the old fashion of amputating limbs, and trepanning heads, in the maimed relics there collected together. In one place, the simple inscription of a date calls up the recollection of the massacres of the Revolution, marking the place where the bones of the victims are deposited:

2 SEPTEMBRE, 1792.

In another quarter, your eye is arrested by a sentence conceived in the worst spirit of French philosophy; and obtruded upon you here in the worst taste—

> Quæris quo jaceas post obitum loco?
> Quo non nata jacent.

At the further extremity of the vault is a pretty fountain, in which some gold fish were sporting about, which seemed to thrive well, unconscious of the horrors that surrounded them.

Though a visit to the catacombs leaves a painful impression, the moral effect is wholesome. You return to the world more disposed to be in good humour with yourself, and with it; and in re-ascending to the "warm precincts of the cheerful day" you taste the whole force of Virgil's exclamation, where he describes the intense but fruitless longing of his departed spirits to return to a world which they had wilfully quitted:—

> ——Quam vellent æthere in alto,
> Nunc et pauperiem, et duros perferre labores!

22nd
To the *Palais Luxembourg*. Here is the exhibition of the paintings of living French artists. The style of the modern French painters is glaring and harsh, and they are too fond of introducing

prettinesses into interesting subjects. In *Guerin's* famous picture of
Phœdra and Hippolytus, you may count the squares of the marble
pavement, and trace all the curious needlework with which the
garments of the figures are embroidered. All the accompaniments
are in the same style. Guerin, however, has finely imagined the
characters of his painting. Phœdra and Hippolytus are admirable;
the nurse absolutely speaks, though perhaps she has too much the
air of a kitchen-maid. Theseus's countenance expresses unmixed
contempt—but surely there should be some mixture of anger. In
the colouring of the French painters there is often great effect—
but then it is almost always an unpleasant effect:—their pictures
are all glare and light; they seem to despise, or to be ignorant of
chiaro-scuro—that delicate management of light and shade which
gives to objects the relief of nature. David is the ringleader of this
style, and he out-Fuselies Fuseli in the overstrained extravagance
of his attitudes. Gerard is the most celebrated artist of the present
day, both in history and portraits. I endeavoured in vain to see
his *Battle of Austerlitz*, which I am told is his best work; but
I saw his *Entrance of Henry IV. into Paris*, and the portraits of
Mademoiselle Mars, and others. There is much merit in his works
in both kinds.

24th

Visited the *Chamber of Deputies*;—a spacious hall of a semicircular
form, handsomely fitted up with a profusion of marble, and
decorated with the statues of Lycurgus, Solon, Demosthenes,
Brutus, Cato, and Cicero. The president's chair, and the desks of
the secretaries, occupy the base of the semicircle; in which the
seats of the members are arranged in semicircular rows, rising one
above the other, facing the president. The two centre benches
on the floor, immediately opposite the tribune, answer to our
Treasury Bench, and are appropriated to the ministers. Above is a
roomy gallery for the public. Their hour of meeting corresponds
with that of our own House of Commons, in less fashionable
times than the present. The doors are opened at half-past eleven
o'clock; the president takes the chair at one; and their debate is

brought to a conclusion by dinner-time. The chamber has not shaken off all the remains of the imperial stratocracy. Drums announced the entrance of the president, who was followed by two serjeants at arms. His dress is the simple uniform of the Chamber—an embroidered blue coat—without wig or gown. These adjuncts may contribute nothing to a native dignity of person, but they are not without their use in supplying the ordinary deficiencies of nature. Nothing could be less dignified than the appearance and manner of the French president, who tripped up the steps of his chair, with the air of a footman in haste to answer his mistress's bell. Private business, and the presentation of petitions, occupied the House till two o'clock; by which time the ministers had taken their seats, and the president announced the order of the day.

The ministers wear a uniform distinct from that of the Chamber; and they have the right of speaking, but cannot vote. The assembly had rather a slovenly appearance; some members being in uniform, and others not; for the *costume* is only strictly necessary to those who mean to mount the tribune. The debate was dull and tiresome; the first speaker read his oration from a written paper, and persisted for half an hour, though it was plain that no person paid the slightest attention to a word that he uttered. Then followed an *extempore* orator, who spoke with considerable force, animation, and effect; but the mounting the tribune—which is placed immediately under the president's chair, so that the orator necessarily turns his back upon him—has a bad effect; it takes away the impression of the speech proceeding from the immediate impulse of the speaker, and gives the idea of a premeditated harangue, which is always tedious.

La Fayette sat on the left side of the Chamber, which is filled by the *Radicals*, or, as the French term them, the *Liberaux*; while the opposite benches, on the right side, are occupied by the Ultra Royalist party. It is impossible not to look with interest at this earliest child of the Revolution—which has been well compared to Saturn devouring his children—for his very existence is a standing miracle; and excites the sort of feeling produced by the sight of a venerable oak, that has outlived the fury of a storm, by which the minor trees of the forest have been destroyed.

The *Count des Cazes*, the popular minister of the day, is not more than thirty-eight years old; being under the age prescribed for a deputy. He is the great hero of the *centre*, which is composed of that party of the Chamber called Constitutionalists, who are supposed to be independent. It will be happy for France if this party be really composed of men who, having no interested views to gratify, are content to "trim the boat and sit quiet;" and by the judicious disposal of their weight, prevent the vessel from leaning too much to the side of the radical royalists on the right, or the radical republicans on the left. It is such a party as this, founded on principles rather than men, and shifting its support as it may perceive danger from the encroachment of either of the ultra parties of the state, that can alone preserve a mixed constitution from being torn in pieces by the madness of democracy, or sinking for ever into the death-sleep of despotism.

Such a body of men is especially necessary in France to temper the excesses of party ascendency; for in France the party in power is omnipotent. Never was there seen such a land for *ratting*;—nothing can equal the rapidity of the contagion; which is shown in an immediate competition amongst all classes to range themselves on the side of the strongest. This utter want of party attachment has often enabled a daring minority, by the semblance of power, to frighten the nation into submission to a yoke, which a trifling effort would have been sufficient to shake off. There is nothing more surprising in the strange history of the French Revolution, than the bare-faced impudence with which a few daring demagogues disposed of the fates of the rest of their countrymen;—unless it be the base and cowardly apathy with which the great mass submitted to the knife of their butchers. Let us hear how Madame Roland—the most amiable and the most enthusiastic of the partizans of liberty—expresses herself in describing the horrible massacres of the prisoners, in September 1792:—"Cependant les massacres continuèrent a *l'Abbaye*, du Dimanche au soir, au Mardi matin; à *la Force*, davantage; à

Bicètre quatre jours. Tout Paris fut témoin de ces horribles scènes exécutées par un petit nombre de bourreaux. Tout Paris laissa faire,—tout Paris fut maudit a mes yeux, et je n'espérai plus que la liberté s'établit parmi des lâches, insensibles aux derniers outrages qu'on puisse faire à l'humanité; froids spectateurs d'attentats que le courage de cinquante hommes armés auroit facilement empêchés.——Le fait est que le bruit d'une prétendue conspiration dans les prisons, tout invraisemblable qu'il fût, l'annonce affectée de l'inquiétude de la colère du peuple, retenait chacun dans la stupeur, et lui persuadait au fond de sa maison, que c'était le peuple qui agissait; lorsque de compte fait, il n'y avait pas deux cents brigands pour la totalité de cette infâme expédition. Aussi ce n'est pas la première nuit qui m'étonne: mais quatre jours!—et des curieux alloient voir ce spectacle!—Non je ne connais rien dans les annales des peuples les plus barbares, de comparable à ces atrocités." It was the same culpable apathy, the same selfish timidity, in the majority of the Convention, which enabled the originally contemptible faction of the Mountain to subdue, proscribe, and condemn all its opponents. The same facility of submission to any yoke has been lately exemplified in the most striking manner in the exits and entrances of rival kings; which have been conducted at Paris after the same quiet and bloodless manner, in which those things are generally exhibited on the stage. Madame de Staël, in describing the French character, does not omit this striking trait. "Les Français," says she, "sont peu disposés à la guerre civile, parceque chez eux la majorité entraine presque toujours la minorité; le parti qui passe pour le plus fort, devient bien vite tout puissant, car tout le monde s'y réunit."

26th

In the evening to the Theatre Français. When a favourite piece is performed, it is necessary to be at the doors some time before they are opened. But the candidates for places have the good sense to perceive the inconvenience of thronging in a disorderly manner, and the established rule is to form *à la queue* as it is called; that is, in a column of two a-breast, and every one is obliged to take his place in the rear, in the order in which he arrives. This is done with as much order and regularity as would be observed in a regiment of soldiers; in consequence of which, the whole business is conducted without the smallest tumult, and with ease to every one. It is true that the *gens d'armes* in attendance have authority to enforce this rule, if there should be any person so unreasonable as to refuse compliance; but still great credit is due to the French for their ready adoption of what is rational. The play was *Joanne d' Arc.* Mademoiselle Duchesnois was the heroine, and a most alarmingly ugly heroine she made; but bodily defects are of little importance if the soul be of the right temper. When that is the case—

     Pritchard's genteel, and Garrick's six feet high.

Her face, however plain, is capable of considerable variety of expression; and, what is of more importance than beauty, there is a great deal of *mind* in her countenance; for this is absolutely necessary to command our interest and sympathy. Who can sympathize with a simpleton, even if it be a pretty simpleton? Duchesnois drew down much applause, and she deserved it;—she feels justly, and has the faculty of expressing what she feels. This is the extent of her merit; but here, where there is so much unnatural declamation, her style appears to the greatest advantage.

Mademoiselle Volnais, for example, with a plump unmeaning pretty face, chants out her part, with no more apparent feeling or understanding than a parrot.

La Fond, who is a great favourite with the audience, played Talbot with something that was very like spirit and dignity; but he can never conceal the actor; he is all "strut and bellow;" and his voice, though it has great compass, is harsh and unpleasant. The political allusions of which the play is full, particularly the prophetic denunciations of Joanne against England, were eagerly seized by the audience, and *rancorously* applauded. It must require all the vanity of the French, to sit and hear, as the audience did with patience and complacency, the most fulsome and disgusting flattery addressed to their national feelings, in the vilest and worst taste of clap-traps. The very gallery in England has grown out of its liking for this sort of stuff.

A new after-piece followed—"*Les Femmes Politiques*;" a pretty trifle, written in elegant language, which was charmingly delivered. Mademoiselle Mars and Mademoiselle Dupuis played delightfully; Baptiste aîné looked and spoke like the old gentleman he represented; and Monrose excited a laugh without descending to buffoonery and caricature. This sort of conversational French comedy is delightful;—it is nature in her best dress—polite—well-bred—and sparkling.

But, in comedies where there is more room for the exhibition of comic humour, the French actors are perhaps inferior to our own. We shall in vain look for parallels of what Lewis was, or what Munden and Dowton are; and even with respect to Mademoiselle Mars, excellent as she is in the first and highest walks of comedy, for which she seems designed by nature—being very beautiful, very graceful, and perfectly well-bred—yet, in characters of archness and humour, she might put a little more heart, and a great deal more mind into her representations. We miss the force, the richness, and the warmth of Mrs. Jordan's acting, and the exquisite point that she had the art of giving to comic dialogue; which only wanted the embellishments and good-breeding of the French Thalia, to constitute a perfect actress.

The point of perfection would perhaps be found somewhere between the styles of the two nations. To take an example from the *Tartuffe*;—the famous scene between *Tartuffe* and *Elmire* is scarcely played up to the intention of the author by Damas and Mademoiselle Mars, and it certainly might be coloured higher, without overstepping the modesty of nature. Dowton, in Cantwell, may go a little too far with Lady Lambert—and yet who can think so that remembers the effect produced by his management of the interview—but Damas, in Tartuffe, does not go far enough with Elmire. The scene "comes tardy off:"—*bienséance*, when carried too far, is a millstone round the neck of tragedy and comedy. Congreve says well, that a scene on the stage must represent nature, but in warmer colours than it exists in reality. It is in Molière particularly, perhaps exclusively, that the French comedians seem to fall short of the author; for Molière is the most humorous of all their writers. He is the Fielding of France, and there is a richness and a raciness about him which are sometimes frittered away in the representation.

It might be curious to inquire the cause of the universal decline of the art of acting, during the present age. France has only two performers that are much above mediocrity; but they are excellent;—Talma in tragedy, and Mars in comedy. As to all the rest, though many have a considerable portion of merit, we may pass them over in silence, except Potier; who is, as he deserves to be, a prodigious favourite in farce and caricature,—but we possess a better edition of Potier than the French themselves, in our own inimitable Liston.

The French Opera is the most splendid theatre in Paris; but protect me from French singing!—especially if it be serious singing. Arthur Young, in speaking of French singing, describes it as the "distortions of embodied dissonance," and Rousseau inveighs against the "lamentable chant Français" as bearing more resemblance "aux cris de la colique qu'aux transports despassions;" and in their choruses there is a grand roar-royal, as if they all had the colic together. The light airs of their comic operas are however very pleasing; and there is at least this merit in their singing, that you can hear what they say. The airs of Gretry are delightful. The ballet of the French Opera is perfect;—in dancing, as well as cooking, I believe we must acknowledge our inferiority, nor attempt to rival, the French in agility of heels. I have, seen, in the gardens of Tivoli, a *pas de trois* performed by two male and one female dancer upon *stilts*. The *pirouttes* on these seven-leagued legs were inexpressibly ridiculous; but, if difficulty be the great desideratum in dancing, this style, of all others, ought to be entitled to the loudest applause.

27th

The Louvre, stripped as it has been of the spoils, which Buonaparte and his myrmidons had collected from all parts of Europe, is still a noble collection. The gallery itself—500 yards in length—lined with pictures, is a magnificent sight.

There are still remaining some beautiful specimens of Raphael, Murillo, Titian, and Salvator Rosa. The gaps, occasioned by the restoration of the spoils of Italy, have been filled up with the Luxembourg pictures of Rubens, who has thrown away a vast deal of labour and fine colouring in hopeless and incurable allegories; and by the sea-pieces of Vernet, which are so beautiful, that we cannot, while looking at them, regret the absence of any pictures whatever. His views of the sea-ports combine all the beauties of painting with the most accurate fidelity of resemblance. But it is in his fancy pieces that he gives the reins to his imagination, and indulges in every variety of tint and contrast; and it is difficult to say whether he is most admirable in the warm glow of sunshine—the pale silver gleams of moonlight—the gloomy gathering of a fog—or the terrific horrors of a tempest.

Nicholas Poussin is the great hero of the French school of painting. There is a hardness of manner in the generality of his works, which injures their effect—but his *Deluge* is sublime. There is a dark and terrible solemnity about it, admirably suited to the subject. The universal desolation is pictured by a selection of a few instances of the most affecting images, which do honour to the heart of the painter; who represents love—conjugal and parental love—as enduring through all trials, exerting its energy to the last, and overwhelmed only in the end—by the destruction of all things. One would almost fancy Poussin had wished to illustrate the sentiment of Solomon—"Many waters cannot quench love, neither can floods drown it."

There is a picture in the Louvre by *Lairesse* from which I think Sir Joshua Reynolds must have borrowed the idea of *Garrick between Comedy and Tragedy*.

The composition and arrangement of the figures are so precisely the same, that the resemblance can scarcely be accidental. The subject is Hercules between Virtue and Vice; and Sir Joshua has not even been at the pains of adding legs to the half-lengths of the originals;—though he has certainly improved upon *Lairesse's* Vice, in his exquisitely charming figure of Thalia.

The Louvre collection of statues may still boast some of the most beautiful specimens of ancient sculpture. The Borghese collection, amongst which are the famous Fighting Gladiator, and the Hermaphrodite, was bought and added to the National Museum by Napoleon.

28th

Before I leave Paris, I ought to record my impressions of the French women; who must, I think, yield the palm to their English and Italian neighbours. They want the freshness, and retiring delicacy of the first; and the dignity, and voluptuous enthusiasm of the second. Whatever beauty there is amongst them is confined to the upper classes, and the *Grisettes*. In passing through the country, I was everywhere appalled by the squalid faces of the peasantry—so unlike the romantic pictures of Sterne. The point in which the Parisian ladies claim the most decided superiority over their English sisters is in the elegance of their *tournure*;—and for this claim there may be some foundation. The French ladies, however, sometimes carry their pretty mincing airs too far; but even this is better than the opposite extreme, which is occasionally exemplified in the striding gait of an Englishwoman. What Rousseau said of the *Parisiennes*, and of the silly spirit of imitation which induces other nations to deform their figures by adopting the deformities of French fashions, may well be applied to the present day; when every Englishwoman is at the pains of making herself hump-backed, for no other reason, as it would seem, than that the native beauty of her form may be reduced to the French standard of symmetry. "Menues," says Rousseau, speaking of the *Parisiennes*, "plutôt que bien faites, elles n'ont pas les tailles fines; aussi s'attachent-elles volontiers aux modes qui la déguisement; en quoi je trouve assez simples les femmes des autres pays, de vouloir bien des modes faites pour cacher les défautes qu'elles n'ont pas."

It is a curious fact that, in 1814, the English ladies were so possessed with a rage for imitating even the deficiencies of their French sisterhood, that they actually had recourse to violent means, even to the injury of their health, to compress their beautiful bosoms as flatly as possible, and destroy every vestige of those charms, for which, of all other women, they are perhaps the most indebted to nature.

The French women appear, what I believe they really are, kind, good-humoured, and affectionate; but light, fickle, capricious, and trifling. Without having thrown off entirely the robe of virtue, they wear it so loosely as to admit of freedoms, which would shock the delicacy of more reserved manners. No woman in Paris, I believe, would feel offended at any proposals, if made *d'une certaine manière, et d'un air bien comme il faut!*—Though it by no means follows that the proposals would be accepted; for, as Mrs. Sullen says in the play, "it happens with women as with men; the greatest talkers are often the greatest cowards, and there is a reason for it:—those spirits evaporate in prattle, which might do more mischief if they took another course." But there can be no descriptions of national characters without exceptions;—Mesdames Ney and Lavalette, in these days, and Mesdames La Roche Jacquelin and Roland, in the days of the Revolution, may challenge a comparison with the fairest names that ever adorned the annals of womanhood.

Matrimony, if one may take the evidence of the journals, seems to be a regular business of advertisement. I select three out of *eight* in one paper;—and all too on the part of the ladies.

"Une demoiselle bien née et aimable, ayant 120,000 francs de biens, desire épouser un homme âgé et riche."

"Une demoiselle de 24 ans, jolie et d'une éducation distinguée, ayant 40,000 francs comptant, et par la suite, 200,000 francs, desire épouser un jeune homme aimable, et ayant de la fortune."

"Une demoiselle, de 19 ans, sans fortune, mais jolie, aimable, et bien élevée, desire épouser un homme âgé, et assez aisé pour pouvoir faire quelque bien à sa mère."

Perhaps *âgé* means no more than our word *aged*, as applied to a horse.

This may suffice as a specimen; on the part of the gentlemen the paper offered no advertisement whatever.

29th

The following document, taken from the *Bibliothèque Historique*, will show the fearful extent to which gaming is carried in Paris at present.

BUDGET DES JEUX PUBLICS.

ETAT DES FRAIS ANNUELS DES JEUX DE PARIS.

7 Tables de Trente-et-un.

9 De Roulette.

1 Passe-Dix.

1 Craps.

1 Creps.

1 Biribi.

——

20

These twenty tables are distributed about Paris; the *minimum* established as a stake, varies from a Napoleon to a sous; so that every man may find a table suited to his fortune. At some, women are admitted, and it is needless to describe the effect which such institutions must have upon the morals of the town. The current expenses of these establishments are calculated at no less a sum than 1,551,480 francs per annum. And in addition to these there is the "*bail*," or duty to government, 6,000,000 francs; and the *bonus* for the *bail* 166,666 francs; making together the enormous sum of 7,718,146 francs.

From documents it appears that the average gain of the tables is 800,000 francs per month, amounting to 9,600,000 francs per annum; which, after subtracting the expenses, 7,718,146 francs, will leave a clear profit of 1,881,854 francs. And yet, in spite of this unanswerable logic of figures and facts, there are every day fresh victims, who are infatuated enough to believe that it is possible to counter balance the advantage which the bank possesses, by a judicious management of the power that the player has of altering his stake. This is a fatal error. For though it is common to talk of the uncertainty of chance; yet, in an unlimited series, chance becomes certainty; and the doctrine of the chances is founded upon the same general and immutable laws which direct all the operations of matter. There is a little pamphlet published at Paris, which ought to be read by every man who needs to be convinced that he who plays against the table must, at the long run, be made a beggar.

30th

The "zeal to destroy" is busily at work all over Paris, in endeavouring to obliterate Napoleon's renown; and indeed to convert the imperial insignia into emblems in honour of the Bourbons. Thus, the N. is universally changed into an H to pay a compliment to *Henri Quatre*, of which he has no need; and the Bee is transformed into a *fleur de lis*. The *bas reliefs* too, which commemorate the achievements of the ex-Emperor, are torn down without mercy. There is something pitiful in this disfigurement, which does little credit to those who ordered it. It is not only ill-judged, as being calculated to engrave deeper on the tablets of the memory the recollection of those exploits, which are thus unworthily treated; but the attempt is manifestly impossible. All Paris savours of Napoleon; for instance—what can be done with the column in the *Place Vendome*?—Can it be supposed that the white flag on the top of it will efface the recollection that this pillar was composed of 1,200 pieces of cannon, taken by Napoleon at the battle of Austerlitz?

   This subject has been well treated in the letter to the Duke of Wellington, which was attributed to Fouché:—"Quand on a été subjugué par Napoléon, il-y-a peu de jugement à la dénigrer plus on cherche à l'abaisser plus on s'avilit soi-même;—le voyageur sourit de pitié en voyant effacer à grands frais les aigles, qui se trouvent sur les monumens qu'il a reparé ou élevés:—comme si la mémoire des faits devait périr avec les aigles!" The same work of destruction has been carried on at the Pantheon, where the fine mythological bas reliefs have been removed, though the example of St. Peter's at Rome might he pleaded in their justification; and the inscription on the frieze of the portico—"*Aux grands hommes la Patrie reconnoissante*"—is about to give place to some more loyal and legitimate motto.

Amongst the unfinished works of Napoleon is the Fountain which he intended should be erected on the site of the Bastile. This fountain was to consist of an enormous elephant, the model of which is now to be seen in plaster of Paris, on the spot where the Bastile formerly stood. It is seventy-feet in height; the *jet d'eau* is through the nostrils of his trunk; the reservoir, in the tower upon his back; and one of his legs contains the staircase, for ascending to the large room within his body. The Elephant was to be executed in bronze, with tusks of silver, surrounded by lions of bronze; who were to expectorate the water from one cistern to another. It is remarkable, how little the persons who live close to the Bastile know of the particulars which happened at the taking of that place by the populace—an event which happened so short a time ago. And, in the accounts which have been published, there is scarcely a circumstance which is told in the same manner by any two narrators.

From the site of the Bastile, I went to the manufactory of *Gobelin Tapestry*. It is extremely curious to see the operations of this manufacture. The material on which the tapestry is worked consists merely of single threads; which are placed upon a frame, over which the workman leans. The outline of the pattern is marked in black chalk upon the threads; and the worsted being ready rolled, the artist then works it in, in the various proper shades, with no other direction to guide him than a coloured model which hangs near him. The extraordinary part of the work is, that he produces the desired effect, using the most brilliant colours and the softest gradations of tints, with the happiest use of light and shadow, without looking at the fair side of his work in its progress;—for it is the inside which is always next to him.

June 5th
Visited the Institution for the Deaf and Dumb;—the most interesting of all the establishments in Paris. The system of

education, invented by the benevolent Abbé de l'Epée for the education of these helpless children, shut out, as it would seem, by nature, from the chief sources of intelligence, has been prosecuted with all success by the Abbé Sicard. The difficulty obviously consists in establishing a medium of communication with the mind of the pupil. The Abbé de l'Epée, who, without preferment, or patronage, or other support than that of his own patrimonial means, devoted his life and fortune to the maintenance and education of a large domestic establishment of deaf and dumb, surmounted the difficulty, and invented a method of conveying ideas to the mind, by means of visible signs. This is done by writing the names of things, and, by a regular system of signs, establishing a connexion between the written words, and the ideas to be excited by them. This ingenious system would appear at first sight to be almost impracticable; but as the Abbé well observed, "the connexion between ideas and the articulate sounds which are the ordinary means by which they are excited in the mind, is quite as arbitrary as that between these ideas and the written characters he used to represent them to the eye."

The mind once stored with ideas, and a channel of communication established, the pupil is soon taught—what may be called the mechanical part of his education—the use and exercise of the organs of speech; and as a privation of any of the senses is found to produce a greater quickness in those that remain, the sense of sight becomes in the deaf and dumb so acute, that they can *see* the answer of the person with whom they converse, by observing the motion of the lips.

Some of the definitions, which are recorded as the *impromptu* answers of Massieu and Leclerc, two of M. Sicard's most celebrated pupils, at public examinations, are at once accurate and beautiful. To instance a few; *Eternité*—un jour sans hier ni demain; *Reconnoissance*—la mémoire du cœur; *Les sens*—des porte-idées.

Many of the definitions of these pupils have been recorded; but there are none more worthy of record than the answers which they made to the following question: "Quelle difference y-a-t-il entre le désir et l'espérance?" *Massieu's* reply is remarkable for metaphysical acuteness, and nice discrimination "*Le désir* est une inclination du cœur; *l'esperance*—une confiance de l'esprit." *Leclerc's* answer displays more imagination, and is indeed less a definition than an illustration; but it is a beautiful illustration: "*Le desir* est un arbre en feuilles; *l'esperance*—un arbre en fleurs; *la jouissance*—un arbre en fruits."

The intellectual attainments of these persons furnish the strongest argument against those doctrines which would persuade us that the soul of man is only the *result* of the organs of sense. If any farther argument were needed to convince us of the immaterial nature of the thinking being within us, we might surely find it in the example afforded by the deaf and dumb; which seems to prove that the soul's existence is independent of the senses;—though their excitement may be required to call out its powers, and a certain material apparatus be necessary to the manifestation of its faculties.

It has been stated, as a singular coincidence, that a deaf and dumb pupil, being asked to define his idea of the sound of a trumpet, compared it to the colour red; as Sanderson, the famous blind Mathematical Professor, used to explain his idea of the colour red, by likening it to the sound of a trumpet.

Drove afterwards to the *Hotel Dieu*, one of the largest hospitals in Paris. Every thing was neat and clean; the furniture of the beds was white, and looked fresh and wholesome. In walking through the wards, though there was much to afflict the eye, there was nothing to offend any other sense.

The French boast much of their surgical attainments; and indeed their campaigns must have afforded them the most ample opportunities of practice and experience.

One improvement, I believe, they may have introduced, which has been found of extensive benefit in military practice;—that of immediate amputation before inflammation takes place; in opposition to the old established system of waiting till the inflammation had subsided.

7th

Left Paris for Dieppe, travelling the lower road to Rouen; which passes along the banks of the Seine, and abounds more in picturesque prospect, than any other which I have yet seen in France—though this is not saying much in its favour. But the view of Rouen, from a height about a league from it, is very fine, and might be admired in any part of England. Normandy, indeed, in many of its features, bears a striking resemblance to England; and the likeness increases as you advance from Rouen towards Dieppe, through the green and fertile valley, rich in pastures and orchards, and peopled with the cotton-workers, by means of whom the French hope to rival our long-established superiority in that manufacture.

Having now arrived at Dieppe, the last stage of the French territory, I would willingly part with them in good humour. There are some amiable traits of character, which are universally prevalent, and must strike the most common observer. They are, almost without exception, a temperate people; and, with wine at command, which may be bought for almost nothing, they rarely drink to excess. It must be confessed too, that they are much kinder and gentler in their treatment of the brute part of the creation, than the lower orders of our own country; and indeed the appearance of the animals confirms this opinion; for you never see those maimed, broken-kneed, miserable objects—the victims of ill-temper and ill-treatment—which so often shock one in England.

Again—if the French have a much greater share of vanity than their insular neighbours, they are at least untainted with that ludicrous sort of pride which thrives so prodigiously in England—setting a fool in fermentation, and swelling him out with inflated ideas of self-importance;—for no one here is above speaking civilly to his inferior, how great soever the distance between them. The French too in many instances exhibit a praiseworthy disregard of outward appearance, to which the English, from pride or *mauvaise honte*, practise so obsequious a submission. In France no man fear sinking in the estimation of his friends from the shabbiness of his coat, the height of his lodgings, or the fashion of his equipage.

If I have seen little else to mention with commendation, it may be that I have been blinded by national prejudice; for I believe it is difficult, if not impossible, to acquire that complete impartiality which is so necessary in the pursuit of truth. It would seem that a man's head was like a bowl, and that he came into the world with a certain bias infixed by the hand of nature herself. This bias in an Englishman's head disposes him to dislike every thing belonging to a Frenchman. I confess, till I had resided in France, I used to think that this prejudice was carried much too far; but I leave it with a most devout wish that it may never be my misfortune to reside in it again; and a very strong hope that the national feeling, which has so long kept us a distinct people in all our habits, feelings, and principles, may long continue to be cherished; and that the sound and sufficient sentiment of love of country may never be laughed out of countenance by the vain and visionary nonsense of universal philanthropy.

9th

Dieppe. Labor ultimus!—Ascended the cliff to snuff up the gale that comes from Old England. "Oh England! England! thou land of liberty—thou climate of good sense—thou tenderest of mothers and gentlest of nurses,"—how I long to embrace thee again! And yet now that I am within twelve hours' sail of thee, and that I can approach thee with amended health and brighter prospects, I feel a strange mixture of apprehension and anxiety. Who has not felt, though parting from friends is the severest of all trials, that meeting again is not without its disquietudes; especially after a long absence from those with whom we have been in the constant habit of thinking, talking, and acting? In such a situation a man fears lest he should find his friends, or lest his friends should find him changed; lest absence should have made such a gap in the chain which united them in the bonds of affection, that it may be doubtful whether the links will ever fit in together again. I believe I was led into this train of thought by a passage in *Atala*, a wild little book of delightfully romantic nonsense, by Chateaubriand:—"Mais que parle-je de la puissance des amitiés de la terre? Illusion! Chimère! Rêve d'une imagination blessée! Vanité des vanités! Si un homme revenait à la lumière quelques années après sa mort, je doute qu'il fût revu avec joie par ceux-là mêmes qui ont versé le plus de larmes à sa mémoire; tant on forme vîte des autres liaisons—tant l'inconstance est naturelle à l'homme!" But the packet is ready, and the wind is favourable.

June 10th
On board. The cliffs of Dieppe are as white as those of Albion; a name which we have been taught was applied to our own island from something peculiar and remarkable in the colour of its rocks. This similarity of materials strengthens the notion that, at some remote period, the sea burst through the straits, and divided us from the continent;—a thought which is well expressed by Mason, when he makes old Ocean tear Britannia

> ——from reluctant Gaul,
> And bid her be his queen.

Long may she retain her sceptre!—and long may she continue to inspire such feelings as now rise within me in approaching her shores, and make me exult in the reflection that I was born an Englishman:—

> Ταύτης τοι γενεῆς τε καὶ αἵματος εὔχομαι εἶναι!

ALSO AVAILABLE FROM NONSUCH PUBLISHING

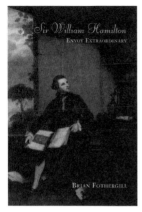

Sir William Hamilton is perhaps best remembered for his involvement in the most notorious love triangle of the time, between him, his wife Emma and Lord Nelson. However, this fascinating account reveals a man whose talent for diplomacy was matched only by his dedication to antiquity, a man who was fêted across cosmopolitan Europe as both art-collector and dilettante.

1 84588 042 0

£18.00

320 pages, 16 illustrations

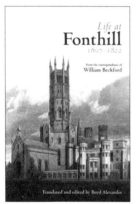

Life at Fonthill contains extracts from the diary of William Beckford, one of the most controversial figures of his time. He is perhaps best remembered as the author of *Vathek* and builder of Fonthill Abbey, his Gothic monstrosity of a house, with its 300-foot-high tower. This book offers an insight into the life of this eccentric and unforgettable character.

1 84588 069 2

£18.00

352 pages, 16 illustrations

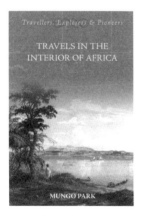

Mungo Park, surgeon, botanist and explorer, was born into a society increasingly fascinated with the dark and largely uncharted continent of Africa. In 1795, at the tender age of twenty-three, Park led an expedition that consisted only of himself and local guides. *Travels* is the explorer's own account of this momentous attempt to chart the course of Niger river, and the perils and wonders that accompanied his journey.

1 84588 068 4

£14.00

288 pages

For sales information please see: www.nonsuch-publishing.com